A Farewell to the Fairways

About the Author

Dermot Gilleece retired in December 2023 as a columnist with the *Sunday Independent*, bringing to an end 63 years as a working journalist. For much of that time, he specialised as a golf writer, including 21 years as golf correspondent of the *Irish Times*.

Since parting with the *Sunday Independent*, he has written two books, bringing his total output to 16. This latest book follows *Links of Love*, on how golf brought Jimmy Kinsella and his wife, Bernie, together. A lengthy period of his tenure with the *Irish Times* involved the struggle for equality in Irish golf-club membership and Gilleece played a prominent role in promoting the women's cause.

In fact, he and Des Rea O'Kelly, honorary secretary of the Golfing Union of Ireland, were responsible for devising the so-called 'three-tier constitution', which formed the basis of an ultimate solution to the issue. And from there, the door was effectively opened for the launch of Golf Ireland.

A Farewell to the Fairways was conceived as a journey back through the highlights of his working career, reflecting his love for the men's and women's amateur game and the progress of such gifted exponents as Pádraig Harrington, Darren Clarke, Paul McGinley, Graeme McDowell, Rory McIlroy, Shane Lowry and Leona Maguire into professional ranks.

Born in Rathcoole, Co. Dublin in 1940, Gilleece married Carlow's Kathy Harding in 1970 and they are now together 54 years. They live in Sutton and have two married children, Tara and Mark, and two grandsons, Harry and Charlie, to whom this book is dedicated.

A Farewell to the Fairways

Dermot Gilleece

Published by
Red Stripe Press
Upper Floor, Unit B3
Hume Centre
Hume Avenue
Park West Industrial Estate
Dublin 12
Ireland
email: info@redstripepress.com
www.redstripepress.com

Paperback ISBN 978-1-78605-237-7
ePub ISBN 978-1-78605-238-4

Typeset by www.typesetting.ie

Printed in Dublin by SPRINTBOOKS

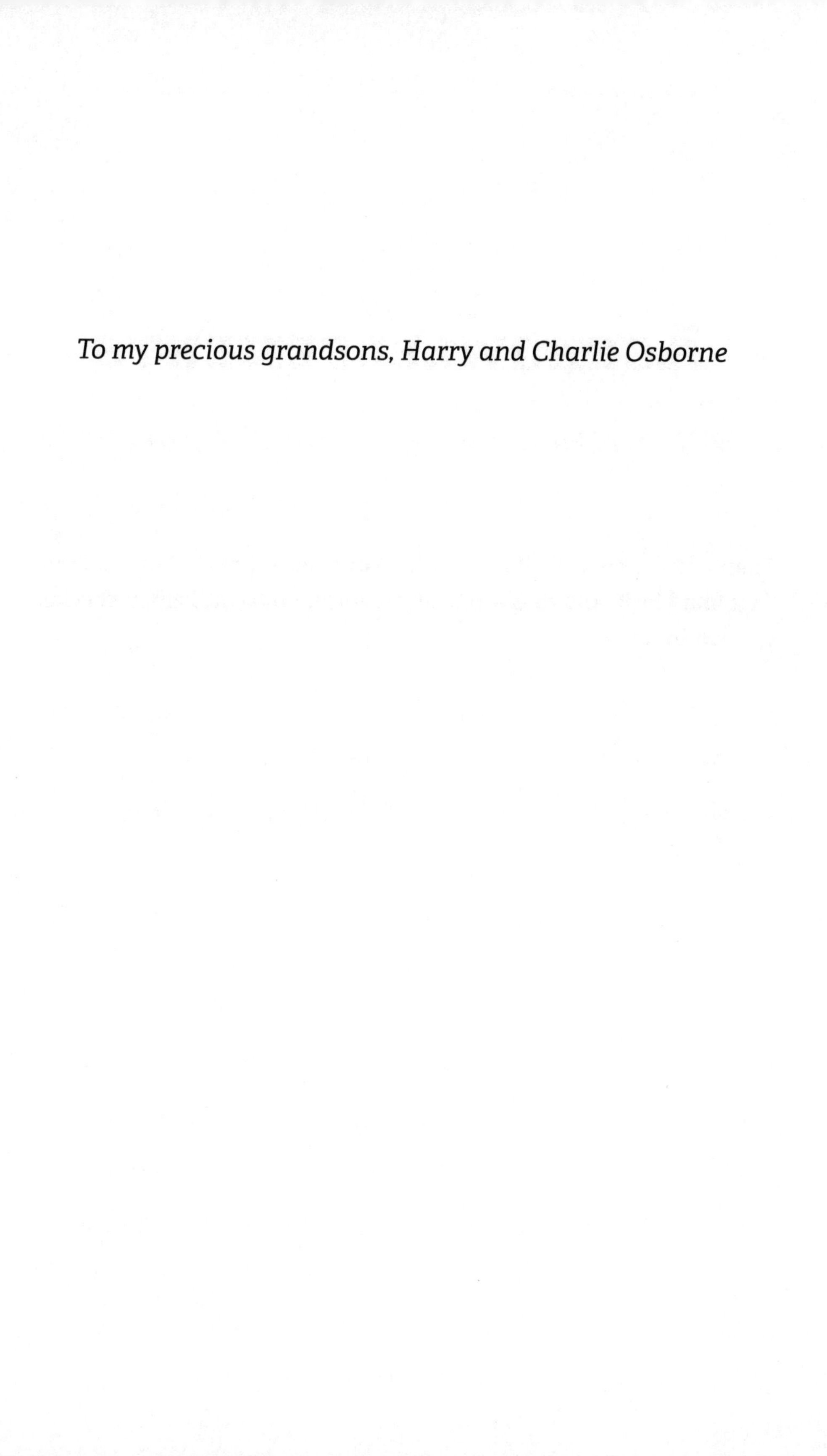

To my precious grandsons, Harry and Charlie Osborne

Acknowledgements

Thank you to my wife, Kathy, for her constant support. To my children, Tara and Mark. And to Clare Lanigan, for her diligent help in checking the text for errors.

Foreword

Back when I was starting off playing amateur golf as a young lad of fifteen years of age, I remember telling my dad after a round that I needed to talk to a certain reporter; whereupon he stopped me and pointed out, 'that man is not a reporter; he's a golf writer, a journalist.' As it turned out, the writer in question was Dermot Gilleece. In those days, I maybe didn't appreciate the difference my father was alluding to, but after nearly 30 years on the professional Tours, I certainly do now.

What was interesting about Dermot and, indeed, all the Irish golf journalists at the time, was that they developed strong relationships with the Irish players. It proved to be a two-way street as they helped the players by providing guidance on how to approach the media. As a consequence, you will often find that the Irish players are considered to be among the best in the world in their dealings with the media, because of those early relationships. Oftentimes during conversations, Dermot would give you time for quiet reflection rather than let you hot-headedly say something that you might later regret. He might then seek confirmation, maybe once or twice, that you really wanted to say it. In addition, you could tell him things in confidence, without worry of any betrayal.

I became more familiar with Dermot from 1988/89 when I was making my way through the Irish amateur ranks. I would see him at the notable tournaments, including my three Walker Cups, before I entered the professional ranks in 1995. When I turned pro, it was striking that this gentleman I knew from my amateur days was now in a different environment, commanding the respect of his peers in the world of golf journalism as a senior figure in the profession. Dermot was a familiar, almost constant face on Tour and at Major championships since then, including the three I won.

He displayed a deep understanding of the game, great pride in what he wrote, and appreciated what the golf writing job entailed. I think he actually loved golf and the intricacies of it, which prompted him to try to get deeper into particular stories.

While I can speak really only of my own era, Dermot had earlier developed relationships with many of the Irish and international golfers of the past, players such as Joe Carr and Christy O'Connor, both of whom became legendary in Ireland, generating stories that you will read in the following pages.

The game has come a long way since those days, with communications changing the way in which tournaments are reported and players are interviewed. Still, quality writing remains fundamental to the craft, while allowing the reader to learn more about the game we love and the intriguing characters involved.

Since moving full-time to golf writing in the 1980s, Dermot has been at the top of his game for over four decades and this book, *A Farewell to the Fairways*, allows him to share those memories with us all and continue to educate us with the quality of his thoughts and insights.

Pádraig Harrington,
August 2024

Contents

Contents

1

My Brother's Clatter

When I made my way tearfully back from the presentation dais at The K Club, the warmth of Paul McGinley's smile was especially welcome. 'We cherish praise from our peers because nobody understands our journey like they do,' he said. With that, my composure gradually returned.

It was the annual lunch of the Irish Golf Writers Association in December 2023 and, totally out of the blue, they had decided to mark my retirement after 63 years in sports journalism. For such an occasion, I could imagine myself making a lengthy, detailed speech interspersed with some working highlights, of which there were many. And there would be genuine appreciation of the kindnesses of fellow scribes over the decades.

Instead, I welled up as the Association's secretary, Brian Keogh, handed me a large reproduction of a rather special back page from the *Evening Press* in July 1960. 'O'Connor's Wonder 63 Won The £1,000', it declared.

There was no byline, but this was my report of a Monday morning play-off in the Hospital Trust Tournament at Woodbrook, where Christy O'Connor beat Ryder Cup colleague Ken Bousfield by eight strokes. It would be more than a month until I celebrated my 20th birthday. As I attempted to absorb the physical and mental impact of this recollection, Brian presented me with a beautiful pen inscribed 'Olive oil'. An expression much loved by the one-time soccer manager Liam Tuohy, which I latched onto as a colloquial substitute for 'au revoir'.

As you will gather, the occasion is all a bit of a blur. In attempting to thank my attending colleagues, I remember mumbling something about it having been 'a great run'. With that, I left the gifts to be collected later and made my way back to my table and McGinley's smile.

In a public acknowledgement of the back-page replica, I mentioned on Twitter/X that it now hangs at home on my landing, sufficiently distant as to be legible only with difficulty. In truth, it wasn't my finest effort – though, crucially, it was factually sound, which wasn't at all bad for a 19-year-old experiencing such an event for the first time.

It had been less than two years since the autumn of 1958, when I was invited to a job interview by the *Irish Press* group. They had written to various schools in the Dublin area seeking suitable applicants for a career in journalism and my name was suggested by my alma mater, St Joseph's CBS, Fairview.

I was born on 30 August 1940, in Rathcoole, Co. Dublin, where my father, Jim, owned a garage. I was still a child when we closed the garage because of petrol rationing associated with the Second World War (or 'the Emergency', as we euphemistically referred to it) and moved to Glenart Avenue in Blackrock. As he had previously been an Army regular, my father was called up as a reserve officer and served out the war years as a captain.

My earliest memory of those Blackrock years was holding my father's hand when we attended a performance of the 'Pirates of Penzance' in CBC Monkstown in which my eldest brother, Colm, sang the role of Mabel as a boy soprano. When the War ended, we returned as a family to Rathcoole where the garage was reopened and my boyhood chores included serving petrol. And I distinctly remember the jockey, Martin Moloney, in a red MG sports model, as one of my customers – and his sixpence tips.

I recall it as a wonderful time of running through open fields during long, hot summers. Even contracting scarlet fever didn't seem to disturb the idyll. My older sister, Maureen, revived memories for me when I consulted her recently as the family's appointed archivist.

She informed me that the scarlet fever epidemic occurred in 1948, when myself and our 18-month-old brother, Declan, were whisked by ambulance from Rathcoole to Cork Street Hospital in the city. She remembered our mother's tears as she washed Declan's little vests, preparing for the great separation.

He and I spent three weeks in Cork Street, which were not especially unpleasant, as I recall. At a time when phones were few and far between, the numbers of affected families were so great, however, that it was deemed necessary to report each patient's well-being by a sort of code in the national papers, including Dublin's *Evening Mail*.

Each patient was given a number and at any given time, their condition could be found in the newspaper with the designated number beside their general status as 'no improvement', 'improving' or 'convalescing', gleaned from a hospital bulletin. I remember feeling like something of a local hero when I returned home to my family and friends, apparently none the worse for the experience.

Remarkably, a certain hospital anthem has remained with me for the last 75 years:

> Mammy, daddy, take me home / From this convalescent home / I've been here a week or two / And now it's time to be with you / Goodbye all the doctors / Goodbye all the nurses / Goodbye all the doctors / And Doctor Daly too.

I've never discovered the identity of this ubiquitous Dr Daly, but he must have been a favourite with the children.

Ten years later, the invitation from the *Irish Press* had a certain appeal, given that I was working as a salesman in the Dublin Fruit Market at the time. And I imagined most of the desirable jobs for Leaving Cert graduates that year had already been taken.

This was a time when the accepted route into a national newspaper was through provincial publications, but the *Press* hit on the idea of taking lads like me directly from school to train them in journalism from square one.

In the event, their decision led to a career that proved to be rewarding in most areas except, perhaps, financially. It provided continuous employment for 65 years.

By way of personal possessions from this lengthy career, I'm left with great memories and two portable typewriters. One is a 'Brother' model, received as an anniversary gift from my wife, Kathy, in 1972, and the other is an East German 'Erica', bought for £45 from the Royal and Ancient after it had been loaned to scribes covering the 1984 Open Championship at St Andrews, where Seve Ballesteros secured an unforgettable triumph.

For more than 30 years, proficiency in shorthand and typing was all I needed for my work. I acquired these skills under the guidance of Douglas Gageby, then editor of the *Evening Press* and later of the *Irish Times*, who also monitored my attendance at Bolton Street College for classes in typography and display.

I had only briefly been in my new role when I was first made aware of Gageby's newspaper skills. With a special, late edition of the *Evening Press* planned for the papal election of 1958, a senior member of staff announced triumphantly that the paper could run; according to United Press International (UPI), the new pope was Cardinal Montini. 'We'll wait for Reuters,' insisted Gageby. It was an agonising fifteen minutes before a news flash from Reuters announced that the new pope was not Montini but Cardinal Roncalli, who would be John XXIII.

My pay was £3, 13s per week, of which I gave my mother £3 and wondered how I could squander the rest. It proved to be excellent training. As a glorified messenger boy, I ran errands to every department in Burgh Quay, many of which no longer survive in newspaper production; like the Creed Room, Case Room, Stereotypers and Clichograph Department.

This was a time of using hot metal, when the sub-editor assigned to the case room would observe compositors creating a newspaper page of lead type, and the uninitiated needed a compact mirror to make sense of typefaces set backwards.

I had not been there long when the prominence of gambling first came to my attention. Part of my job was to run messages for senior members of the staff. This included regular trips to the local bookmaker placing bets for the group's main racing expert, Maurice Ring.

Though Ring, known as The Ringer, enjoyed only moderate success, I was still fascinated by the idea of using one's acquired expertise to make handy money. So I asked him why it was that he didn't quit working and take up punting full time. Peering up at me over a pair of horn-rimmed glasses, he paused for a moment before saying gravely, 'Young man, you must remember that horses are only human.'

More importantly, my job also entailed going to the Scotch House pub each day for Gageby's lunch, generally a ham salad costing two shillings and sixpence. I've often wondered if he remembered those formative days after being told that I had won the Sports Writer of the Year Award for 1985.

On the road, the philosophy at the *Press* was to trust a reporter's coping skills, which explained my first assignment. Covering a race meeting was totally new to me, but at the tender age of 22, I became coursing correspondent of the *Irish Press*, which involved travelling to the Waterloo Cup, outside Liverpool.

Meanwhile, my office environment was very different to what might be experienced these days in a Dublin city workplace. An awful lot of drinking was done at the hostelries on Burgh Quay. Given the modest earnings of us foot soldiers, this led inevitably to much borrowing and lending and I relied heavily on the kindness of Mick Dunne, the paper's GAA correspondent. At a time when there was no problem in parking one's car on Burgh Quay, day or night, Mick used to drive to his home in Clontarf for lunch and there was always a lift for me to my home in Fairview.

In 1965, a national printers' strike led to the journalistic staff receiving a month's protective notice. Being an ambitious 24-year-old, I decided to accept the notice as severance and try my luck in London.

Within a few days, I was working for Hayter's Sports Agency in Shoe Lane, off Fleet Street. That was in June and it proved to be a remarkable experience. For six guineas per day, my knowledge of my craft was broadened extensively through covering mainly soccer and rugby union in the Greater London area. And as colleagues and I headed from our Shoe Lane office to the local pub for lunch each day, the owner, Reg Hayter, expressed surprise at how well-behaved I was where drink was concerned. I don't really know what he expected, but the remark contained an Irish inference.

My first assignment was being sent to Craven Cottage for an interview with Vic Buckingham, the Fulham FC manager, and I was left entirely to my own devices. Though I later discovered that Buckingham was to become acknowledged as one of Europe's leading coaches, especially when moving to Barcelona, he was in a decidedly playful mood when I met him, sitting in his office with his secretary on his knee.

In rugby, it wasn't unusual for me to do up to 13 reports on a Saturday match in the London area and I especially remember my first visit to London-Welsh. The post-match bar seemed fairly normal until, as if by magic, the place burst into song. This was no come-all-ye sing-along, but three-part male-voice harmony that made the hair stand on end on the back of my neck. Unforgettable.

When the strike back home was resolved, Hayter expected me to return to Dublin, but I had already decided to stay in London.

That was when Bill Hicks, sports editor of the *Daily Mail*, phoned and asked if Patrick O'Kelly would visit his office. This prompted quite a bit of laughter, except for the few members of staff who were aware of the name being a pseudonym bestowed on me by Norman Giller of the *Daily Express*, who clearly found it easier to pronounce than my given name. I suppose I could have insisted on being addressed correctly, but I decided not to become an awkward Irishman in a strange city.

Having explained all of this to Hicks, I observed an array of Irish newspapers on his desk. He wanted me to suggest a suitable candidate as the *Mail*'s sports representative in the Republic of Ireland.

It suddenly dawned on me that there was an attractive position on offer. 'Do you want the job?' asked the sports editor. 'Yes,' I replied. 'Then it's yours.' It was the simplest job appointment I would ever have, ending with both of us expressing our respective tastes in classical music.

Joining the *Mail* made a huge impression on me. Having just turned 25, I remember being delighted at the arrival by post of a first-class rail ticket to Manchester at my Holland Park apartment in London. And when I later disembarked the train, I was met in Manchester by a *Daily Mail* company car, a Humber Super Snipe, with a liveried driver who took me to the company's north of England headquarters in Blackfriars.

Our Dublin office was a lot more modest, suitable for four of us – news reporter, Don Turner, office secretary, Bea McMunn, and Dublin manager, Jos Brown. But the sense of opulence was maintained by regular visits from the company's leading British-based writers. Notable among these was Vincent Mulchrone, an award-winning feature writer who projected an appropriate image by drinking only snipes of champagne in Higgins, the local Upper Abbey Street hostelry.

He expressed a great affection for this country and was far too young when he died in 1977, at 54. Interestingly, he returned to the news in fascinating circumstances in 2022, when BBC news presenter Nick Robinson quoted Mulchrone's celebrated 'two rivers' metaphor without attribution.

Mulchrone had coined the phrase in a famous *Daily Mail* article in 1965 following the death of Winston Churchill. 'Two rivers run silently through London tonight and one is made of people,' he wrote, describing the former prime minister's lying-in-state at Westminster Hall for three days from 26 January. During a BBC Radio 4 Today programme in September 2022, Robinson described the queue to see the late Queen Elizabeth as a 'vast river of people'. 'London has not one but two rivers this morning,' he said.

For his part, Ian Wooldridge also liked to take trips to this country as part of a globe-trotting regime. He took in his stride such sharply contrasting activities as the 1,200-mile husky race in Alaska, a white-knuckle ride with the Red Arrows air-display team, a round of golf with the Australian prime minister (which he won) and three rounds in the ring (diplomatically lost) against former heavyweight boxer Idi Amin, the notorious prime minister of Uganda.

There was always a memorable quote from his writings, like when he observed in the wake of a wretched first-round 83 by Jack Nicklaus in the 1981 Open Championship at Royal St George's: 'The only equivalent plunge from genius I could think of was Ernest Hemingway's tragic loss of ability to write. Hemingway got up one morning and shot himself. Nicklaus got up the next morning and shot 66.'

When he died in March 2007, aged 75, he had been with the *Mail* for almost 50 years. And a measure of his remarkable appeal was that his passing was felt at a remove from Fleet Street as unlikely as a small village in Co. Limerick.

Bridget Gleeson-Healy, who lives in Ballingarry, near Adare, once had a celebrated golfing encounter with the *Daily Mail* scribe, in which I happened to have an involvement.

Like Mulchrone, Wooldridge would travel here in his enthusiastic pursuit of the unusual. So it was that I pointed him to Killarney in April 1975. There, in a level match, he had the nerve to pit his modest, 18-handicap skills against an 11-year-old schoolgirl, who stood 4ft 9 ¾ins and weighed less than five stone.

He later reported:

> Miss Gleeson (favourite author, Enid Blyton; favourite food, rice pudding; pet hate, long division) did not, as they say, mess about at it. She splashed out of a canyon-sized bunker at the 13th, stroked down the subsequent four-foot putt, extended one diminutive hand and offered falsetto condolences for having won our match 6 and 5. ...

> Between times, she had five single putts in thirteen holes, hit both par-five greens against the wind in four shots, struck her drives a consistent 135 yards, her three-woods an equally consistent 120 yards and strayed from the fairway only once. Off her 18-handicap, she finished three shots over regulation figures and that was wholly attributable to a sudden hailstorm which shrieked in off the Atlantic.

His delightful 1,200-word piece concluded:

> What I meanly never let on was that I'd played just about as well as I damned well can. It just never looked like being enough against a child I must rate as the finest 11-year-old player of any ball game I have ever seen.

Bridget, who went on to represent Ireland in 1980 and 1982, now plays only infrequently, because of back problems. But we both enjoyed a very happy reunion in Killarney GC in June 2023, when attending a special function in honour of Michael Guerin, winner of three successive South of Ireland titles in 1961, 1962 and 1963.

And naturally, her little escapade with Wooldridge was given a fresh airing.

There were other visits here by the celebrated scribe, but all travel to Ireland ended on 27 August 1979, when Lord Mountbatten was killed at Mullaghmore. As it happened, I had only been a short while gone from the *Mail* at the time, but I became aware of Wooldridge's anger and sorrow at the outrage. Much as he enjoyed his visits here, this was more than he could stomach as a proud Englishman.

I don't know if he stuck rigidly to that pledge, but I remember being interviewed on RTE by Marian Finucane, who found it difficult to understand Wooldridge's decision. As far as I can recall, I could readily empathise with him as somebody who had to make contact with British employers, even against the background of outrageous happenings during the Troubles.

Meanwhile, the return to my Fairview home with an enhanced salary and expenses made me very comfortable financially, which led to an undisciplined lifestyle culminating in serious abuse of alcohol.

The first warning sign was a run of car crashes in which, fortunately, the only injured party was me and my pride. And they were decent cars, including a Mark II Jaguar 3.8 automatic and a Citroen DS 21, the one with futuristic hydropneumatic suspension and a dramatically tapered front like a duck's beak.

On an icy road in the early hours of the morning, the Jaguar was wrapped around a lamppost on the North Strand, prompting the arrival of two Gardaí. Having surveyed the scene, one of them concluded, quite perceptively, 'I think he's done enough damage for one night.' The accuracy of that statement can be gauged from the fact that the car realised a modest £50 when towed away for scrap.

Through all of this, the *Mail* was remarkably tolerant, especially the Manchester-based Northern sports editor, Bryan Webster, who later became a dear friend. In fact, he and his wife accepted invitations to Dublin when Kathy and I got married in March 1970. Our daughter, Tara, was born twelve months later. There were visits to the Webster home outside Manchester where I shared Bryan's affection for the great operatic bass Owen Brannigan, who hailed from his part of England's north-east.

****

Despite all the good that was happening in my life, my drinking still caused my employer to administer warnings, verbal then written. Distressing low points included the Ireland rugby coach, Syd Millar, having to abandon a post-match press conference at Murrayfield because of my drunken interruptions.

This episode led to a stay in St Patrick's Psychiatric Hospital, after which I sought Millar out, who graciously accepted my apology. Later, I made a similar – if overdue – apology to rugby's Mike Gibson, who playfully responded: 'You didn't leave any marks that I'm aware of.'

Another shameful incident occurred during a rugby weekend in Paris, where I found myself at 5.00 in the morning on the Champs Elysees, the worse for wear and with no idea as to the hotel I was booked into. Racking my addled brain, I eventually figured out the colleague who was likely to have imparted such information to his wife: Tom Keogh of the *Daily Mirror*. So, oblivious to the fact that it was 4.00 a.m. in Dublin, I phoned Tom's wife, Mary, and asked her where Tom was staying. 'Hotel Solferino,' came the reply. Complimenting myself on being so wonderfully resourceful, I put the phone down, hailed a taxi and was in my hotel in a matter of minutes.

After inflicting considerable pain on myself, I eventually responded to the unstinting help of some extraordinary friends and left the glass down in June 1977. That was four months before Kathy had our second child, Mark.

At this stage, I suppose my general attitude could have been characterised as somewhat arrogant. Indeed, I saw myself as being remarkably gifted at what I did and the independence of operating effectively on my own and being answerable only to voices on the other end of a phone in Manchester wasn't ideal training. Circumstances, however, would force me to change.

This was a time when my copy was transmitted from Dublin to Manchester in two ways, either by teleprinter from the *Mail*'s Dublin office in Middle Abbey Street, or by telephone. In the 1970s a postal strike meant I had access to neither.

With a rugby piece for publication, I seemed to have no way of getting it to the *Mail*'s sports desk. Then I hit on an idea. Putting the typed copy in an envelope, I drove to Dublin Airport. There, I joined the queue for an Aer Lingus flight to Manchester.

Picking a young, business-type passenger, I decided he would be my courier. Handing him the envelope with a £5 note I asked him to take it to Manchester where he would leave it at the airport information desk. He would then phone the *Mail* (number supplied), who would have it collected. Remarkably, it worked perfectly and my copy duly appeared in print the following morning.

Meanwhile, successive winters of discontent in Britain eventually caught up with the *Mail*, which closed down its Irish operation in 1979, making me redundant. I now faced the challenge of seeking a job in an environment where a prospective employer might be generous enough to look beyond my general attitude and reputation.

Generously, Adhamhnan O'Sullivan, sports chief in the *Irish Press*, saw fit to offer me a job, which I regretfully declined. I had set my sights on Independent Newspapers, which I considered to be a more secure option long term.

In 1980, I had my first experience of serious journalism from beyond these shores. I was to report for the *Evening Herald* from the British Amateur Championship at Royal Porthcawl where a group of strong Irish challengers included Ronan Rafferty, Philip Walton, Pat Mulcare and Arthur Pierse. I always enjoyed watching Pierse, who was such a wonderful driver of the ball. I remember him telling me how his father, Gerry, a Tipperary dentist, was a great devotee of Ben Hogan, and that when Arthur was perfecting his skills as a teenager, his dentist father gave him Hogan's *Five Lessons: The Modern Fundamentals of Golf*, indicating that this was the only tuition book he would need on the game.

Gerry Pierse could never have envisaged his son learning so well. A generation later, Pádraig Harrington felt moved to remark:

> Arthur Pierse was unquestionably the best driver of a golf ball that ever played in a left-to-right wind. And it was just uncanny how straight he would hit the ball in that wind. It was like it was on a tightrope. A great swinger of the golf club, he was unusual in terms of players of his era in that he had an orthodox golf swing.
>
> His ability to swing club and strike the golf ball was as good as any pro's was or is. Arthur had a strong presence on the golf course too. You worried about playing Arthur Pierse; you didn't want to give him the upper hand.

I was seriously excited to report for the *Herald* on the progress of certain Irish players at Porthcawl. The week began with Rafferty gaining a first-round win over Michael Bonallack, five times a winner of the title, who was then a veteran of 45. 'This lad is amazing,' he said of Rafferty. 'He plays golf like a computer.' Then there was a particular visit to the practice ground where Walton was trading shots with the local favourite, Philip Parkin. Apparently, they were trying to establish who could achieve the greater distance out of a sand wedge and Walton eventually edged clear with an effort of 150 yards, to which an experienced Scottish player remarked acidly: 'Who wants to hit a sand wedge 150 yards?'

The stories kept flowing for me with Rafferty reaching the quarter-finals and then Pierse going on to the semis, where he faced the eventual winner, Duncan Evans of Wales, a 6ft 5ins giant of a player.

I remember hearing whispers at the time about Evans, even from Welsh officials, who needed to be watched like a hawk, especially when he happened to go into the rough. Which probably explained why Pierse asked me to keep an eye on him when I followed their semi-final clash. As it happened, he beat Pierse by 2 and 1 and went on to beat the South African David Suddards by 4 and 3 in the 36-hole final, played in wretched conditions.

From an Irish perspective, there was a wonderful warmth to the week, not least because a Dubliner, Bob Davitt, happened to be captain of the host club. And with an annexe built behind his house, he gave accommodation for the week to a few of the Irish contestants, Pierse included.

Pierse went on to win the Senior British Amateur in 2007 as a delayed compensation for his disappointment at Porthcawl. In fact, he still plays the game off a scratch handicap, having celebrated his 73rd birthday in April 2024.

Meanwhile, as a local hero and the first Welsh player to win the Amateur, Evans received the BBC Wales Sports Personality of the Year award and went on to win the Welsh Amateur Strokeplay Championship in 1981. Then he earned a place in the Walker Cup side which played at Cypress Point that year, when his last match was a halved singles against Corey Pavin. He proceeded to turn professional but was later banned for cheating.

More seriously, in 2003 Evans was jailed for three years after being found guilty of money-laundering by Birmingham Crown Court. He was later returned to jail in 2009 for his involvement in a £20 million tax fraud. Pierse retains vivid memories of his match with Evans, not least for the fact that Porthcawl was his first appearance in the British Amateur and his caddie in the semi-finals happened to be an Irish colleague, Pat Mulcare, who was beaten in an earlier round.

Later that summer, the *Independent* sent me to Muirfield, again to work for the *Herald* for the Open Championship where I grabbed the opportunity to interview the American Jay Sigel, who was emerging as a serious amateur at the time. From there I went on to Dusseldorf for the *Independent* to cover the European Junior Team Championship, which Ireland won. As it happened, Gerry Noone, Sports Editor of the *Irish Times*, covered both these events because Edmund van Esbeck was on tour with the Irish rugby team in Australia. At the end of the year, Noone offered me the role of golf correspondent in the *Times* and I moved across the Liffey in March 1981.

Later that year, my first US trip was to California, to cover the 1981 Walker Cup at Cypress Point. We're talking about a time when the amateur was king and Ireland had unquestioned golfing royalty in teenagers, Rafferty and Walton.

A whole new world had opened up for me, even at a difficult time for business in this country. I must admit, however, that trips away were often faced with mixed feelings. Strange hotels in strange environments could be lonely places. Still, I found myself totally absorbed in what I was doing, while the sociability of golfers and golf officials made for a lifestyle that gradually grew on me.

Indeed the golf writer's life made me the envy of my friends, especially when it came to the big occasions.

I especially remember that Walker Cup trip for the splendid story it delivered on the opening day. In the top foursomes, visiting captain, Rodney Foster, did something that Joe Carr wasn't prepared to gamble on as captain of Ireland: he paired Rafferty and Walton at number one against Jay Sigel and Hal Sutton, arguably the world's best amateurs at that time.

It seemed a disastrous decision when the Irish teenagers lost the first three holes. With their prospects written off, however, Rafferty and Walton staged a remarkable recovery to be two up after fourteen. Then they completed the most extraordinary finish imaginable.

When Rafferty missed the green at the short 15th, Walton chipped in for a winning birdie. Then, at the famous par-three 16th with its elbow over the Pacific, the exploits were reversed. This time Rafferty chipped in from the dreaded ice plant for another winning birdie and a stunning 4 and 2 victory.

Even with an eight-hour time lag, the outcome should have allowed me to comfortably make my first edition back in Dublin, but it was a close-run thing. This, remember, was a time before laptops, when my typewritten copy was phoned to Dublin where a copy-taker, armed with a desktop typewriter and a roll of paper, would type what I dictated. It would later be typed for a third time by a linotype operator before eventually seeing print.

On this particular occasion, I was halfway through dictation when the voice on the other end piped up: 'Well, that's me done. I've got to catch my bus.' My protests about being on the far side of the US were to no avail. Eventually, one of the sub-editors took over and finished the job.

The 1980s proved to be a lavishly productive period for Irish team golf. It ended with a first away Walker Cup triumph in Atlanta where Eoghan O'Connell and Garth McGimpsey were involved. In between, Mary McKenna, Claire Dowling and Lillian Behan featured in the first Curtis Cup triumph across the pond. Then there was the memorable 1988 Dunhill Cup victory by Des Smyth, Eamonn Darcy and Rafferty at St Andrews, a year after Darcy had played a key role in the historic Ryder Cup breakthrough at Muirfield Village.

By this stage, our country seemed to be becoming more conscious of its European identity, which led to major golf championships being covered in the US, including the Masters. My first such trip in 1989, when Nick Faldo won the first of two successive green jackets, remains memorable, however, for an entirely different reason.

It marked the last occasion the Masters media were accommodated in a corrugated Nissen hut, housing a dense pall of cigarette smoke and the incessant clatter of typewriters, to which my 'Brother' contributed. Within a few years, these factors were to undergo the greatest transformation of my working career. Smoking became increasingly unacceptable while the change to new technology, which I had been observing from British and Irish colleagues during the 1980s, came late to the *Times*.

Teething problems, however, seemed common to most outlets and instead of the clatter of typewriters, we now had agonised outbursts from pressurised scribes whose copy had somehow disappeared into the ether. I later learned that newspapers used their sports writers as pioneers in this revolutionary process.

My first Open Championship with a laptop was at Muirfield in 1992, and the week didn't start well. On the Tuesday, I had two hours of failed attempts at transmitting my copy electronically. In the process, I missed Joe Carr's address at the annual Association of Golf Writers' dinner as captain of the Royal and Ancient.

But happily, there would be smoother times ahead.

2

Precious Guidance from Gifted Old Hands

The process of writing fascinated me. Not because I considered myself any good at it but curiously, I linked it to my love of mathematical subjects: I was always especially strong in maths, and the importance of structure in putting a piece of writing together held its greatest appeal.

As a trainee in the *Irish Press*, I was fortunate to have some old hands on the sub-editors' desk who took a particular interest in my work. When handling my copy, they would call me aside and indicate how the point of the piece could work far better with a slightly different approach.

Two men who were especially helpful in this regard were David Guiney, a one-time star shot-putter in his own right who went on to work for the *Sunday Mirror*, and Frank van Esbeck, brother of Ned, who would become the highly regarded rugby correspondent of the *Irish Times*.

Apart from suggesting changes in structure, they would also point out corrections like the use of an 's' in the verb 'to practise', as opposed to the 'c' in the noun, 'practice'. Then there were simple instructions, such as 'unique' being an absolute; in other words, there could be no such thing as degrees of uniqueness. Also, 'presently' refers to the future.

This may be viewed as fairly obvious knowledge for a national journalist, but I found it to be extremely helpful. And I've no doubt that it improved my basic writing skills. On this point, my Fleet Street experience with Hayter's Agency had been a considerable boost.

Having arrived there as a relatively raw 24-year-old whose basic knowledge of written English did not extend beyond the Leaving Certificate, I was surprised at how highly regarded I became among English colleagues of similar age.

For instance, I had only been there a few weeks when I was called aside for a particular assignment. The agency had a working relationship with a publisher named Bagenal Harvey, whose ancestors could be traced back to the insurgent of the same name from the 1798 Rising. He had got a young journalist, no longer with the company, to write a book on Jimmy Greaves, and wasn't especially pleased with the outcome. The upshot was that as part of my daily duties, I was to 'knock this thing into shape.' In other words, I was to adjust it into readable English. Which I did, apparently to their satisfaction.

While working for the *Irish Times*, it wasn't unusual to have correspondence about my writing. On reflection, there were quite a few occasions when such comments dealt with grammatical soundness rather than style of writing. And I came to accept this as a treasured compliment.

So I was greatly gratified to receive a letter on 21 April 1989, on my return to the office after my first experience of the Masters at Augusta National. Handwritten by Conor Brady, editor of the *Irish Times*, it read: 'Dear Dermot, Just a brief note to say how well-received were your US reports. I've had a lot of enthusiastic comments from golfer/readers! So you're appreciated!! Yours ...'

Against this background, it was especially pleasing and indeed surprising to receive a letter on 12 September 1996 from Tom Mullins, Lecturer in Education from the Department of Education at University College Cork. He wrote:

As you may be aware, a committee of the National Council for Curriculum and Assessment has been revising the Leaving Certificate English Syllabus for some time and its work is now nearing completion. Besides drafting a new syllabus, the responsibility of this committee is to produce a comprehensive set of Teacher Guidelines on the teaching of language to facilitate the implementation of the revised syllabus.

The preparation of the Teacher Guidelines is a major project and the Department of Education, University College, Cork has been commissioned to research and produce the guidelines. It is in my capacity as Director of this project that I am now writing to you ...

In specific terms, he requested a piece of between 500 and 1,000 words on the topic 'Why I write' or 'My approach to writing' and 'A short commentary on an exemplar of your work.'

This is how I replied:

Firstly, let me make it clear that I consider myself to be a craftsman rather than a creative writer. In other words, I'm someone who applied himself to the actual business of writing, without having had any great talent in that direction.

In that context, the most important tools I took with me from school – honours English and a pass in Latin in the Leaving Certificate – were an ability to spell and a solid grounding in grammar. I later discovered that spelling was not all that important if one had ready access to a dictionary.

While on this point, it may be appropriate to add that I rely heavily on a dictionary and would never approach a serious piece of writing without one. Strangely, my children find this difficult to understand, despite their obvious problems with spelling!

I found myself in journalism largely by accident but was extremely fortunate to join the Irish Press *in 1958. It happened that at the time, the journalistic hierarchy in the* Press *thought it would be a good idea to take lads like me directly from school and teach them journalism from square one: the accepted route into a national newspaper was through the provincial press.*

Douglas Gageby, who would later edit the Irish Times, *was then editor of the* Evening Press *and he took me under his wing. This meant that I was encouraged to dabble in some modest freelancing for one of the three newspapers in the group, while actually working as a glorified messenger boy.*

I started out doing small reports of Dublin inter-club GAA matches. One paragraph (about 45 words) to start with, followed by two paragraphs and, eventually, three- or four-paragraph pieces. With such relatively few words in which to tell my story, I found I had to think a piece through very carefully before committing anything to paper. The process also made me conscious of picking out the most newsworthy elements in a match.

Eighteen months later, I was appointed to the staff as a junior sports reporter. Now I could write seriously on a daily basis, through match reports at the weekends and shortish news items on weekdays. This was when I first became aware of the reporter's nemesis: the sub-editor.

As with all jobs, there were good sub-editors and some dreadfully infuriating ones. I was fortunate in that much of my early work was handled by one or two enlightened practitioners who invariably changed it for the better. And I studied those changes to see where I had gone wrong. Usually, it was in a simple matter of grammar or repetition or a lack of proper emphasis on the nub of the story.

By this stage, I had come to appreciate some of the key ingredients of newspaper writing. The most important one was to grab the reader's attention and then try to hold it until the final full point. As with the early one-paragraph pieces, I became keenly aware of the importance of thinking things through.

If I were to hold a reader's interest, I realised that I would have to spread attention-grabbing facts through the piece, while saving an appropriate tailpiece for the end. So, effectively, the story had to have a top, middle and end.

I also learned the importance of how it was written. For instance, long sentences – of more than 40 words – were to be avoided. And where unavoidable, they should always be followed by a short sentence, otherwise the overworked reader would soon lose interest.

Then there was the challenge of achieving a flow to the writing. When great composers such as Mozart, Handel or Beethoven worked on a piece of music, they first established a basic melody. Later, so-called grace notes were added with a view to achieving a sense of rhythm to the musical line. These grace notes were superfluous to the melody but essential to the listening ear.

I believe that one should adopt a similar approach to writing. Adjectives, adverbs and conjunctions, superfluous to the actual meaning of a sentence, can be included purely for the purposes of rhythm, bearing in mind that the objective must always be to facilitate the reader.

This extract from a piece about Muhammad Ali [by Patrick Collins in the Mail on Sunday*] at the 1996 Olympics is a good example: 'The sporting summer has run its crowded course and its images scurry by like the leaves of autumn, yet that single image remains as sharp and as poignant as it did on a July evening in Dixie.' It would be possible to cut that sentence in half and still retain the meaning, but at what cost to its readability?*

Having graduated to more lengthy pieces, sometimes as long as 2,000 words for a feature article, I found the overall planning of the piece to be absolutely critical towards its success. What do I want to say? How do I plan to say it? Am I absolutely clear about the subject matter before I write the first line? Do I know how the piece is going to end, before I start?

Then, when I start, do I construct the opening paragraph in such a manner as to heighten the reader's interest, even curiosity? Am I conscious of having little nuggets on hand, to be introduced at those stages when the story might be in danger of flagging? Above all, I must remember never to underestimate the intelligence of my reader. Patronising prose is extremely difficult to stomach.

There have been countless times, when facing tight deadlines, that I have had to cope with the horror of a totally blank mind. In these circumstances, I have learned to write something, anything, simply to get the process started. These words of desperation will probably undergo radical change before the piece is completed but they have served their purpose of unblocking the mind.

In this context, the word processor has been a tremendous boon to writers of all categories, largely for the scope it affords to fiddle around with phrases. Writing by hand is similarly adaptable, compared with the strictures imposed by the typewritten sheet and the bottle of Tipp-Ex.

Finally, I rarely enjoy the actual process of writing, which can be tedious and tiring, depending on one's mood. But when finished, a well-written piece is immensely satisfying. Indeed, more often than not, it's the hope of ultimately delivering a well-crafted story, that gives one the enthusiasm to make a start.

My own work

When David Graham was sixteen, he announced to his father that he would like to drop out of school to take up a career as a professional golfer. His father warned, 'If you do, I'll never talk to you again.' He held to his threat: they never exchanged another word.

Years later, when the older Graham died, it was months before his son heard about it. 'Most definitely it made me more determined,' he said, while contemplating his 50th birthday next Thursday. 'I went on a personal mission to prove to him and some others that I could make it in golf.'

After Graham captured the US Open at Merion in 1981, some wicked wag suggested that he had eventually become as good as he thought he was. Now, though inactive for five years, he is set to prove himself all over again on the US Seniors' Tour, starting in the BellSouth Senior Classic in Nashville next Friday.

Irish Open enthusiasts will remember Graham's appearance at Portmarnock in 1977 when he shot rounds of 75 and 76 to miss the cut. And they will recall that in 1981, two months after winning the US Open, he returned to Portmarnock, this time playing all four rounds for an aggregate of 284 and eleventh place behind Sam Torrance. 'I felt I owed it to the sponsors,' he said at the time.

Graham has always been his own man. Which explains why, on being asked as a long-time friend of Jack Nicklaus what he thought of Muirfield Village, he replied: 'It looks like they copied a bunch of holes from other courses.'

Now, with sadness in his voice, he says: 'That comment was devastating to my relationship with Jack.' But typically, there was no apology. Graham, beaten 69–74 by Ronan Rafferty in the final of the 1988 Dunhill Cup, remains one of a kind.

****

That piece was written by me in the summer of 1995 for my 'Golfing Log', which appeared in the sports pages of the Irish Times *on Saturdays. I recall being pressurised for space at the time, so it had to be tightly written, which, at 315 words, it is. Looking back on it now, the piece pleases me because:*

1. *The writing is clear and simple.*
2. *Despite its relative shortness, there is a wealth of information about Graham's career.*
3. *The anecdotes about his father and Jack Nicklaus provide valuable insights into the make-up of a complex man who has always been unpopular with his peers.*

Its topicality at the time lay in the fact that Graham was going to celebrate his 50th birthday the following week, which would make him eligible for competition on the US Seniors' Tour a day later. But, through research on the Irish Open and the Dunhill Cup, I was able to give the piece an Irish relevance.

Those cynics who would dismiss sports writing as semi-literate, cliche-ridden hyperbole should consider the simple beauty of these opening four paragraphs by Patrick Collins on 8 October of 1996.

> *On a sultry night in Georgia, he came shuffling from the side of the stage, blinking in mild surprise as the arc lights tracked him down.*
>
> *He seemed almost timid, a stranger to celebrity. But we knew better.*
>
> *Muhammad Ali peered out at the world with the shadow of a smile flickering across his face, as if recalling some private joke. His left arm was shaking with uncontrolled urgency. His right arm was holding high a torch.*
>
> *The audience rose, united in astonishment, as the greatest athlete of the century stood before them. A roar came rumbling across the stadium, wavering for a few seconds as Ali fumbled with the fuse, then rising once more in full-throated relief as the Olympic flame burst into life.*

That is what I sent to the good lecturer. And now, almost 30 years on, there is little I would change, except perhaps to emphasise the benefit of brevity. In my view, long sentences have become something of a plague in newspaper writing. As a consequence, I find myself almost worn out by the time I've waded through the first four or five paragraphs of a piece.

In heading towards retirement at the end of 2023, I was struck by the significant impact on my working life of what we initially described as new technology, more than 30 years ago. As I have indicated, for the pressurised scribe, the laptop offered the opportunity to fiddle around with phrases, compared with the strictures imposed by a typewritten sheet.

But there then emerged the challenge of composing a piece without the comfort of a cigarette. For me, the fag's death knell was sounded during the 1992 US Open at Pebble Beach, where a state trooper appeared beside my desk in the media centre and ordered: 'Put that out.' When I protested that the US Golf Association, organisers of the championship, had no problem with my smoking, he snapped: 'But the State of California does.'

Indeed, a measure of how much my life had become tied to golf can be gleaned from experiences during The Open at Royal Lytham in July 1996. The first incident happened when I was heading on foot from the media centre to my hotel nearby, over a hump-backed bridge.

Laden with various pieces of equipment, I suddenly felt a tightening across my chest. The pressure eased when I stopped, but returned when I began walking again.

At the end of August, I underwent heart bypass surgery in the Blackrock Clinic under the gifted hands of Maurice Neligan. It wouldn't be an exaggeration to suggest that his timely intervention effectively mapped out the remainder of my life, until this day.

There were other, positive aspects to this particular Lytham weekend. It marked the delivery of a wonderful performance by Paul McGinley; it was also when I happened to wear the blazer of the host club captain, Dr Steven Reid, to lunch. And it was when I first met Steve Stricker and his wife.

On the Sunday, I found myself donning a shirt, tie and Lytham blazer belonging to Dr Reid, so I could join him and other guests for lunch in the clubhouse.

His fine book, *Get to the Point*, was an unashamed labour of love about Co. Sligo GC. Sensing my reluctance to sacrifice a few hours around lunchtime on the final day of an Open Championship, he insisted: 'Just think of it, you will have worn the blazer I'll be wearing when I present the trophy to the winner later today.' Which he did, to Tom Lehman.

McGinley sent Irish hearts aflutter when, on the second day, he holed in one on the short ninth en route to a sparkling 65, equalling the course record set by Christy O'Connor Snr, among others.

McGinley's exploit later prompted some serious reflection by Dr Reid about the most punishing bunkers in championship golf. And while those on the last four holes inflicted cruel torment on Adam Scott in his failed challenge at the 2012 Open, those on the short ninth have proven to be the most vicious of them all.

That was the scene of Lytham's current record holder for bunker bother, whose identity we will protect, other than that he played off eleven.

Determined to avoid a 'no return' in a club competition, he battled bravely, if not very fruitfully, until the fateful ninth. There, where McGinley served his memorable ace, the hapless member hit a reasonable tee shot and completed the hole with two putts. In between, however, he played no fewer than 27 strokes and incurred a one-stroke penalty for a total of 31 on the hole.

Most of the shots were played in four of the nine bunkers encircling the green. And I'm informed the most unkind cut was that having escaped successfully with his seventeenth stroke, his ball landed on a bare, sandy lie from where he proceeded to skull it back into the sand. He eventually signed a card for a wretched score of 135.

But to Stricker: I met him and his wife Nicki on the Tuesday of Open week, which also happened to be 17 July, the eve of their third wedding anniversary. It was also his Open debut and, as had been the case when he captured the Western Open in Chicago ten days previously, Nicki was caddying for him. Though Stricker was tied 22nd at Lytham, Tom Watson was moved to remark: 'He has the whole package. He reminds me of how I was at that stage of my career.'

Meanwhile, Stricker and Nicki's affection for each other was obvious. It was also enduring, as we saw in her presence at Whistling Straits in September 2021 when he captained the US to a runaway Ryder Cup triumph over a European line-up led by Pádraig Harrington. Still, it had taken courage to have her as his caddie back at Lytham. As he said at the time: 'People remarked that I would have a tough time winning with her on my bag, but I'm glad she's with me all the time. Apart from being my wife, she happens to be my best friend.'

For her part, she saw it as making the best of 'the freedom to be together.' But the former two-handicapper added: 'Obviously that would change if we happen to have a family.' Two years later, in 1998, shortly after her husband was runner-up to Vijay Singh in the US PGA Championship at Sahalee, Washington, she gave birth to a baby daughter, Bobbi Maria. They had another daughter, Isabella Nicole (Issy) in October 2006.

Clearly, those who criticised their golfing partnership conveniently ignored any link between the serious decline in his tournament fortunes over the following two years and the fact that Nicki happened to be at home looking after their first-born. However, Stricker's torment was well documented in the wake of a marvellous $1 million victory in the 2001 Accenture Matchplay Championship.

Meanwhile, during the two months of my recovery from heart bypass surgery, I caught up on some reading, including a book of golf quotes from a friend in the US. In it was this beauty from the mercurial American golfer Tommy Bolt, expressing his outrage at the media: 'Only half the lies you bastards told about me are true,' he declared. You will gather that I had become suitably thick-skinned by then.

This period of profound change coincided with the decline of the great Seve, which was a source of immense sorrow to his countless fans, myself included. I can still picture the scene behind the eighteenth green at Oak Hill in the aftermath of the 1995 Ryder Cup, where Philip Walton secured a glorious winning point sometime after Ballesteros had struggled heroically in losing to Lehman.

'You must be very proud of Philip,' Seve said to me while holding a magnum of champagne. Whereupon Walton interjected: 'There's nothing wrong with your swing, Seve. Your only problem is lack of confidence.'

It turned out that Seve's problems were indeed between his ears, though in the form of an incipient brain tumour, which would ultimately kill him sixteen years later. 'Don't worry about my swing,' he instructed Walton. 'Here, have a drink.'

At a time when equality in golf had become a very active and contentious issue in the game here, I remember pointing out that Ireland wasn't alone in grappling with this issue. I referred to the story of Wirral Ladies, which was founded in 1894 by the all-male preserve of Royal Liverpool GC five miles away, for the benefit of their womenfolk. For economic reasons, they took in men as associate members before admitting them as full members in 1952 for a subscription costing, significantly, £1 less than women's.

Echoing the Irish scene, however, the law intervened in the mid-1990s when the Licensing Officer for the Wirral District threatened not to renew their liquor licence unless they revised their treatment of men. Which eventually they did.

It seems that the timespan of seven years has been critical in my working life, like spending seven years with the *Irish Press*, fourteen years with the *Daily Mail*, then twenty-one years with the *Irish Times* up to 2002. So it was perhaps predictable that I began to get itchy feet, especially when a redundancy scheme was brought in.

By that stage, technology had tortured me for the last time. With an eight-hour time gap, Sunday's report on the 2000 US Open at Pebble Beach remained challenging, even with Tiger Woods coasting to victory by a staggering fifteen strokes. In the event, I had been issued with a change of laptop, with the delete button in a position strange to me.

Though I managed to get my first-edition story away on time, my piece for the city edition disappeared into the ether. I had accidentally hit the delete button. Panic! 1,200 words gone. I phoned the desk in Dublin. Could they indulge me in my hour of need by stretching my deadline? Starting from scratch, I eventually got the job done in probably the most pressurised circumstances of my career.

When the publication of my final 'Golfing Log' in May 2002 indicated my imminent departure from the *Times*, I received a phone call from Adhamhnan O'Sullivan.

This was the long-time friend who, in 1979, had kindly offered me a reporter's job in the *Press*. Back then, I regretfully declined but when we met for lunch on this occasion, my mood was very different. Now Sports Editor of the *Sunday Independent*, he offered me a job as a golf columnist and I gratefully accepted.

Little did I realise I was about to experience this country's most exciting period of competitive golf. The build-up to the 2006 Ryder Cup at The K Club was already in full swing and by way of confirming Ireland's stature in the world game, we had El Tigre capturing the 2002

American Express Championship with rounds of 65, 65, 67 and 66 at Mount Juliet.

By this stage, we could tell that Ireland's leading professionals were thinking differently. Following a time when they simply didn't believe themselves capable of taking on and beating the best at the highest level, Pádraig Harrington and Darren Clarke were projecting an image of serious self-confidence.

It's not difficult to revive memories of 2007 at Carnoustie where the intrusive eye of the television camera picked up every wince and wobble of Harrington negotiating the fateful 72nd hole. We witnessed the deeply disturbing spectacle of a decent, dignified man being stripped bare before Carnoustie and the world.

It was the price he had to pay in pursuit of the 136th Open Championship.

Typically, he admitted afterwards: 'I think far too much for my own good. Nothing in golf has ever come easy to me. I've always taken the difficult route.' Which is probably why we took such delight in the spectacular ease of his Open triumph at Royal Birkdale twelve months later. And for me, the best of them all was his PGA Championship win at Oakland Hills, the following month.

In the process, Harrington created what Bob Rotella described as a powerful contagion, which was to inspire Graeme McDowell, Clarke and most recently, Shane Lowry to Major success. In between, Rory McIlroy outdid them all with four Majors, but it seemed this was the very least he would deliver by way of a very special talent.

I had the good fortune to witness all these successes while attending a total of 105 Majors, along with Paul McGinley's hugely impressive Ryder Cup-winning captaincy in 2014.

Meanwhile, there has been a special joy in seeing childhood skills come to glorious fruition, such as those of 11-year-old Leona Maguire in Clarke's Foundation at Moyvalley where, after chipping from off the 16th green to within two feet of the flag, the organiser instructed his diminutive charge: 'Get inside that if you can.'

This brought the response of an eight-iron running shot of 30 feet for a holed-out birdie on the toughest hole on the course.

When I was set to leave the *Irish Times* in 2002, colleagues in the Association of Golf Writers presented me with a signed photograph of Jack Nicklaus on the Swilcan Bridge at St Andrews. On it the great man wrote: 'To Dermot. It's been a great run for both of us.'

As it happened, it was to become a long goodbye for us. After bidding farewell to the US Open at Pebble Beach in 2000, it felt as though Nicklaus had also played his last Open at St Andrews a few weeks later. But the irresistible appeal of the Old Course brought him back for what seemed certain to be a last hurrah.

That was the 2005 Open Championship when his bag was carried by his son, Steve. Meanwhile, the Royal Bank of Scotland took the extraordinary step of placing the great man's likeness on a five-pound note, to mark the occasion. A unique print of the Road Hole, measuring 76cm by 135cm, was also produced to commemorate his final bow.

'I'm kind of a sentimentalist, I suppose, but it was the same course when I played there in May [2005],' he said. 'You'd expect it to be soft, but it was as hard as a rock. And I thought of all the people who played there and how it's still a competitive challenge after all the years.'

He didn't finish on the Sunday of the Open Championship, as he would have wished. Still, on a pleasant Friday afternoon, the widest fairway in golf was surrounded by thousands of adoring fans as Nicklaus bade a final farewell. And he did it in appropriate style with a closing birdie before walking off to embraces from his loving family.

Two days later, Tiger Woods would join Nicklaus as the only two players in the post-war era to have won two Open titles over the Old Course. T prompted me to ask Peter Thomson if he had felt any sympathy for Doug Sanders on the occasion of his crushing loss to Nicklaus at St Andrews in 1970. 'I think it would have been inappropriate if Sanders had won, because the championship was set up to produce the best winner,' said Thomson, who never shared a tee with Nicklaus in the Open. 'And Nicklaus was the best.'

While other tributes flowed freely, McGinley recalled having dinner with Nicklaus, his son Gary and Roddy Carr in Spain some years previously, when he asked Nicklaus how confident he was when at his best.

Pausing to give the matter some thought, he turned to the eager Dubliner and said: 'It's like this. On the morning of a tournament I would go to the practice ground and I'd look up and down the line of players. And I knew I was better than every single player on that range. But I also knew that each one of those players knew I was better than them.' 'That,' said McGinley, 'summed up his remarkable sense of superiority, even though he never came across as an arrogant person. Self-belief was the key.'

3

From Family Warmth in Ringaskiddy to Tragedy in Alaska

On a wild, wind-blown weekend in April 2024, the notion took me to head for Ringaskiddy on the west side of Cork City. I had been thinking of James McCarthy, who had talked lovingly of his birthplace when we met many miles from home. Now seemed like a good time to wrap up his story, which contained all the elements of a thrilling adventure yarn.

Intending to sort out some loose ends, I contacted Angela Foot, who seemed to manage everything at Raffeen Creek, the charming nine-hole stretch where McCarthy once plied his craft. Relatively new to the Cork golf scene, it was founded in 1988 to a typically imaginative design by Eddie Hackett, with its treacherous eighth and ninth holes over water – 'It's what God put there, you see.'

I had my first shock when attempting to establish a contact number for McCarthy. In an exchange of e-mails, Angela referred to the 'late' James McCarthy, while giving me a mobile number for a Richie O'Flaherty, the husband of James's sister, Trina. When I made the call, Trina could not have been more cooperative. Having processed the news of James being dead, I was quite prepared to head back to Dublin without further ado, but she wouldn't hear of it. 'The story you wrote about James is framed and hanging on the kitchen wall in my parents' home,' she said. 'They would love to meet you.'

So it was that my wife, Kathy, and I planned an overnight stay while Trina insisted that she would call for us at our hotel at 10.30 the following morning. She would be our guide to Ringaskiddy.

Back in November 2005, James McCarthy had reluctantly concluded that he would have to call an end to a two-year flirtation with professional golf. So it was that, with his dog Murphy by his side, he left the bright lights of Las Vegas and headed for decidedly chillier climes to resume a hazardous life, deep-sea fishing in Kodiak, Alaska.

The mini golf tours had been good, but he had dreamed of grander things. There had been two failed attempts at local qualifying for the US Open, but with a third apparently out of the question, everything changed. Following a phone call from a former tournament colleague, he found himself bound for Oakmont, Pennsylvania, one of America's most iconic golfing venues. There, he would live his US Open dream walking inside the ropes, though instead of hitting shots, he would be carrying a bag of them as a caddie for an American dreamer, Michael Berg. For McCarthy, memories of teenage golf at Raffeen Creek might well have been from another world.

'I remember that drive from Vegas,' he mused, as we talked under a burning sun on the practice ground at Oakmont. 'I covered the 3,700 miles to Anchorage in less than four days, in a Toyota Corolla.' Sensing my disbelief, he smiled and went on: 'I've a heavy foot. Up the Alaska-Canadian highway in the middle of winter. No cops. Drop the hammer as fast as you can go. At one point I was driving in 10 inches of snow and if I'd stopped I'd have frozen. So I kept trucking.'

On arrival in Kodiak, he went fishing again with his brother Peter. And while we talked, I soon understood how his player, Berg, had been attracted to McCarthy's fun-loving, adventurous nature, as in the name of his dog: 'I called him Murphy because he's black with a white head, just like a pint of stout.'

With sunglasses and a neatly groomed goatee, James was a perfect model of the modern caddie – both in golf and fishing. 'For one of them you put on nice clothes; for the other you're covered in you know what,' said the Corkman with a thin smile. His native accent was still there, though softened appreciably by an American overlay.

'My home in Cork was where the ferries are,' he went on. 'And though I played a little golf, fishing was my thing. At 16, I went to the fishing school in Greencastle, Co. Donegal and a year later, in May 1994, I was off to Alaska to join my brothers.' John, the eldest, was running a boat in Kodiak.

There were three fishing McCarthys in Alaska: Peter, James and John. John decided to emigrate to America, ended up in San Francisco and became involved in fishing there. About two years later, he heard that the serious money was to be made in Alaska. So that's where all three of them headed.

'Just like the apostles,' James remarked with a smile. When asked if their work resembled the TV series *Deadliest Catch* about Alaskan crab fishermen in the Bering Sea, he replied:

> Yeah, we're pretty close to that stuff, except our boats are half the size. It's tough, especially in winter. Freezing. Bleak.
>
> If we get days we can fish, we go. Minus-10 with a wind-chill sometimes bringing it down another 15. It's really tough on the women. At least we men can go out to work, but they're stuck back in the house, on their own.
>
> But being a loner doesn't bother me. It's always been my way. Anything I've ever done, I've done it alone. And even for three guys on a 58-foot boat, you can still get away from each other. When two guys are sleeping, the other is watching the wheel.

Kodiak Island is located in the Gulf of Alaska, 250 miles south of Anchorage. Interestingly, it is known as Alaska's Emerald Isle, where

Kodiak City has a population of 6,273. As a break from fishing, McCarthy turned to golf on public courses in the area and improved to such a degree as to gain a US Golf Association handicap of two. For three years he saved money for a grand plan and late in 2002, the time had come to execute that plan.

> After eight years, I had got tired of fishing and moved to Vegas where club jobs at Rhodes Ranch and later Dragon Ridge gave me free golf while allowing me work on my game. By the start of 2004 I felt I was ready. So I turned pro.
>
> This led me into mini-tours covering North and South Dakota, Minnesota and Iowa. For an entry fee of $400, we played for up to $10,000 in three-day tournaments while first prize in a four-day event could be $20,000. I met Mike Berg in the second tournament of the year. There was a group of eight of us including a few Canadians, some Americans and me, the lone Paddy. We became friends; roomed together and had fun.

Back in Kodiak, his perspectives changed once more. Tired of working for other people, he got involved in his brother Peter's purchase of a $300,000 boat in June 2006. 'At 58 foot by 19 foot wide, it's the smallest trawler in the Kodiak fleet,' he said. 'We painted her bright yellow, so she'd get noticed.' All the while during idle hours at sea, he kept in touch by mobile phone with his friends from the Dakotas Tour.

In early June 2007, McCarthy was on the second tee of the Bear Valley course in Kodiak when Berg called and asked if he'd caddie for him at Oakmont. Without a second thought, he booked a flight to Anchorage that night. The next morning, he flew to Minneapolis, rented a car and drove to Berg's home.

On the following Wednesday, the final practice day at Oakmont, McCarthy and Berg talked with boyish optimism about the challenge ahead: a brutally difficult examination, especially on greens where Stimpmeter speeds of 14 weren't unusual. Tougher than anything either of them had known. As Berg said: 'I don't know how you can prepare for something like this, except by going to Augusta National. And I haven't been able to get there yet.'

On Thursday morning, the big test was at hand. In the event, Berg struggled to a round of 81 which contained 35 putts, two double-bogeys and seven bogeys. 'It was a lot, lot tougher than we expected,' McCarthy admitted. 'Mike was nervous and he wasn't helped by the wind. You couldn't tell which way it was blowing. But there's always tomorrow.'

Friday brought an admirable recovery, though it wasn't quite good enough to ensure survival in an event in which Argentina's Angel Cabrera won with rounds of 69, 71, 76 and 69 for an aggregate of 285. After their second round of 75 for 16 over par, the pals from the Dakotas Tour left the scene, justifiably proud of their effort.

'It seems a pity to have to part with this,' said McCarthy of the luxurious, top-of-the-range Lexus 460 which was at their disposal for the week. Still, there would be some wonderful memories for the dark winter nights in Kodiak. He had made it to the US Open not knowing that another, potentially life-changing experience was lying in wait for him down the road. But first, there would be golf, this time as a player.

In September 2009, McCarthy made headlines in the *Kodiak Daily Mirror* for setting a course record in the island's 23rd championship.

With a sizzling 36-hole score of 132 – 12 under par – he beat his closest challenger by no fewer than 17 strokes over the Bear Valley course. Not one for hyperbole, McCarthy had a simple, brief reply when interviewed. 'That was the goal – coming back,' he said. His 65 on the second day, including a front nine of 30, was a course record. This proved that the six weeks he had just spent on the Dakotas Tour had left their mark. His reference to 'coming back' was connected to back-to-back titles, set up by a winning 139 the previous year.

Then, in circumstances a lot more frightening than anything the slick greens of Oakmont could threaten, he was fortunate to escape with his life in March 2013.

The weekend storm had abated somewhat as Trina drove us the scenic route through Passage West in fairly quiet Sunday morning traffic. She began relating how James had come home in 2014 and that he didn't look great. 'To me he wasn't himself,' she said. 'And I thought he seemed very quiet in himself. But I put that down to the shock of his fall overboard.' There was a pause before she went on about how the brothers had gone back fishing, and how they were doing up Peter's boat.

In what was potentially a lethal accident in 2013, James lost his last remaining keepsake from Oakmont when a logoed t-shirt was cut from his body. Rescuers fought to save his life in highly dramatic circumstances while he was close to death in freezing Alaskan waters. Here, we might have had a real-live episode of the TV series *Deadliest Catch*, with a Corkman centre stage.

James had been swept overboard while fishing in the Gulf of Alaska. Fortunately, Peter managed to haul him to safety after a 20-minute battle for survival culminating in an airlift to hospital, where he had to recover from lung damage.

Later, in emphasising the importance of golf in his life, he told Trina during a phone call to Cork about an interview he had done with me on the practice ground at Oakmont, six years previously.

Meanwhile, the *Irish Examiner* of 22 March 2013, reported:

> The Irish fisherman who survived a fall overboard into one of the world's coldest and most treacherous oceans has spoken for the first time about his survival. James McCarthy, 36, felt he had breathed his last and was prepared to die after falling from his brother's trawler into the icy waters of the Gulf of Alaska.
>
> The Kodiak-based fisherman, who is from Ringaskiddy in Co. Cork, spent 25 minutes without a floatation device or survival suit, in near-freezing water. Experts said the survival time should only have been about 15 minutes. However, James said that as he felt life slipping away, his brother Peter, 44, and fellow crewman Makodo Odlin, 26, did everything they could to save him.

He proceeded to talk of Mak and his brother becoming his heroes for the remainder of his life. By way of explaining how he had beaten the odds, James said: 'I suppose my brother just wouldn't let me go.'

The *Examiner* went on:

The men were fishing on Peter's boat, the 17-metre *Stella*, in the Shelikof Strait – a treacherous area of ocean featured in TV's *Deadliest Catch* series. They were hauling 50-ton of pollock at around 5 p.m. when one of James's legs got caught in the net. He was pulled up towards the net reel and was flung head-first into the frigid ocean. 'There was no shock, no instantaneous loss of breath,' he said. 'I suppose the adrenalin just kicked in. Panic didn't set in. I just knew what I needed to do.'

A non-swimmer, James was pushed by the boat's wash away from the vessel as the mayday call of 'man overboard' went out. In a remarkable twist of fate, James and Peter's older brother, John, 46, was among several skippers in the Kodiak fleet who heard the distress call over the radio.

John was just leaving port, and when he heard the coast guard scrambling a rescue helicopter, he decided it was best to head back to port to meet the chopper when it landed, not realising it was his own brother who was in trouble. In the meantime, Mak had thrown a life ring to James and Peter battled to turn the boat as the 50-ton bag of fish began to sink. James grabbed the life ring, took slow deep breaths, and stopped moving to conserve energy.

'I could see the boat, and could see them trying to turn the boat, and Peter was yelling to hold on,' he said. 'I didn't feel cold or anything, but the sea changed. It got choppier and I said to myself if I'm going to make it, I've got to do something so that they can get me, or get my body. I was fighting as hard as I could but I felt there was a good chance I wouldn't make it.'

James tied his left leg to a rope on the life ring and pushed his leg through the ring so that, even if he drowned, his body would float. As he tired, it became more difficult to breathe. 'I couldn't take a breath without swallowing water and I started to fade,' he said. 'I felt my grip loosening and I proceeded to drown. I thought, this is it. This is how you're going to go. Damn it! My dog is going to outlive me. Then I went under and blacked out.'

By this time, Peter and Mak had managed to cut the net and turn the boat towards James. As they neared, Mak tied a rope around his waist and dived in and swam six metres to grab James's body. He attached a line around James's waist and Peter hauled him, upside down, on to the deck of the trawler. James wasn't breathing and had no pulse as Peter and Mak struck him hard on the chest and began CPR. They battled for five minutes before James finally gasped for air.

'Am I alive?' James asked. 'In my head, I was gone. I had breathed my last. I knew I had. It was very confusing and I was wondering was this the next life.' Peter and Mak stripped James of his wet clothes, wrapped him in blankets, and stuffed hot water bottles around his body. As Peter liaised with the coast guard, Mak kept talking to James, keeping him awake and alert. 'I was absolutely frozen at this stage, and my core temperature had plummeted,' James said.

The coast guard chopper arrived over the vessel soon afterwards and a rescue swimmer airlifted James for the flight back to Air Station Kodiak, where an ambulance, and his brother John, were waiting.

James fought back tears as he recalled the moment John said: 'It's OK. Your big brother is here.' He was rushed to Providence Kodiak Island Medical Center in a critical condition.

James later commended the doctors on having done a great job while his brothers ensured that he kept up the fight. Remarkably, the hospital discharged him within 24 hours with nothing worse than minor back and leg injuries and he was soon back on the *Stella*, preparing her for three and a half months in dry dock.

'They tell me I'm headed towards a full recovery,' he said later. 'I have no problem being around the boat, or water. It's what I do, what I'm good at, what I love. I've been fishing here for 20 years and all that training the coast guard make you do, paid off.'

After such an extraordinary escape, it felt desperately sad to realise that James was no longer with us. I was to discover that while the passing years had eased the pain of that crushing episode for Trina and her parents, there was more severe heartache to follow.

Confidently guiding her SUV along familiar, narrow roads, Trina reached the Ferry Boat Inn in Ringaskiddy, where she turned right. We then progressed up a hill and past a blue wall on the right when the McCarthy bungalow came into view, with its distinctive yellow squares of cement on the outer walls.

All the while, Trina was filling in some family history:

> At one stage, Peter came home here for two years and took a factory job, but he couldn't stick it. All he wanted to do was fish. On returning to Alaska, he hired a nanny to mind the children from his first marriage. She was a Dublin girl, and they developed such a great relationship that they ended up married. John has been married to an Alaskan for 30 years. For James, it was golf and his dog Murphy. He was 39 when he died.
>
> After the accident, we sensed that he could never be right.
>
> He went back to Las Vegas to meet up again with his golfing friends there and his long-time golfing buddy, Mike Berg, looked after him.
>
> When he came over here early in 2014, things had seemed back to normal for him after his accident. But we learned that on returning to Alaska, he was on the golf course one day at Kodiak when he fell ill. I'm not sure if he collapsed or not, but he went to hospital where they diagnosed bile-duct cancer. A later diagnosis established it as pancreatic cancer. That was in July 2014.
>
> My parents travelled over there when he underwent surgery in August of that year and I went over in October. James was really grateful for that. He liked my parents being around. It's a long, long trip, nearly 24 hours, to New York and Chicago and on to

Anchorage. Or it could be via Seattle. Either way it involved four flights, ending with an hour's trip from Anchorage to Kodiak.

Before we experienced her parents' hospitality, there was another shock: Trina told us that the middle of the three brothers, Peter, had also died. He had been diagnosed with brain cancer on his birthday, 12 March 2015. Trina explained how he had gone to San Francisco for an operation, 'but the surgeon told him he didn't get all of the cancer. Which obviously wasn't good. When he died at the end of the following year my parents made another trip over. It was like we were over and back all the time.'

With the framed article from the *Sunday Independent* on the kitchen wall helping to ease our initial exchanges, Dick and Val McCarthy offered a smiling welcome. The heading on my piece read: 'From the shores of Alaska to the greens of Oakmont'. Their anxiety to maintain any contact, however tenuous, with their departed sons, was reflected in correspondence I received from them to my home a month later.

The envelope contained cuttings from the *Kodiak Daily Mirror*, which they had since come across in 'James's Box,' along with a eulogy delivered on the occasion of his death.

The newspaper report of his death highlighted his golfing achievements locally. 'He was probably the best that ever played on the island,' said long-time Kodiak golfer, Peter Allan. 'He was a wonderful guy to play with. He had a great attitude and a lot of charm.'

'James phoned from Oakmont to tell me he'd met you and that there might be a piece in the paper,' said Val. 'On the Sunday morning, I ran down to the shop and started looking through the paper for a small mention of James. Not what appeared! I never expected that!'

Throughout more than an hour with them, there wasn't the slightest sense of awkwardness, no difficult silences, as they proceeded to bare their souls about what they had been through, even to the point of explaining how both of them had fought their own battles with cancer. They further acknowledged that all the memorabilia helped them to cope with their loss. That was when we were shown around their home, to take in the various keepsakes associated with their fishermen sons.

The hall was dominated by an image of the *Stella*. This was Peter's third boat, following on the *Eskimo Princess* and the *St Anthony*.

I learned that the three brothers were regarded as pioneers among Alaska's fishing fraternity, setting standards for the fleet. It was unheard of when Peter decided to widen his boat by two feet on either side. People questioned whether this revolutionary development would work, but not only was it successful, it even performed so well as to become the standard for boats of that particular size. James, we were told, was especially proud of his hands-on involvement in the project.

Back at the family home, the lounge contained an array of mementoes, including little carvings in walrus ivory, the sort of activity a sailor might engage in during idle moments at sea.

Though their role as hosts must still have been terribly painful for Dick and Val, they remained remarkably composed through it all. This was something they needed to do for their departed boys and the only tangible emotion was Val's silent tears at one especially painful moment.

Then they talked about the remarkable solidarity of the local community, which we like to believe is a uniquely Irish thing. A special fund-raiser night was organised in neighbouring Carrigaline so the family could travel to Alaska. Almost €20,000 was raised. 'My father [who, at 82, still works as an auto-electrician] would be well known,' said Trina. 'It was phenomenal.' She added: 'Then, when James's ashes were brought home, we had a service in the local church and the crowd was enormous. I don't think we'll ever see such a crowd around here again.'

The three of them talked, I imagined therapeutically, about the fate of James and Peter. About 'how great James was for coming home', not having the family ties of the other two. And how Mike Berg met the parents in Anchorage when James was undergoing surgery there. 'The other two were married, but James had nobody, so we went out there to look after him,' Dick explained.

'A couple of years after James died, Mike Berg and his wife came here to visit us,' said Val. 'We had spent four months out there when James had his surgery in Anchorage and met Mike at that time. He and his wife were here for about a week. My brother, Robert McCarthy [Val was also a

McCarthy before marriage], is a member of Kinsale Golf Club. He met up with Mike Berg and they played there and a game was also arranged at The Old Head. Mind you, the weather was so bad that day you couldn't hit a ball. But he tried it just the same.'

As if their painful loss wasn't more than enough to bear, they had to cope with the additional headache of red tape. Visa complications arose when they found themselves heading back to Alaska following Peter's death towards the end of 2016, having been there for James's passing in January of that year. 'We eventually had to go to the American Embassy in Dublin to sort things out,' said Dick.

Then, as the clock approached lunchtime, he said: 'There are two plaques out on the wall which we'll show you before you go.' With that, Kathy and I headed out into the back garden where James had indulged his sporting dreams, having been a fine hurler and Gaelic footballer during his teenage years. There, on the end wall, were cement plaques beside each other, indicating two lives and the fishing vessels that dominated their work, many miles from these shores.

James McCarthy 30-11-1976 ~ 01-02-2016. *Fiddlers Green.*
Peter McCarthy 12-03-1969 ~ 29-12-2016. FV *Stella.*

Their ashes were spread close by, in accordance with the boys' wishes. As we viewed those memorials, I wondered what Dick thought of losing his beloved sons so far from home.

'The experience they got in Greencastle Fishing College, where they all topped their classes, was very important to them,' he replied, taking a practical view of their career choices. 'Then they went away to make their own lives. And I was proud of them. The way I look back on it now, that's life. Whatever happens, that's life. James was in the water for 27 minutes and to all intents and purposes, he was dead when they pulled him out. He was very determined.'

Dick clearly remembered every detail of the rescue. Innate pride in their individual achievements was evident when he added: 'Peter bought his boat, the *Stella*, for $1.5 million and spent another $1.5 million on it. It's now worth up to $5 million and his wife owns it. John remains skipper on the same boat he has worked for years.'

At that, Val piped up: 'John was going out fishing at the time he heard the news on the radio about James going overboard. Then he phoned us to tell us the news. And contacted the coast guard. He said nothing about James's chances of survival.'

During the six weeks in hospital fighting for his life, James had a final request. He wanted to be taken to the local Bear Valley golf course, where he had relished so many precious experiences, hitting heroic shots when the weather permitted. Like Raffeen Creek, where it had all started for him, Bear Valley is a modest, nine-hole layout which wouldn't officially open for another few months – in May. But he went there just the same, in his brother Peter's car. As Trina put it: 'He needed that before he left us.'

With that, she headed back to Cork City and our hotel, but not before making another call. As we drove into Raffeen Creek, it became clear that play on the golf course had been suspended because of the storm. But there was plenty of action on the pitch-and-putt course on the left side of the entrance road, where Trina knew she would find her husband, Richie, involved in a competition.

Soon we were back on the road to our hotel, whereupon Trina blurted: 'I think James still holds the course record at Raffeen,' – in the way that golf has of preserving memories.

4

The Making of Golf Ireland

When Mary Robinson became the first woman to be elected President of Ireland, it fell to me as golf correspondent of the *Irish Times* to make the phone call. Given the assumption that all Irish presidents were automatically granted honorary membership of Portmarnock Golf Club, my superiors would need to know the situation regarding Mrs Robinson.

I suspected that the club had been waiting for the call. Straight off, their honorary secretary, David Keane, pointed out that Dr Patrick Hillery, Mrs Robinson's predecessor, was so honoured 'because of his active involvement in the game and his existing membership of certain clubs [including Portmarnock].' This did not apply to any of the other five former presidents.

It was further pointed out that honorary life membership was limited to 'existing members of the club or to personalities who have given a specific service to the game.' If Mrs Robinson was to be honoured, she would first have to become an ordinary member of the club, which 'would have been impossible under the rules which restrict membership to gentlemen properly elected.'

I felt like shouting my approval which, of course, I couldn't do. I was journalistically bound to maintain a neutral view of golf's most controversial topic of the time. And this was just one instance in what became a seriously lengthy process.

Through decades of relatively quiet, orderly development, the Golfing Union of Ireland (GUI) headed towards their centenary having survived the trauma of the Troubles with their all-Ireland integrity admirably intact. Dramatic change beckoned on both sides of the fairway ropes, however, in the unprecedented success of Ireland's senior international team, and the serious challenges posed by the issue of women's equality in golf.

If I could claim to have made any worthwhile contribution to the administration of golf on this island over the last 40 years, it would be in promoting constitutional change by participating clubs. The first serious move on the issue occurred back in 1985, during Frank Bowen's presidency of the GUI. That was when representatives of the GUI, the Irish Ladies' Golf Union (ILGU) and the Women in Golf pressure group, spearheaded by Marguerite Martin of Bray GC, aired their views before the government's Joint Oireachtas Committee on Equality, chaired by Máire Geoghegan-Quinn.

It was an ambitious undertaking which promised much and delivered little. In fact, the most significant move towards recognising the plight of the nation's women golfers was made two years later by the GUI. That was when an annual general meeting of the Union removed an infamous clause from their constitution.

Section 9(3) was a clumsily worded directive threatening disaffiliation from any club which permitted women to attend or vote at annual general or special meetings. Ironically, such a ban would still have remained valid up until the emergence of Golf Ireland. The problem for women was that, for the most part, the GUI members of golf clubs were also the beneficial owners of these facilities, a reality which was later addressed by the so-called three-tier constitution.

In practice, the abhorrent clause made sense in that it protected men's rights to exclusive control over the running of their own game and could have been equally applicable to the ILGU, but there was no doubt that it caused offence. So, in a conciliatory gesture to his female counterparts, the then honorary secretary of the GUI, Des Rea O'Kelly, negotiated to have it removed. Though hailed in certain quarters, particularly by Women in Golf (WIG), as a notable triumph, it was clear that for all practical purposes, nothing had changed. As Gerry O'Brien, the 1987 President of the GUI, pointed out: 'Our constitution was written for the sole purpose of the administration of men's amateur golf in this country. The clause at which offence was taken was relevant solely to the men's section of a golf club.'

However, the key factor bolstering discrimination in clubs, i.e. the constitutional right to free association, remained an insurmountable hurdle. Still, there were other encouraging developments from the women's perspective. The so-called three-tier constitution effectively separated the golf course and clubhouse from the actual playing of the game, making way for women to become involved in administration.

In lengthy chats about the issue, I had suggested it to O'Brien as a possible solution. And he agreed.

Meanwhile, the ILGU played their part by maintaining pressure on all concerned. As opposed to polls in which the opinion of male officials of clubs was sought, they surveyed the women themselves. In January 1997, Lansdowne Market Research produced the results of a survey in which 277 out of a total of 341 clubs took part.

Among other things, it showed that women were still largely excluded from the more important club committees and that only one third of the clubs included women on the general administration or finance committees. In half of the clubs surveyed, the women's committee was not consulted on the election of new women members.

In effect, this confirmed what most of us already knew: that no meaningful progress could be achieved on a national scale without some way of forcing the clubs to toe the line. To put it simply, a solution would have to be imposed.

The passage of the Equal Status Bill (1999) through the Oireachtas suggested that such a solution had been reached, concerning the vast majority of clubs. Its function was to deal with all areas of discrimination, including the fairness of any payments which a club might consider appropriate when a woman changes from associate to full membership.

A club would also have been deemed guilty of discrimination if it provided 'different terms and conditions of membership [for men and women] for members or applicants for membership.' In other words, a club couldn't have full membership for men and not for women, nor, for that matter, an associate membership category for women and not for men.

The crucial point came in section 10 which ordained, in effect, that any club found guilty of discrimination would lose its certification of registration. That, in turn, would cause it to forfeit its liquor licence. On the assumption that the legislation did what it set out to do, any non-compliant golf club would have about a year to put their affairs in order. And if they still refused to change, their members would almost certainly find themselves without a 19th hole, in any meaningful sense. Of course, it was quite possible that certain establishments might be prepared to go down that particular road, rather than bow to change.

When this legislation was brought before Dáil Éireann, however, it was found to be unconstitutional. The key issue of free association had not been circumvented. Still, the vast majority of clubs accepted the inevitability of change. They acknowledged women's rights to equality, without being forced to do so through legislation.

In a way, it seemed sad that matters had come to this; but it simply reflected the general selfishness of modern living. The sort of selfishness which had led to ever-increasing incidences of road rage by people determined to have their own space, even on a public highway.

Certain male golfers expressed fears of their course being overrun by 'these bloody women'. Without a doubt, there was going to be more congestion on the tee, especially in Dublin's busier clubs, but the more sensible members saw this as an inevitable price to be paid for the overall affluence that afforded our citizens greater leisure opportunities.

It was felt that the principle of equality should be accepted without all the usual red herrings being thrown onto the top table. From this conciliatory base, men could sit down with their female equals and hammer out a way of making the arrangement work. As my late mother liked to insist, where there's a will, there's a way.

Crucially, a new section in the 1999 Bill stated that a club would 'not be considered to be a discriminating club if it caters only for the needs of persons of a particular gender, marital status, family status, sexual orientation, religious belief, etc. ....' The general opinion was that it would be extremely difficult to justify in law a refusal to renew, for instance, the Freemasons' certificate of registration, which is based not on any drink-related ground, but on a refusal to admit women.

Then came the government directive, through Fáilte Ireland (Bord Fáilte), which established that no European Union aid or any other form of grant aid could be disbursed to clubs which did not offer equal status to women.

On 14 April 2000, Seamus Given, a solicitor with the Dublin law firm of Arthur Cox, expressed the view that an amendment to the Equal Status Bill 'put single-sex clubs beyond the reach of the law, insofar as the refusal of admission of females to membership is concerned.'

Five years on, his opinion was roundly endorsed by a justice of the High Court – at a cost of about €500,000 to the Irish taxpayer. And when the Equality Authority proceeded to take the case against Portmarnock Golf Club to the Supreme Court, the bill rose to close on €1 million.

Strange things have been known to happen when taxpayers' money is applied to golfing matters in Ireland. Like the decision of An Bord Pleanála to take The Old Head of Kinsale to the Supreme Court, where the board's case was dismissed in its entirety in December 2002. Indeed, the five judges ruled that the state body had acted in 'a manifestly unreasonable' manner.

The amendment to which Seamus Given referred was Section 9 of the Equal Status Bill and was intended to protect clubs 'whose principal purpose is to cater only for a person of a particular gender ....' And in a transcript of the Seanad debates, Mary Wallace (then junior minister at the Department of Justice) said: 'I stress that these changes have been included on the advice of the Attorney General and have been carefully formulated to pass constitutional muster.'

Since the attorney general at the time happened to be a certain Michael McDowell, it was hardly surprising that he was happy with the findings of High Court Justice Kevin O'Higgins. This was his ruling in June 2005, which was to become something of a milestone in the history of golf in this country. His decision stated 'in terms of registered clubs, it is permissible to have exclusively a bridge club for Bulgarians, a chess club for Catholics, a wine club for women and a golf club for gentlemen.'

There would be no immediate moves to amend the law, which made it almost laughable for Green Party spokesman, Ciarán Cuffe, to be calling on Minister McDowell to support further action by the Equality Authority.

It was also interesting to reflect on the alacrity with which Niall Crowley, chief executive of the Equality Authority, instituted legal proceedings against Portmarnock. The action came only a matter of months after John O'Donoghue, the government minister responsible for putting the Equal Status Act on the statute books, expressed the view on national radio that the membership structure of Portmarnock GC was not at odds with equality legislation.

Pádraig Slattery, then captain of Portmarnock GC, talked of his club's 'relief and vindication' at the outcome. And he insisted: 'There is absolutely no sense of triumphalism. For us, it has always been a far wider issue than the concerns of our club. The argument is about the right to free association.' This was a deeply held view especially for long-standing members of Portmarnock who also felt, without any prejudice towards women, that they simply preferred to play golf in the company of men.

On this point, they did a considerable favour to their neighbours down the James Larkin Road in Dollymount. At that time, Royal Dublin was the only other all-male club in the Republic of Ireland, though its membership was not specifically defined as 'gentlemen', as Portmarnock's is. It effectively evolved into an all-male establishment.

Meanwhile, it was somewhat disingenuous of the Authority to claim credit for the very significant progress evident in the treatment of women in Irish golf clubs. Much of it was down to admirable work by the GUI, which encouraged a change of attitude within the clubs themselves.

Nevertheless, as evidence of ongoing antagonism, alleged breaches by golf clubs of the Equal Status Act were still prominent. In actual fact these complaints, eleven in all, represented only two per cent of the 540 cases which had been referred to the Equality Authority by the end of September of a particular year. It was also notable that most of them were resolved without recourse to the District Court. But as usual with the issue of equal rights in golf clubs, I remember finding it necessary at the time to sift through much misinformation in pursuit of the truth.

During the worst of the Troubles in Northern Ireland, beleaguered tourist officials desperately pointed out to potential visitors that what they were shown on their television screens was a small minority of the population hell-bent on creating mayhem. What they didn't see was the vast majority who were not planting bombs nor throwing missiles.

I tried to point out that golf clubs had become victims of a similarly negative image. While undoubtedly problems arose during the transition to equal status, no mention was made of the majority of clubs which accepted change in a positive, even generous manner. And there were some notable shining lights.

For instance, a special general meeting of Baltinglass GC unanimously passed a motion granting women full playing rights, without the payment of any entrance fee. 'Our lady associates were made full members back in 1996, when they agreed not to play at weekends until our new, 18-hole course was up and running,' said club captain Fintan Doyle.

There was no question of any entrance fee and with the condition of no weekend access, women accepted the deal at a reduced membership fee of €240 – half of what the men were paying. When the full 18 was up and running, Baltinglass made good on its promise of full playing rights, albeit for full subscriptions, to the satisfaction of all concerned.

Then there was Howth GC, which also granted full membership to its women with no question of an entrance fee. But the club went considerably further in that it allowed women a phased transition to full fees over a period of five years, without relinquishing any of their rights. This meant that men paid a subscription of €820 compared with €680 for women.

'It worked perfectly, without even one dissenting voice from the ladies,' said Don Mahony, who was honorary secretary when the process of change began in February 2000. 'We cracked open champagne when matters were finalised at the men's AGM in November of that year and the women joined us in celebrating, later in the evening.'

For the record, the Act listed nine grounds for complaint – gender, marital status, family status, sexual orientation, religious belief, age, disability, race and membership of the Traveller Community.

An enduring memory of the movie *The Agony and the Ecstasy* is of Michelangelo painting the ceiling of the Sistine Chapel and an exasperated pontiff standing on the floor below, pleading: 'When will it be at an end?' After decades of negotiation, it would have been easy to make the same point about the equality issue in golf.

As a golf correspondent, I became aware of campaigning journalism, where the objective is to right a grave wrong, as a lively issue. On the matter of equality, certain scribes seemed to delight in pursuing a populist agenda which involved guiding editors along a road of spicy controversy.

When equality for women in golf was gaining national exposure, I regularly became appalled at the exaggerations and plain disinformation peddled by pressure groups who quietly admitted, off the record, that this was a standard strategy in grabbing attention.

I feel I could honestly claim to have been on the women's side, but I knew I also had to tread warily. And I have to admit to becoming seriously angry at the politicking on the issue, especially by the Equality Authority.

In the *Sunday Independent*, when serious nonsense was being spouted about the staging of the 2003 Nissan Irish Open at Portmarnock, I stated that the club had a perfectly legal right to exist under our Constitution. And if the Equality Authority disputed this status, they should take them to court. Which they did. And lost. And lost again.

The fact is that Portmarnock were viewed as a soft target in what was essentially a national issue. Since then, of course, they and Royal Dublin have opened their doors to women. And there is no doubt that this was greatly facilitated by the establishment of Golf Ireland, whose existence makes it possible simply to absorb both genders into the same establishment, without the need to create a separate ladies' club.

Portmarnock always held the view that certain responsibilities fell to them as the acknowledged leading course in the Republic. They were almost duty-bound to make their links available for significant international events, which they did, with the 1960 Canada Cup, 13 stagings of the Irish Open, the Alcan Tournament of 1970 and leading amateur events such as the 1991 Walker Cup and the British Amateur Championship of 1949 and 2019.

Commercial pressures on the R&A, however, forced them to thoroughly review how to stage their events at single-gender venues. And the European Tour went down the same road. These decisions caused the Irish government to follow suit, which meant that High Court and Supreme Court rulings in Portmarnock's favour were no longer relevant.

Meanwhile, significant change also occurred at administrative level. When Pat Finn took over from Seamus Smith as general secretary of the GUI in May 2011, John Treacy, CEO of the Irish Sports Council, suggested that Finn should engage with Sinead Heraty, his counterpart in the ILGU, with a view to creating a closer working relationship between the two Unions.

The GUI had shown themselves to be in a strong financial position, especially when moving to new headquarters in Carton House in 2005. Though the move involved an outlay of €7.6 million, it was done, remarkably, with absolutely no borrowing. And given the financial difficulties that lay ahead internationally, the timing could hardly have been better, not least for the fact that the existing headquarters in Eglinton Road realised €2.9 million at auction. A further €2.6 million, incidentally, was raised through a one-off contribution of €15 by every golf-club member.

The sod at Carton House was turned on 28 January 2005, by Albert Lee, his last official function as President of the GUI, and the new facility, including a splendid 22-acre Academy, was officially opened on 4 July 2006. Little more than a year later, the first rumblings were heard of an impending world financial crisis.

In January 2012, the dramatic announcement came that officials of the GUI, ILGU and the Irish Region of the PGA were coming together to commence work on 'a new strategy for golf in Ireland.'

Through the newly formed Confederation of Golf in Ireland, they would discuss how to work together in preparation for golf's return to the Olympic Games in Rio de Janeiro in 2016.

A development plan for golf, to cover the years from 2014 to 2020, led to a close working relationship between Finn and Ms Heraty. These circumstances culminated in a national ballot on 19 January 2019 in which 94 per cent of GUI members and 100 per cent of the ILGU voted for unity.

With Golf Ireland set to take shape, Finn and Ms Heraty duly stepped down from their respective roles, prompting Ms Heraty to remark: 'I believe that if myself and Pat hadn't worked so well together, we wouldn't have got such overwhelming support from the clubs.' So it was that two great institutions edged towards a structured demise.

The eventual ease with which the process of unifying Irish golf was finally accomplished stood as a glowing testament to patient endeavour. And one realised that all it ever required was a healthy sprinkling of goodwill on both sides.

It was a situation light-years away from the struggle which once confronted the ILGU when they attempted to fulfil their expected role in an international capacity. Most notably, there was the financial challenge of staging the 1979 European Women's Team Championship, which eventually went ahead at Hermitage in 1979. I remember Anne Tunney, their centenary president in 1993, detailing the nature of the undertaking.

'Quite simply, it was going to be a huge challenge from a financial standpoint,' she said. 'We were greatly encouraged, however, by a formal agreement that was already in place with the Ladies' Golf Union (LGU). They promised they would split the cost with us 50–50.'

She went on:

> We encountered quite incredible generosity. With courtesy cars from Mazda and help from other sources, the figure eventually worked out at £5,400, with the result that ourselves and the LGU paid £2,700 each. Yet it remained a daunting challenge at a time when we had only 21,000 members in 223 clubs.

There were special situations, apart from those caused by the large galleries:

> At an individual level, there was the problem of one of the visiting players being whisked off to Holles Street Hospital with a miscarriage. And her team captain instructed that she was to bring her clubs with her because she would be needed for play the following afternoon. Which she did.
>
> I remember the German team being captained by a man, and an albatross being scored at the long second by a 14-year-old Austrian. And I recall the fact that none of the 126 caddies let us down. But, of course, the crowning glory of the week was that Ireland won. From fourteen competing nations, we emerged to beat West Germany by the wide margin of 6–1 in the final.

To demonstrate what could become possible when the two Unions came together, there was a highly successful staging of the 2018 World Amateur Team Championships and the Espirito Championship at Carton House. Simply by observing competitors from all over the golfing world, it was immediately evident that Carton House was not only an excellent venue but admirably cost-effective.

As a joint venture, it presented two golfing bodies working splendidly together, with the GUI helping the staging of the women's Espirito Santo event and the ILGU then rowing behind the men's Eisenhower Trophy at the same venue. GUI chief executive Pat Finn explained:

Ground transport was a key part of our responsibilities. About 90 per cent of the players stayed in the Maynooth University campus with the remainder split between Carton House and Dunboyne Castle. Their commute was straightforward enough, but the tricky part was getting them to and from Dublin Airport. On the Sunday and Monday, about 300 of those involved in the Espirito Santo were transferred to Dublin Airport while the 300 competitors for the following week's Eisenhower arrived between Friday and Sunday.

With key elements so closely integrated and volunteer drivers such a help, our outlay of €700,000 was roughly half the staging cost of $1.5m in Mexico in 2016.

Two national unions working together represented a very different scene from the bitter point-scoring of previous decades. It was the first time that I could appreciate the dramatic changes in the administering of the game during that period.

Against this background, Tim O'Connor, chairman of the transition board, was optimistic. 'For the first time ever, we will have a single grouping of people focused on the future and well-being of Irish golf in all its aspects,' he said. 'We want to bring all the talents, all the energies, all the expertise together under the one roof.'

A native of west Limerick, who went on to serve in Foreign Affairs, O'Connor approached the transition assignment armed with considerable skills acquired when negotiating the Good Friday Agreement. In fact, he belatedly took up golf as a member of Edmondstown GC in the summer of 1998, 'as an antidote to involvement in that process.'

'This is a much more positive experience,' he said of the prospective formation of Golf Ireland. 'When I was appointed, the hard decisions had already been taken after a four-year process by the discussion group. The future is to have men and women working together. Single-gender endeavour has no future, especially where you can have people working against each other.'

By this stage, O'Connor's negotiating skills had been enhanced by distinguished company, such as US senator George Mitchell. 'I remember him calling us all together in mid-March 1998 and saying: "I've really enjoyed your stories and there have been many of them. In the meantime, a son has been born to me in New York and I would like to see him before he goes to college." With that, he nominated April 9 as the day we must bring our talks to a conclusion.' Which is what happened.

With the launch of Golf Ireland on 1 January 2020, the death-knell was sounded of both the GUI, which became the oldest men's national union in the world when launched in 1891, and the ILGU, which held the same distinction in the women's game, from its foundation two years later.

As a footnote, my various journalistic activities in recent decades happened to include the role of editor of a splendid magazine called *Golf Ireland*, owned by Greg Francis. Though the magazine bit the dust, its registered title lingered on, to the point where Francis received a settlement of €100,000 so that the new body could bear its name. Even for a title, money is at the heart of things!

5

The Thrill of Inter-Club Competition

Nenagh's Pierce Purcell Shield treble

More than any other event, the national finals of the Cups and Shields have become invaluable, bridge-building competitions in terms of maintaining golf as an all-Ireland sport. And from my experiences over the years, none exemplified 'hands-across-the-border' better than the Pierce Purcell Shield of 1991, when Nenagh GC captured the pennant for a second time, in the club's centenary year.

The finals that year were in Malone GC, where the members had never before witnessed celebrations to match the Tipperary way. Recalling a remarkable week, Nenagh's Liam Gleeson, who partnered the club captain and local solicitor, Noel O'Meara, told me:

> It was absolutely incredible, there was so much excitement. Our last pairing came to the 18th, where there's water on the right. And one of our chaps, Brendan Galvin, played a brilliant bunker recovery towards the water to about six feet from the hole, and his partner, Gary Howard, knocked in the putt to win the title.

I'll never forget the scenes at Malone, as we sang 'Slievenamon' and 'Tipperary So Far Away', above in the clubhouse. And the way the champagne, of which I drank my fair share, kept flowing, long, long after the golf had ended.

Later that year, when the accounts were presented at the club's AGM, others took a rather jaundiced view of the whole episode. But they wouldn't have seen the great goodwill which we experienced. To the eternal credit of the members of Malone, they shared the celebrations with us visitors from the deep south, assuring us that it was one of the great occasions in the recent history of their club.

And the Good Friday Agreement was still seven years away!

Singing was very much to the fore once more when Nenagh completed the treble, by way of marking said agreement. This time, their triumph took place against the backdrop of majestic Lough Ree, shimmering under an autumn sun.

Almost predictably, the air around Athlone GC was filled with the unmistakable strains of 'Slievenamon'. It was September 1998 and Nenagh's Pierce Purcell Shield team and their supporters were in full voice. Many of those present would have remembered another day of rousing celebration in Malone GC, where a bastion of Belfast conservatism resounded to that much-loved ballad, along with 'Tipperary So Far Away.'

A glorious journey had started, in fact, at Woodbrook GC in 1989 when Nenagh captured the higher handicappers' national pennant for the first time. Now, with their third triumph, they had become undisputed masters of a competition often described as the Fierce Purcell Shield, because of the intensity of its foursomes battles.

Along the way, their teams had included players more noted for their achievements in other sports, such as Eamonn Cregan, the gifted Limerick hurler, and Liam Gleeson, who won a total of 11 national athletics titles, nine for the pole vault and two for the javelin. And from soccer, there was Tommy Gaynor, who won English League Cup medals with Nottingham Forest in 1989 and 1990 and was on the losing team in the FA Cup final, a year later.

Then there was Brendan O'Shea, a rather special member of Nenagh's 1989 and 1991 teams. 'When I caddied for Brendan at Woodbrook in '89, he explained why our win meant so much to him,' recalled honorary secretary, Tony Murphy. 'You see, he was a distant cousin of Pierce Purcell, through his mother, and they were both natives of Kilkenny.'

There were other mighty men on the Nenagh roll of honour. In wonderfully expansive language, Noel O'Meara informed me about Jimmy Gleeson, 'who owns the biggest piggery here in Tipperary'; Willie Duff, 'the biggest potato grower in North Tipperary'; Joe McGrath 'who hurled with Toomevara, along with his brother Pat', and about the left-handed Sean Minogue, 'who came from the pitch-and-putt era'.

Another set of brothers, William and Paddy Harty, shared in the Purcell triumphs. And Tony Grace could claim to have been involved with all three victorious teams, though he has only two medals, from 1989 and 1998. Pat McGrath, meanwhile, went on to win a Jimmy Bruen Shield medal with Nenagh at Dundalk in 1997.

As it happened, Sean O'Donoghue reversed the established trend by going from that Bruen Shield win to a share in the Purcell triumph of 1998 at Athlone. Dinny Ryan, a Tipperary all-Ireland hurling medal winner, also played in the 1998 team and another all-Ireland hurler, Noel O'Dwyer, was in the Purcell panels of 1989 and 1991.

O'Meara himself gained the remarkable distinction of playing in the triumphant team in 1991, which happened to be his year as centenary captain of the club. And he was more than ready for the considerable flak which came his direction at the following annual general meeting, over the amount of money spent on that particular venture. He recalled:

> To be honest, it cost us a fortune, but the fact that I got stick from the club doesn't upset me in the slightest. I don't give a fiddler's damn. You'll win nothing unless you make the proper preparations and before the national finals at Malone, we must have gone up

> there on about six daytrips to play the course, at our own expense. That's what it takes to win things.
>
> So if we celebrated well, it was no more than we deserved. The club were always complaining about spending money and on this point, I was quite happy to stand up and be counted. We had set our hearts on winning the Pierce Purcell in our centenary year and we saw it through. And weren't we entitled to be drinking champagne?

Indeed. And however much may have been spent on lighting up the North, wasn't there enough in club funds several years later to extensively upgrade the course to a design by leading architect Patrick Merrigan? In fact, the work included no fewer than 13 new sand-based greens.

In the event, O'Meara, who had been club captain in 1979, won two Pierce Purcell medals with the 1989 and 1991 teams. He also left his mark on the local rugby scene, as centenary president of Nenagh Ormond RFC in 1984 and as a long-time representative on the Munster Branch IRFU.

'We like to think of ourselves as a friendly, homely club, where the visitor is always made welcome,' said Murphy. 'And while our Pierce Purcell opponents would make the usual complaints about handicaps, I believe that the key to our success was the tremendous competitiveness of our teams. And we had our share of luck, which is crucial.'

Success with Nenagh came as a rather special bonus for Cregan, who savoured all-Ireland hurling triumphs at colleges level with Limerick CBS and with the Limerick senior team in 1973. As he suggested himself, it made for a most unusual treble.

Manager of Limerick in 1987 and 1988 and from 1998 to 2002, Cregan also managed his own club side, Claughaun, before going on to take charge of Offaly from 1993 to 1996. But there was still a gap in his sporting life when he happened to be working in Nenagh, in 1987. 'I had finished with club hurling and suddenly found myself with nothing to do for about six to eight months,' he recalled.

It dawned on me that I should take up golf but, to be honest, I didn't like the game, which I considered to be slow and boring. So I became a reluctant convert but before I knew it, I was hooked. I played left-handed, partly because my wife's first cousin, a priest in America, gave me a set of left-handed clubs. It was mainly, however, because I believed that as in hurling, my dominant hand [right] should be at the top of the shaft. As a 15-handicapper, I partnered Tony Grace in the '89 Pierce Purcell team.'

When I played hurling against Tipperary or Cork, the rivalry was so intense that you didn't want to talk to your opponents, but I found that golf was entirely different. I met Tipperary guys at Nenagh GC that I played hurling against and I enjoyed their company immensely. In fact, we had Cork, Kilkenny, Tipperary and Limerick people all playing golf together.

The pressures were also a lot different, much worse than in hurling where there was always somebody likely to cover for your mistakes. In golf, you're on your own.

Cregan continued:

In the Pierce Purcell final at Woodbrook, Tony and I had a dreadful start – four down after four. And I remember the vice-captain of the club, Gerry Quinlan, coming to me and pleading. 'Will you for God's sake crack a joke to make Tony relax a bit.' So I told Tony about The Three Bears and was so nervous that I made a complete bags of it. With that, we looked at each other and burst out laughing.

The upshot was that we went from the fifth to the 17th hole in two under par to draw level. A guy from Cork GC had told me that one-over would win most holes, but he was wrong. That day, it took either a par or a birdie. Finally, with a four-footer for the match on the 18th, I was horrified to see my putt horseshoe in and out of the hole. And as a consequence, I knocked down my drive at the 19th, where we were beaten. Fortunately, the last match on the course went our way.

By 1991, Cregan was down to six handicap and the Pierce Purcell competition had become a cherished memory.

Liam Gleeson, who won his first two all-Ireland titles as a member of Nenagh Olympic on successive days in 1961 – the year he was married – didn't take up golf until 1975. 'I joined Nenagh GC and became involved with a lot of my friends who would have been former hurlers, men like Mick Burns and Tony Tierney,' he recalled. 'By the time the 1991 Pierce Purcell came around, I was playing off 14.'

With fond memories of a remarkable week at Malone, where he partnered O'Meara, Gleeson enthused: 'It was absolutely incredible, there was so much excitement.' As an accountant, Gleeson took more than a passing interest in O'Meara's perceived profligacy. 'I had the suspicion that Noel was determined we'd win, if only so it couldn't be repeated for another 100 years,' he said. 'And to his credit, he set his mind to it and saw it through.'

From 1989 at Woodbrook to the club's first Northern adventure two years later, Nenagh went on to give vibrant expression to the heart of club golf, with their Purcell triumph at Athlone. There, they dominated the middle order to lead Woodbrook by 2–1, leaving the fourth pairing of Paul Maloney and John Hickey with the chance to secure victory.

One down after 16, the Nenagh pair levelled with a par at the short 17th. And on the 18th, looking down the line of a nine-foot putt for the title, Hickey, a Clareman from Parteen, considered it to be 'fairly straight.' Then, in the best tradition of a great competition, he successfully willed the ball into the hole.

Old hands at the heart of golf had found new heroes.

Paul McGinley and a rather special Senior Cup match, Sept 2013

There was no inkling of a future career as a European Tour caddie when JP Fitzgerald had what was arguably his finest amateur moment. It happened in the 1987 Irish Close Championship at Tramore GC, where he and Darren Clarke crossed paths competitively for the first time.

That was where Arthur Pierse, encouraging Mick Morris prior to a forbidding second-round match, famously observed: 'This fella Clarke is only a flash in the pan. You'll take him easy, Mick.' Also, the Portmarnock member, later reeling from a 7 and 6 thrashing, suggested that as a judge of golf, Pierse should stick to the motor business, or words to that effect.

In the event, Clarke won through to the semi-finals where he met none other than the bold JP, a Baltray member who, against all odds, brashly informed anyone who would listen: 'My greatest asset is my mouth.' And he would have got no argument from those of us who had been exposed to his amusing, boyish chatter.

When beating Clarke at the 20th, it could be said that Fitzgerald produced golf to match his mouth. No matter that he went on to lose to local man, Eddie Power, in the final: priceless bragging rights had been secured.

'Yes, we've known each other for a long, long time,' Clarke has since admitted about his one-time caddie. 'And OK, he beat me when we were amateurs. It's there in black and white in the record books. But no matter how often he gets at me about it, he knows in his heart it was a fluke; that he got it up and down from all over the place.'

Still, didn't it leave Clarke in the embarrassing position of being the only leading professional to have lost to his caddie in a championship match? 'That I don't know,' the victim replied defensively. 'But all those years ago in Tramore, we could never have dreamt of ending up as a partnership on tour.'

As it happened, Paul McGinley was in the opposite half of the draw to JP on that occasion, though it hardly mattered as he lost in the second round to Paul Bray. However, they were to meet four years later in a Bulmers Senior Cup match which McGinley still remembers vividly, and which Fitzgerald is never allowed to forget.

Among other things, the occasion marked Paul's most successful Senior Cup run with Grange GC, though where the Cups and Shields were concerned, he quit amateur ranks without ever matching the achievements of his father Mick or younger brother Michael. McGinley

Snr had reached the all-Ireland finals of the Barton Shield with Naas in 1985, the year he was captain of Dunfanaghy.

Having defeated Tullamore in the Leinster final at Carlow, Naas went on to outscore a formidable Cork team in the national semi-finals at Kilkenny GC. The key performance in that particular match was by the partnership of Mick McGinley and Turlough Boylan, who beat Hugh Mackeown and Denis O'Sullivan. But as things turned out, the all-Ireland pennant went to Shandon Park.

Michael, who captured the North of Ireland Championship in 1996, was to match his father's Barton Shield achievement when Grange won the Leinster pennant in 1998 at Powerscourt, beating Greystones by four holes in the final. At the all-Ireland stage, however, they lost by five holes to Co. Sligo, with Michael McGinley and Niall Ruane going down by one hole to Ken Kearney and Seryth Heavey.

He was also in the Grange Senior Cup teams which lost 3-2 to Portmarnock in the Leinster final at Skerries in 2001 and by 3½ to 1½, again to Portmarnock in 2002 at Baltray. Mick McGinley recalled:

> Over the years, I watched an awful lot of these matches. Paul would be back on holidays from university in the States and there would be great excitement at the club.
>
> I've never really got nervous watching himself or Michael play. I suppose that's because I have confidence in both of them as good players, while being a little envious that I could never hit the ball the way they do, especially off the tee and with their long irons.
>
> I've often found myself thinking, 'if only I could do that.' But my forte was the short game. On a broader level, I took pride in having got them into golf as a pastime early in their lives. My biggest thrill would be to stand behind the tee and watch their drives fly like arrows down the middle of the fairway. That would sometimes give me a greater buzz than any honours they might achieve.

Though he was Irish Close champion in 1989, Paul McGinley was generally overshadowed by Leslie Walker in the Grange Senior Cup team. 'Leslie was number one and I was usually played at number five,' he recalled. 'It was only in my last year as an amateur that I became the number one player at Grange. Prior to that, Leslie was the man.'

He went on:

> Though we had a useful Senior Cup team over a period of about three years, we never did anything at national level, mainly because I reckon we were short at least one player. So, instead of winning pennants, we usually had to settle for quarter-final or semi-final places in Leinster. For instance, we lost 4–1 to Co. Louth in the Leinster quarter-finals at Tullamore in 1988 and were beaten by Milltown in the provincial final of the Barton Shield at Portmarnock that year.

McGinley paused, obviously satisfied about the next bit: 'When we eventually managed to reach a Leinster final in the Senior Cup, it became quite a story.'

Warming to the memory, he continued:

> The final was against Co. Louth and the playing order was arranged in such a way that I played JP Fitzgerald. It became a big talking point because I also happened to have been a member of Baltray, where I first went as a junior every Saturday with my dad during the winter months.
>
> That's when I got to know JP and we became such good friends that my last three amateur summers were spent in his company. And when I was away at college in San Diego, he would come out to me now and again to get away from the dismal Irish weather.
>
> But friendship was forgotten when we got to that particular Senior Cup final. He was up to all his old tricks, shouting his mouth off as only JP can do, about how the team captains would have to set it up so that we met. And how he planned to beat me, just like he had done to Darren four years previously.

I can tell you he knocked serious mileage out of that win, making sure that his audience were aware of how Darren was then the country's top amateur, by miles. And for anybody who was prepared to listen, he promised the same treatment for me, now that he had me on his home track and in front of a home crowd.

Anyway, however it was arranged, we ended up playing each other and I remember being determined to give it my best shot, if only for the fact that this would be my last Senior Cup with Grange, before turning professional that autumn.

McGinley then recounted in remarkable detail how JP hit a four iron to four feet at the first, but that they halved it in birdie after he himself had holed from 20 feet. They also halved the long second in birdie. Game on.

McGinley took up the story again:

At the long third, both of us were short of the green in two, but I chipped on and holed the putt whereas JP had to settle for a par. I was one up and at the risk of sounding brash, I remember thinking at the time that I had him. It was game over as far as I was concerned, even at that early point. In the end, I hammered him 5 and 4.

From the moment of victory, McGinley was in no doubt about the significance of what he had done. 'While JP would have been considered the hometown boy, I was probably the number one amateur in the country at the time,' he said. 'For sure, there was a lot of pride and honour at stake.' He continued:

Even now, it remains an important match, especially when JP gets on his high horse and starts shouting the odds as only he can do. I must admit that I found it funny when he would have a go at Darren over the Tramore match. But anytime he dares to try it on with me, I promptly throw that Senior Cup match at him. So it was very important.

Yet I remember leaving Baltray that day with very mixed emotions. Though I'd won my match, Grange lost overall by 3–2. And the team aspect of these events was always so important to me, that I was really disappointed. I desperately wanted Grange to win a pennant before I moved on.

Three years later, in the 1994 World Cup at Dorado Beach, Puerto Rico, Ireland were represented by McGinley and Clarke. And the Dubliner's caddie was none other than JP, who would remain with him until the end of the 2002 season, when he joined Clarke with McGinley's blessing. Having arrived at Dorado Beach without accommodation, JP happily accepted my offer to share my chalet for the week. He was the perfect guest, most appreciative. A lasting impression, however, was of a tube of toothpaste which he squeezed so vigorously as to leave it akin to a blade by the end of his stay. I've often thought of that enforced economy when JP talked some years later of the 'tsunami of dollars' which tumbled into his bank account as his caddie's share of Rory McIlroy's first bonanza FedEx Cup triumph. As it happened, professional ranks would deliver more team success for McGinley than he had ever managed in the Senior Cup with Grange. Along with strong performances for Ireland in the Dunhill Cup, he and Harrington won the World Cup at Kiawah Island in 1997. It's interesting to recall that he was marginally the stronger of the pair, with a four-round aggregate of 272 to Harrington's 273. And, of course, there was the 2002 Ryder Cup when he had the honour of sinking the winning putt for Europe in a halved match with Jim Furyk.

'Great as those team successes undoubtedly were, there are still times when individual bragging rights are even more important,' McGinley concluded with a smile. 'That's why the Senior Cup win over JP will always be very special to me.'

Eddie Power and the Barton Shield

In the best tradition of Lahinch caddies, the instructions were clear and precise and would be ignored at one's peril: 'See that little bush down there? Now, hit it for that and hit it firm.' Without realising it, Martin Garry was shaping a sparkling future for Eddie Power as a competitor in the Bulmer's Barton Shield.

They met in September 1987, when Power made a memorable debut in Ireland's first-ever Triple Crown triumph in the Home Internationals. And the Tramore player remembered Garry when taking a key role in Barton Shield successes for his club, especially at a national level in 1992 and 1994. Power recalled:

> Martin was so authoritative that he took the decision-making off you. And that's what I was prepared to let Mick Burns do as my foursomes partner. Mick took me under his wing and I honestly believe that having a dominant player in each pairing was a key element of our success with Tramore. And the absence of such an approach seemed to create problems for Tiger Woods and Phil Mickelson in their famous Ryder Cup partnership at Oakland Hills.

But what of playing with his younger brother Peter? 'Myself and Mick were already established by the time Peter came along,' he replied. 'And they weren't about to split up their top pairing.'

The year 1992 was highly significant in Power's life, whose championship breakthrough had come on his home course five years previously, when he beat JP Fitzgerald in the final of the Irish Close Championship. In February, he married Eileen Rose McDaid, who had been Irish Women's champion in 1988. As it happened, she would regain the title in 1992 at The Island, where her new husband would lead Munster to success in the Interprovincial Championship.

From a Tramore standpoint, however, the most precious prizes were to come in September at Killarney, where the club achieved the almost unthinkable distinction of completing an Irish Senior Cup and Barton Shield double. Unthinkable, that is, to observers other than those associated with Tramore.

'To be honest, we saw it as a reward for several years knocking at the door,' said Power.

> For instance, the same panel of players had got to the final of the Senior Cup in Kilkenny in 1985, only to lose to Clandeboye. In fact, I can still vividly recall John Mitchell being beaten on the 21st by Edmund Quiery in the decisive match.
>
> By the time Killarney came around, the panel had been together for about 10 years, during which time we had great support from backroom men such as Michael Murphy, Seamie Kiely and Noel Jackman and from club officers like Tom Healy. Mind you, I remember not being considered good enough to get into the Senior Cup side, the week before I was runner-up in the Irish Close in 1983. But I was still happy to plod along in the shadow of Mick Burns.

In fact, when Tramore lost in Kilkenny, Burns was number one in a line-up which also included Power, Paddy Butler, John O'Brien and Mitchell. By the time the 1992 Barton Shield campaign got under way, Peter Power had come on the scene.

'With Mick and I playing well and a solid partnership behind us, nobody was going to touch us,' Power went on. In this context, Tramore's confidence received a considerable boost in the 1991 Barton Shield campaign, when they crushed Fermoy and Clonmel, each by 10 holes, before losing to Douglas in the provincial final.

The structure of the national finals, with the Barton Shield semi-finals and final being played on the opening day, made the big double less daunting than it might otherwise have appeared. So it was that with their eye on both trophies, Tramore maintained their focus over what became the three most rewarding days in the club's history, certainly from a competitive standpoint.

In the semi-finals against Ulster specialists Shandon Park, Power and Burns gained a crucial two holes win over the international partnership of Neil Anderson and David Long. It meant that Butler and Peter Power could be called in, with Tramore five holes up with three to play.

The final against Claremorris was even more one-sided. 'Mick and I lost the first where I was a bit jumpy and skied my drive left,' recalled Power. 'But we then won the next eight holes in a row.' After Tramore had secured a combined 10-hole lead with eight holes to play, both matches were called in.

Those of us who observed this brilliant triumph could see an inescapable irony in the fact that where the Power brothers were split, the Killeen brothers, Pat and John, played together at number one for Claremorris.

Meanwhile, with a coveted trophy secured, Tramore could reflect on a campaign in which none of their pairings had lost a match. In fact, they were never even behind. This remarkable dominance gained fresh emphasis when Mitchell and Noel Cunningham joined the Power brothers and Burns in a Senior Cup triumph two days later. By that stage, they had won 32 out of the 35 matches played, and two of those defeats were in the national semi-finals against Co. Sligo.

An amazing run of victories then extended into 1993 and ended only in the national final at Woodbrook, where they lost to Portmarnock. That was when Adrian Morrow and David Kelleher secured an extremely rare three-holes win over Power and Burns.

Another winning sequence, however, started in 1994, when they took revenge on Portmarnock in the national semi-finals at Co. Sligo, before going on to defeat Cairndhu in the decider. This second national Barton Shield pennant in three years sparked off a winning sequence which continued into 1995, before they eventually lost again, this time to Killarney in the Munster final.

In 1989, Power's work took him to Kilkenny, where he became technical manager of Ormonde's Brick company in Castlecomer. As an honorary member of both Tramore and Kilkenny golf clubs, he made himself available for Kilkenny teams in 1998 and has been ever since.

'We've had some success at provincial level and I got a bit of a run going until Noel Fox [Portmarnock] beat me at Mount Wolseley,' he said.

Having turned 40 and with three Irish Close titles to his credit, Power couldn't find the same enthusiasm for battle which had once fired Tramore to wondrous heights. He and Eileen Rose also had to care for a young family, which included Mark, a future Walker Cup representative. Either way, as Power explained it, Tramore had been a rather special team.

'There were no imported players,' he said. 'All five of us were home-grown in Tramore. That's what made our success so important to the club.' As well it might.

Downpatrick win the Junior Cup

Looking towards the 1987 season, one of Warrenpoint's more gifted golfers believed he had an irresistible way of strengthening their Senior Cup and Barton Shield teams. 'Why don't we invite Darren Clarke to become a member?' Jim Carvill suggested to Rory McShane.

The idea clearly had merit, not least for the fact that Clarke, who was on the verge of full international honours, faced the prospect of yet further disappointing campaigns with Dungannon. But the 1986 Warrenpoint club captain, who was set to lead the two category-one teams, would have none of it.

'I knew where Jim was coming from,' McShane acknowledged. 'Darren's talent shone like a beacon in the various scratch cup competitions throughout Ulster at that time, but I insisted that we had enough talent of our own.'

As things turned out, Dungannon failed to reach the match play stage of the Senior Cup in Ulster that year and were eliminated by none other than Warrenpoint in the second qualifying round of the Barton Shield. Meanwhile, Downpatrick were quietly expecting great chances at the Junior Cup, after failing at the All-Ireland stage in 1977 and 1979.

'There were times when you felt it was harder to get off the teams than it was to get on them,' recalled Godfrey Clarke, Darren's father, who became the club's head greenkeeper in 1983 and moved some years later to Ballycastle. Darren's memory is somewhat different. 'I knew we didn't have much of a chance of winning a provincial pennant,' he said. 'But on the credit side, I was never really conscious of any pressure. I remember our main objective was simply to give the club a boost by winning a couple of rounds. That was the height of our ambitions and I looked upon it as terrific fun and great experience.'

Father and son played in both the Senior Cup and Barton Shield but never partnered each other in the foursomes event. 'Maybe we felt it would have put too much strain on family relations,' conceded Godfrey with a chuckle.

One of the more interesting aspects of their involvement was the fact that Darren's club had to waive a regulation to allow him compete in the Senior Cup and Barton Shield. This stemmed from his status as a juvenile member. He played off scratch at 14 but was more interested in rugby at Dungannon Royal.

Meanwhile, Ken Armstrong, the former Irish rugby international who was coach to Dungannon Royal at the time, could see the enormous potential of young Darren Clarke as a loose forward. So, he was understandably anxious that one sport should not interfere with the other. Darren recalled:

> When the crunch came with regard to opting for either rugby or golf, the choice between a physical contact or walking pursuit was effectively made for me. As a 15-year-old, I broke my arm during rugby training and on medical advice, golf became my sport of choice from then on.

Godfrey took up the story:

> I was a member of Dungannon and playing in the Junior Cup team before taking over the greenkeeping job. Then, by the mid-eighties, I would have been playing off four while Darren was down to plus one or plus two and would obviously have been the backbone of

> both teams. With a very small pool of category-one players, we could generally put him down for a win in the Senior Cup, but the Barton Shield was obviously less predictable.

He continued: 'After a lapse of almost 20 years and as a poor eight-handicapper, my involvement in both competitions entered a new phase.' That was when Godfrey became captain of Rathmore GC, which automatically made him the non-playing captain of their Senior Cup and Barton Shield teams.

It meant a remarkable double for the two Clarkes. When he was made an honorary life member of Royal Portrush some years later, Darren became the only professional since the great Fred Daly to be accorded that distinction. And on a different level, Godfrey also followed in the footsteps of Daly, being elected captain of Rathmore for 1953–54 and 1954–55.

While Godfrey Clarke was plying his craft as greenkeeper at Dungannon, John Moore was assistant greenkeeper at Downpatrick. It would be some time before Clarke moved to the same position at Ballycastle GC, but Moore actually took over as head greenkeeper at Ardglass in 1987, while remaining a member of Downpatrick for a few more years.

This meant he could spearhead one of the most notable Junior Cup triumphs in the history of the competition.

Moore, Raymond Madine and Eugene Lynch had each known the bitter taste of failure in the national finals of the Junior Cup at Hermitage in 1977. The same trio were again on the losing Downpatrick side two years later, this time by the narrow margin of 3–2 against Limerick at Royal Portrush.

'Though we continued to have a strong Junior Cup squad during the following years, the all-Ireland pennant remained elusive,' recalled Moore. 'And when it eventually came, it was only after a hell of a battle in the '87 final against Killarney.'

The greenkeeper had been the rock of the team, winning all his matches except for the Ulster final, in which he lost on the 18th. In the all-Ireland semi-finals at Clandeboye, he thrashed Dermot O'Brien of

Grange by 9 and 7 and went on to win his top match in the final by 5 and 4. In fact, Downpatrick never went beyond the 15th green in the top two matches.

They knew they had a good side, if only from their experience in the local Senior Cowdy, which was a singles scratch match play competition between eight-man teams. 'We had some great matches against Warrenpoint, who had Senior Cup boys such as Jim Carvill, Kenny Stevenson, Gary McNeill and Paddy Gribben in action,' said Moore.

Still, Killarney made them fight all the way. Indeed, the remaining three matches of the final, due to be completed on the Saturday, had to be held over until 7:30 a.m. on the Sunday morning because of torrential rain. And all three went to the 18th, with Killarney winning at numbers three and four before Colm Coyle, the youngest member of the Downpatrick side, secured victory with a courageous nine-foot putt.

'I haven't played Junior Cup golf since then, because my handicap has been too low,' said Moore. 'But I've had the considerable pleasure of playing against Darren Clarke and his sister [Andrea] in mixed foursomes. And some years previously, there were Fred Daly Trophy matches against the likes of Ronan Rafferty and his brother Stephen.'

Darren Clarke made his debut for Ireland at Lahinch on 11 September 1987, the last day of the Home Internationals. And with a half-point in his singles match against Scottish veteran George Macgregor, he contributed to a major breakthrough – Ireland's first Triple Crown triumph.

Still, he had no involvement a week later at Clandeboye, where Warrenpoint brilliantly dominated the national cups and shields. The only trophy they didn't win was the Junior Cup, which went, as we have seen, to their Co. Down rivals.

'And you know, the Junior Cup breakthrough remained elusive,' said McShane, who was later honorary treasurer of Warrenpoint. 'I can't explain it. Even when we appeared to have good sides, it remained our Achilles heel.' Not surprisingly, he prefers to remember more rewarding times:

Our '87 success really had its beginnings at the national finals in Galway the previous year, when we were challenging for the Pierce Purcell Shield and the Jimmy Bruen Shield. Though we lost to Kanturk in the final of the Purcell and to Castletroy in the semi-finals of the Bruen, a major objective began to take shape.

Having inspired the gifted Warrenpoint players to share his wild dreams, McShane was rewarded with an unforgettable few days of unique achievement over that wet September weekend on the Dufferin course at Clandeboye.

With four out of five national pennants, they had set a new benchmark for competition in the Cups and Shields. And in the process, they unwittingly drew excessive attention to the efforts of Downpatrick, who had quietly secured the one that got away.

Portarlington win the Bruen Shield

With eight relatives in a squad of players, you would expect a rather special quality of team spirit. At Portarlington, however, the sort of togetherness which delivered a Bulmers Jimmy Bruen Shield triumph at Royal Portrush in 1999 went to the very roots of the club's existence.

The catalyst was Liam McMahon, a building contractor born and reared in the town. He had been one of the prime movers in the club's expansion, from a nine-hole layout with 280 members to 18 holes with more than double that number. And he went on to contribute handsomely as a player to the inconceivable prize of a major national pennant.

When Liam's brother, Noel McMahon, set about bringing the 1999 Bruen Shield squad together in his role as team captain, it became very much a family affair. Two of Noel's sons, Colm and Shane, were involved, along with four cousins: Conor and Seamus McCusker, Colm Murphy and David Lawlor.

Indeed family focus gained further emphasis through the inclusion of Mark Kennedy, son of the team's vice-captain, Tom Kennedy. Mark, who later studied medicine at UCD, was only 16 when he partnered with

54-year-old Liam McMahon in the crucial anchor position, where they lent a fascinating dimension to the notion of youth and experience.

'That was the strategy in all our pairings,' said Tom Kennedy. 'Another thing was a determination not to get ahead of ourselves; to concentrate on each match as it came. And we were still thinking that way when we got to the all-Ireland stage at Portrush.'

He went on:

> We stayed in a lovely little hotel called the Anchorage in Portstewart, where the owner promised to break open the champagne if we beat City of Derry in the semi-finals, not thinking we'd go all the way. But when we captured the trophy, he provided an upstairs room for ourselves and our supporters. Then he placed a crate of champagne in the middle of the floor and said, 'Go ahead boys.' It was a lovely gesture, and we didn't need second bidding.

Portarlington had taken over the hotel from the Tuesday of competition week until the following Monday, when they eventually headed south with their coveted prize. The more monetary-minded officers of the club had only come to terms with the £10,000 cost of the venture when they embarked on planning and building a new clubhouse worthy of their progressive spirit.

In recalling a period of remarkable development, Liam McMahon, who had been club captain in 1982 and was later made an honorary life member, said:

> When we got to thinking about expanding to 18 holes, we asked Eddie Hackett for a plan. His initial idea was that we should have eight par-threes but I disagreed and showed him a layout I'd done myself, which would give us a par of 71.
>
> The upshot was that Eddie went along with my plan, which meant that he charged us only £500. That was the last we saw of him. I then hired in all the machinery and took charge of the construction, and we did it all for £108,000, which included

tree-felling, laying out our own greens and putting in our own watering system.

All the members rowed in. I remember one particular evening having 88 people picking up stones off the fairways. With that sort of team spirit, how could we possibly fail when we went in search of a national pennant?

McMahon responded again to the call of the club by designing and building the new clubhouse. 'And I don't think I robbed them,' he added with a chuckle.

To encourage youngsters like Mark Kennedy and Conor McCusker to develop as serious players, Portarlington came up with a fascinating concept. Normally, these juniors would be restricted to their own competitions, but it was decided they could play in all the official club events, provided they got their handicap down to single figures. The only limitation was that they would not be eligible for the first net prize, only from second downwards, along with the gross prizes.

It worked wonderfully well. For instance, Mark Kennedy came down from 21 handicap to seven in two years and others followed suit, giving Noel McMahon the idea of combining teenagers with seasoned players in their fifties in his Bruen Shield partnerships. 'We all did our bit,' said Tom Kennedy. 'I remember during the summer holidays, I would take Mark down to the golf club at 9:30 in the morning, give him the price of sausages and chips for lunch and then go out and collect him in the evening. Sometimes in the dark.'

The renowned Dunluce stretch was unforgiving when Portarlington met City of Derry in the all-Ireland semi-finals, that wet, windy September. 'Those Derry guys were the nicest people I have ever met in golf,' said Liam McMahon. 'They even went so far as to come back on the morning of the final to wish us luck.'

Mark Kennedy, who was starting his Leaving Certificate year at the time, took up the story:

> I really enjoyed playing with Liam, who had introduced me to inter-club golf in a South Leinster competition a few years previously. I was off seven and he was 10, but his experience was very important.
>
> I remember in the semi-final we were two down after two and at the short third, Liam missed the green on the left, leaving me down a bank. We had never been down so early in a match and it came as a bit of a shock. But even with the pin cut close to the left, I managed to get my pitch within a foot of the hole, for a half in par. That gave us the impetus to go on and dominate the match, which we did.

In fact, they won by 5 and 4 in a 3–2 victory overall. And the anchor pair were even more dominant in the final, winning by 8 and 6 as Portarlington beat Athlone by 3 ½ to 1 ½. 'I imagine the memory of those days in Portrush will stay with me for the rest of my life,' he added. 'It was a great achievement for a small club; something we look back on with fond memories.'

Portarlington were no longer a small club, timid about treading such a formidable path. Rather had they become seasoned combatants who had quite correctly placed their store in the irresistible balance of youth and experience.

Memories of Bosco

Bosco McDermott had just driven back from Enniskillen. Bridging a gap of 53 years, he and nine others had journeyed in hostile weather to honour a colleague from the Leaving Certificate class of 1952, at St Mary's Galway. It was the sort of solidarity which characterised his extraordinary record in the Bulmers all-Ireland Cups and Shields.

The classmates gathered at Brewster GAA Park for the formal dedication of the stand to John Vesey, a native of Achill, who had become a great servant of Gaelic football north of the border. On their return, the next game at Galway GC beckoned for McDermott, who appeared to be at his most comfortable with a golf club close at hand.

'You know I'm like a kid with a comfort rag, a bit of blanket,' he said with disarming simplicity. And recalling the words of a friend, he went on: 'He would talk about this king who used to go down to the cellar every day. Nobody knew why. Only later was it discovered that he went down there to put on the old working clothes he was used to before he was made king. He felt more comfortable in them than in his regal attire.'

Remembered as the brilliant right full-back in Galway's famous three-in-a-row Gaelic football team of 1964, 1965 and 1966, McDermott went on to apply the same enthusiasm to the royal and ancient game. And it brought him a further six All-Ireland medals – four in the Bulmers Pierce Purcell Shield and two in the Bulmers Jimmy Bruen Shield.

'I love team golf,' said the former schoolteacher. 'I always viewed it as a natural extension of the team sports I played when I was young. Individual competition never did much for me, but the JB Carr Trophy [for seniors] was wonderfully fulfilling. I just loved to be part of a team, any kind of team.'

Remaining seriously competitive, he found that his sporting ambition wasn't dulled by the passing years. 'I'd love to be still playing Pierce Purcell with Galway, but I probably wouldn't be considered good enough.'

McDermott retained painful memories of his last Pierce Purcell appearance at national level in 1993, when Galway won at Woodbrook. That was when he was deemed the weak link in a beaten semi-final partnership with the late Martin Greaney, so he was dropped for the final.

'It was probably the only time I was ever dropped from a team, but I had to take it on the chin,' he recalled. 'I had played badly and it was a fair decision. John Flaherty was the captain and do you know, we fell out over it. How many years is that?'

There was a pause. Suddenly McDermott started laughing heartily. He knew he had caught me with his wicked humour. 'Believe it or not, I got over it,' he added, still laughing. 'And like any good team man, I did my thing by going out and caddying for one of the other lads.'

A second great sporting adventure began for him when, on retiring from inter-county football, he took up golf as a member of Galway GC. Success came quickly.

In 1974, he partnered Christy Tyrrell in the victorious Pierce Purcell team at Royal Dublin. 'I thought it was great; just like football again,' he recalled. 'I can still remember playing the short, par-four 16th in the final. Christy, who could hit a great ball, found the green with a long-iron tee-shot. Having seen that, our opponent put his wood back into the bag, took out an iron and was well short.' Another chuckle.

A drop in handicap meant missing out on Galway's Pierce Purcell triumph of 1982. By that stage, however, McDermott had added Jimmy Bruen Shield medals from 1980 and 1981 to his all-Ireland haul. His partner in 1980 at Lahinch, incidentally, was former Gaelic football colleague Jimmy Duggan, with whom he had a memorable 6 and 5 victory in the national semi-finals.

'I found those wins very satisfying, especially since Galway had done so much to promote the idea of the Bruen Shield in the first place,' he said.

The Pierce Purcell called to him once more in 1988, when he and his partner, Tom Greene, experienced the joy of winning both their matches at Little Island. And by the time they reached the national finals yet again in 1992 at Killarney, Galway were widely acclaimed as the Dream Team, a nickname borrowed from the famous US basketball line-up from the Barcelona Olympics of that year.

In partnership with Jackie Carroll – 'he sank an awful lot of putts' – McDermott shared in crushing victories by 8 and 7 and by 8 and 6. This, he had to concede on reflection, lent an element of overkill to the intense preparation of his teammate, Pat (Pateen) Donnellan.

'Pateen's partner was Johnny Walsh, an Army man who was used to meticulous preparation, whatever he was about,' said McDermott. 'But he never reckoned with Pateen, who had him out at the crack of dawn, getting ready for the fray. Going right through the bag. Serious stuff. Senior Cup players weren't as well prepared. What I remember most, however, was how much fun we had.'

He then paused before referring to another Galway Golf Club member, Tommy O'Connor, who departed to divot-free fairways in May 2022. 'Tommy was a first cousin of Christy Himself', he said:

> He was a member of the Senior Cup team and played off four-handicap well into his seventies. And I guarantee you that he spent more time on the putting green than any other member of the club. I was definitely on that wavelength. I know fellows in their eighties who still practise. They're still looking for the magic.
>
> When we were playing football, I remember Martin Newell getting the man-of-the-match in an All-Ireland we'd won. And he told me that on the morning of the final the following year, he prepared in exactly the same way, in the hope of rediscovering that special feeling. But he couldn't find it. Golf's like that. The magic can be so elusive.

He remembered some of the other players from Killarney in 1992. 'We always had wonderful team spirit – that's what made the difference,' he claimed. 'Without it, you're not going to perform either as a team or an individual.'

Warming to the subject, he added, as an indisputable expert: 'It's something you create and it means your ego has to go out the door a bit. I know some people who will play better for others than they would for themselves. They're the kind of people you need on a team.'

6

Golf in Strange Places

In classic missionary fashion, officials of the Golfing Union of Ireland were attacked by angry natives while attempting to play their part in promoting the development of the game in Iceland. It was a vicious onslaught, totally without warning, leaving our intrepid adventurers extremely grateful for the relative peace and calm associated with the game on their own island.

Let me explain how it happened. The Union hierarchy – president John McInerney and president-elect Fred Perry – were enjoying a leisurely game on the nine-hole Ness Course situated on a peninsula about seven kilometres from Reykjavik when suddenly the air was rent with a strange bird cry. At first, it sounded not unlike a common seagull, but the Irish officials became somewhat concerned when this was accompanied by a rapid rat-rat-rat, such as a woodpecker might make when attacking some defenceless tree.

Attack is an appropriate word, for suddenly, the birds came swooping down as eagles might pounce on their prey. It was only with some extremely adroit footwork, and wild swinging of a midiron by Perry, that injury to both officials was averted.

Arctic terns, which migrate to that particular part of Iceland to breed, are dangerous birds, particularly when their nesting areas are threatened. Smaller than a seagull and with a black head and long beak, they will dive like miniature heroes and attack without warning.

It was only after this frightening incident that the Irish officials learned it is common practice at Ness for players to walk along the fairways with a club held over their heads to ward off the terns. But even experienced campaigners have sustained head injuries, while cuts to arms and legs are a common occurrence.

Originally from Wexford, Perry was never at a loss for words. 'Jaysus! The boys back home would get a quare shock if these lads started coming down on them in the middle of a quiet, Sunday-morning fourball,' he said. 'I'll tell you they'd make it shockin' difficult to keep your head down in the middle of a stroke.'

Despite this unfortunate incident, however, the Irish were delighted to have made an important contribution to the 21st staging of the European Junior Team Championship, defending the title won in Dusseldorf the previous year. This time, it had come to the Grafarholt Course (hill of graves) near Reykjavik, which was the country's only 18-hole course.

I travelled there directly from covering the Open Championship at Royal St George's, where Bill Rogers was the surprise winner. It meant flying from London to Glasgow and from there to Iceland, which I was excited to be visiting for the first time.

It also made a considerable impact on Perry, who displayed a boyish enthusiasm for the assignment. Later, I discovered that tucked away on top of a press in his Boyle home, he kept a piece of whale meat which had first come into his possession during that Icelandic trip of 1981.

'It sort of dried out and cured itself over the years, so it doesn't stink anymore,' he said when we chatted shortly before his unexpected death in March 2018. Indeed, the same piece of meat had been the source of considerable amusement when Perry insisted on bringing it home in his carry-on luggage. It most definitely smelled in that early state.

Perry was an industrious official for whom I had the utmost respect. Still going strong at 84, he spent the last week of his life rescheduling a meeting of the GUI's Constitution Review Committee, which he was due to chair. He had previously served as convenor of this committee from 2009 to 2012.

It may be that as an enthusiastic fisherman, the Icelandic whale stirred in him wild notions of becoming a latter-day Captain Ahab. Either way, it seemed appropriate that he should be laid to rest in the hillside grounds of his parish church overlooking Lough Key, where he loved to venture when the Mayfly was up.

He became President of the GUI in 1982 but it was as a front-line official, likely to be found more often on the golf course than in the comfort of the clubhouse, that he made his greatest contribution to the game he loved. As you will gather, he had an innate stubbornness which was frequently expressed in his favourite saying: 'I might be wrong but I know I'm not.'

Up in Iceland, Spain won the title by beating Ireland by 5.5 to 1.5 in the final. The highlight of the decider was the 4 and 3 victory by Spain's top player, Jesus Lopez, over potential Walker Cup representative Philip Walton in the leading singles. Lopez, who was beaten by Walton in the final of the Spanish Open Amateur Championship at Torrequebrada in March of that year, went on to capture the British Boys' title in August 1981.

I remember Walton for his youthful enthusiasm in coping with the challenging conditions. For instance, a local rule permitted the moving of volcanic rocks if your ball happened in or beside them.

Unhappy experiences turned to physical pain when Walton carded a 75 in the final round of stroke-play qualifying. He injured the middle finger of his left hand while attempting to move a rock out of the way of a misdirected tee-shot on the 10th, getting his finger caught between two rocks which inflicted cuts above and below and caused blood to seep through his leather glove.

Ultimately, however, his main problem was connected with putting on difficult, bumpy greens where, if memory serves, he was reduced to using a three-iron in desperation.

It cost the Icelanders £25,000 to stage the European tests and they considered it money well spent. The main objective of Reykjavik Golf

Club and the Icelandic Union was to publicise golf in their country. However, despite the previous best efforts of all concerned, golf remained inferior as far as Icelanders were concerned to swimming, handball, football, athletics and a traditional style of wrestling called glima.

At the time of my visit, there were 2,200 golfers in 21 clubs playing 18 courses in Iceland, several of which were in very poor condition. Gunnar Torfason, the Reykjavik club secretary, told me:

> Our first golfers were professional people who went abroad to be educated and brought the game back to their native country. When our course was opened in 1963, we had 150 members, but the figure is now 550, at £100 membership fee per year.
>
> The problem is that we have too many golfers trying to play our course during a limited season from May until October. During that period, the course is in use for up to 20 hours each day. We are forbidden by law to restrict membership, so the only option as we see it, is to introduce an entrance fee of £200 which is double the annual subscription. But the ideal solution would be the building of more courses. If the European Championship succeeds at achieving this objective, then it will have been a marvellous success.

Icelandic golf has been given an update since then; the country now boasts 60 courses with 40,000 members. These include Ness, which remains a challenging, nine-hole layout, and Reykjavik, the country's oldest. We're told that it now has 2,500 members with access to 36 holes. One is at Grafarholt and the other at a location called Korpa.

To cope with increased demand, the second course was built in 1993 to a design by Hannes Þorsteinsson, a member of the British Institute of Golf-Course Architects. There had been a small 12-hole course on the land for several years, available to members. The 18-hole Korpa layout was formally opened in July 1997 when it held the national championships.

Meanwhile, Grafarholt continues to stage international events, as in the Nordic Team Championships three times, the European Team Boys Championship once and The European Senior Amateur Championship once. This more than anything shows the level of recognition that the Grafarholt golf course and Reykjavik Golf Club have gained overseas.

It will come as no surprise that building a golf course in Grafarholt was a very difficult task. There was hardly any depth of soil usable for cultivation, let alone building a golf course. Nevertheless, the club members persevered and under the guidance of Sweden's Nils Skold, sufficient topsoil was transferred to the site to make for a workable layout of remarkable variety. All of which makes for a remarkable story.

'It's not that big of a deal,' said Damian Mooney, with the nonchalance of a seasoned professional, 'just another golf course where the objective is still to get the ball into the hole.' It was May 2005 and we were in the Azores, of all places, looking towards a modest golf event.

The scene was the Batalha course, host venue for the 54-hole Verde Golf Azores Championship. And of the 11 Irish players competing for a prize fund of €100,000, only the 37-year-old Northerner had got a precious place in the Nissan Irish Open at Carton House later that week, when the money would be mouth-wateringly different.

As indicated by the tournament's title, we were in the Azores, a two-hour flight due west of Lisbon and set to become a serious golfing destination within a few years. This was the declared ambition of Drogheda-born Gerry Fagan, director of Oceanico Developments, which was already familiar in the golf tourist industry at that time for Amendoeira, a prestige project in Portugal's Western Algarve where Christy O'Connor Jnr and Nick Faldo were designers of a 36-hole complex.

The Azores is a nine-island archipelago in mid-Atlantic with a population of 240,000. While remaining a Portuguese dominion, its largely autonomous government was totally supportive of Fagan's €700 million investment plans, including the building of a third golf course on the charming island of Faial.

The two existing courses at the time of my visit were of admirably high quality, Batalha (27 holes) and Furnas, on the island of San Miguel.

Furnas, on less inviting, elevated terrain in the east of the island, was originally a nine-hole layout designed in 1936 by Turnberry's creator, Philip Mackenzie Ross, and expanded 50 years later. But the Batalha complex was seriously impressive, by any standards.

It was designed by Cameron Powell and opened for play in 1992, located on lush, delightfully rolling terrain with a generous covering of mature trees. Measuring 7,079 yards off the back tees, it had the unusual climax of a 208-yard par-three 18th, which brought to mind such celebrated American venues as Congressional.

To find golf in the Azores was surprising enough, but to find golf courses of the design and condition of Batalha and Furnas was utterly unexpected. And Fagan and his partner, Mancunian Simon Burgess, were determined that the new, third course, about a 25-minute flight from San Miguel, would be a worthy flagship.

'Our objective is to stage three European Tour events between the Portuguese mainland and the Azores, over the next four years,' said Fagan back in 2005, when a world recession was in nobody's thoughts. 'It may be the Portuguese Open or a new event entirely and the venues will be Amendoeira, Batalha and a new development we're doing north of Lisbon at Óbidos, designed by Seve Ballesteros.'

He went on: 'I believe that a tournament in the Azores could do much to heighten its appeal as a tourist destination, just as the Madeira Open has done for another Portuguese island. And to attract Irish visitors, we're obviously looking at direct flights from Dublin.'

Within a few years, these ambitious plans were to fall victim to the economic downturn which was to have a devastating effect on such developments. As I recall the Azores, the weather lacked the appeal of the Iberian Peninsula. In fact, I found myself comparing them to Connemara on a decent summer's day, though an absolute culinary delight was a local stew cooked in the ground, presumably by a submerged geyser.

The latest information is that the Azores have three golf courses, Batalha and Furnas on São Miguel island and Terceira Golf Club on Terceira island. All are to be found in the middle of the Atlantic Ocean, between Europe and North America.

Former amateur colleagues Noel Fox, Ciaran McMonagle and Timmy Rice were among those who joined Mooney back in 2005 on a modest stepping-stone in their patient quest for a professional breakthrough. And I could tell it wasn't easy. Though sponsored, a substantial portion of the prize fund still came from entry fees of £275 from each competitor.

'I played five EuroPro events last year, made all the cuts and then ran out of money,' said Mooney, who had qualified for Carton House by finishing eighth in the PGA Irish Region Order of Merit.

Meanwhile, all 11 participants would remember their first visit to the Azores. And in time, they might even see themselves as golfing pioneers, where pirates once sheltered from less benign authorities.

Barbados

A little-known historical fact is that under the Cromwellian repression of the 17th century, thousands of Irish men, women and children were transported to Barbados where they were sold into indentured servitude. As a consequence, hundreds of black families in the current population have surnames such as O'Connor, O'Carroll, O'Dowd, O'Duffy and Fitzgerald. Now, 350 years on, their descendants were benefiting from a golfing revolution, spearheaded by two leading financiers and a former Walker Cup player from the mother country.

The principals in this remarkable Irish story from 2002 were Dermot Desmond and J.P. McManus, major shareholders in the Sandy Lane resort, and Roddy Carr, who became the driving force behind Barbados Golf Club.

Perhaps the most exciting element of these dramatic developments in the Caribbean was the construction of Sandy Lane's Green Monkey Course, which was set for completion by the end of 2002. That is when the sale of 111 residential sites of one and a half acres, bordering the course and at a cost of $3 million each, commenced. This totalled a tidy $333 million.

The spectacular nature of the layout, designed by Tom Fazio, the leading architect who would go on to upgrade Adare Manor where the

2027 Ryder Cup will take place, had already attracted international attention at the time of my visit. 'It's a fantastic site – unbelievable,' enthused Darren Clarke of the Green Monkey. 'When completed, I have no doubt it will become one of the world's all-time great courses.'

As it happened, Desmond, as chairman of the Sandy Lane company, had already been approached to stage a major international tournament there. 'A sponsor is in place and there is also outline approval for the event from the European Tour and the US PGA Tour,' he told me. 'In fact, they've even set a date.'

He went on: 'It will be a new, world event with an exciting format but for reasons of confidentiality, I'm not in a position to divulge further details at this stage. I can say, however, that we are going to consider it.'

The attraction of the Green Monkey, named after the species indigenous to the island, lay in the nature of the quarry-dominated site and the expertise of the designer. This was where extensive amounts of coral rock were quarried to build Bridgetown Harbour, and the huge gaps in the landscape that the excavators left in their wake made for dramatic changes in elevation, up to 150 feet in places.

At $30 million, it was one of the most expensive courses ever built at that time. During my visit in June 2002, I was especially taken by how Fazio heightened the existing spectacle through the additional movement of earth. For instance, he extended the 22-acre quarry to achieve a sheer face, 30 feet high, to the right of the par-five, ninth fairway. And further on, he cut a channel through the rock for the 11th and 12th holes.

The overall impact was of a decidedly angular layout rather than the seductive curves one normally associated with his work. The signature hole and one certain to be greatly photographed was the short 16th, where a cliff face provided a backdrop to the green which had a monkey-shaped bunker to the front, on the right. Irrigation was supplied from the company's own desalination plant.

Fazio was often in the news at the time, through his much-acclaimed, seamless lengthening of Augusta National, but this happened to be his first project outside of the US. Explaining the reasons for choosing him, Desmond said:

> It's very simple: we researched those we considered to be the best designers in the world and in our view, Fazio came out on top for lots of different reasons.
>
> Who made the changes to the world's premier courses such as Cypress Point, Pine Valley and Augusta National? Fazio. Then there are the number of his courses which are ranked in the top 100 in the world.

Among these was his 1989 creation, Shadow Creek, which had become part of golfing lore, certainly in the US. Effectively, it entailed transforming an utterly barren area of the Nevada desert on the outskirts of Las Vegas into a breathtaking oasis of rolling terrain with glistening streams and ponds, mature trees and lush gardens. Fazio described it as: 'One of the grandest experiences of my life.'

His brief for the Green Monkey was: 'If you owned this site, what would you do?' And having been given total freedom, he was, understandably, reserving judgement until the project was complete. But apart from Clarke, it drew lavish praise from Mark O'Meara and fellow US tournament professional, John Cook.

Meanwhile, the plan was that Sandy Lane would have a total of 45 holes, including the original nine and the new Country Club 18 which, another design by Fazio, was very much a resort course. 'Our objective was to have a course where people would score well if they played well and another, more challenging layout,' added the chairman. And his verdict on the Green Monkey? 'Fazio has surpassed what he said he would do.'

The overall investment by Desmond, McManus and their fellow shareholders in Sandy Lane stood well over $400 million at the time. Much of that would be recouped through the sale of sites around the Green Monkey, though Desmond pointed out that they would probably sell no more than 14 or 15 sites per year.

Meanwhile, Carr and Michael Davern, who was then general manager of golf and property before moving to The K Club, were working closely with the Barbadian government looking to promote the island (only 21 miles long) as a golfing destination. Carr anticipated dramatic expansion, which has culminated in the recent spectacular Apes Hill establishment, designed by the sadly departed Ron Kirby.

'The exciting thing is that the government, through the recent launching of Golf Barbados, are determined, with our help, to make this the leading golfing destination in the Caribbean,' said Carr.

After ending his association with Seve Ballesteros in Spain, Carr found an intriguing new challenge for his organisational skills on the Caribbean island. There, with government support, he set about redesigning and rebuilding the existing Barbados GC course which had lain dormant for 20 years through lack of interest.

With the help of Kirby, an old friend who had worked with Jack Nicklaus on Mount Juliet and actually completed the routing of the Old Head of Kinsale, Carr opened the first Barbadian public course in July 2000. During my visit, the quality and condition of the layout reflected considerable credit on everybody concerned.

MIDNIGHT FINNISH!

All sane golfers, especially from these parts, know that their great game was invented by Cúchulain, up there in the Cooley Mountains many moons ago. Then the Romans tried to claim it for themselves, along with the Dutch and, of course, those inferior Celts from north of Hadrian's Wall, the most brazen copyists of all. Now, it turns out that the Finns, of all people, also attempted to get in on the act.

Down in Enniscrone back in 1999, I remember talking with Mikko Korhonen, an 18-year-old from Helsinki, who lost to Garth McGimpsey in the opening round of the West of Ireland. In the course of our chat, he enthused: 'In the middle of June, the light is good enough to play 72 holes in one day, which I have done.' Ah, for the energy of youth. I didn't have the nerve to tell him that even then, on the gentle, tree-lined terrain of Clontarf GC, 18 holes was generally as much as I could manage.

Apparently, it's not enough that Mikko Ilonen should have wiped the eyes of our brave amateurs by capturing the West of Ireland title at Enniscrone in 1999, only to return 15 years later to win the Irish Professional Open at Fota Island. Just think of it, in every club he visits, the bold Mikko will be able to boast a double that only elite Irish practitioners such as Pádraig Harrington, Rory McIlroy and Shane Lowry have managed to achieve.

As it happens, a popular story around golfing circles in Helsinki concerns two young reindeer herders, Paarvi Tuulvitskoog and Olaaferinn 'Ollie' Ruukinaanaluu, who took to batting around a frozen herring with a finely polished antler. The idea was to see which of them could slide the slippery kipper into a far-off, empty vodka bottle in the lowest number of strokes.

They called their game 'paar en fisken', which means hit the fish. Or paar for short. When the lads discovered that the Scots had been playing a similar game for several centuries, however, they immediately sold their animals and moved to Glasgow, where they became besotted with the royal and ancient pursuit.

The upshot of this episode was that 'paar', or 'golf' as it soon became known, found a permanent and revered place in Finnish sports consciousness. Indeed, it led to the founding of the Helsinki Golf Club in 1932.

A likely story, I hear you mutter. But whatever the truth of these antler-waving antics, golf in Finland can have a fascinating side to it. One of the most intriguing of its 180 courses is the Green Zone GC, located directly on the border with Sweden. The result is that roughly half the holes are in either country.

At one time, clubhouse attendants were only too happy to supply visitors with stamped customs forms. Especially interesting is the fact that the short sixth hole actually traverses the international boundary and time-zone. Which means that your fourball could tee off in Finland at 12.50pm and putt out in Sweden at noon.

Having visited the scene of midnight golf on the trip to Reykjavik for the European Junior Championship in July 1981, I was delighted to be given the opportunity of actually playing in such conditions 26 years later. That was when I found myself looking down the fairway of my final hole into gathering gloom.

I could still make out the desirable landing area for a drive, between bunkers right and left, about 220 yards away. Further into the distance, cars with their headlights on were approaching from the clubhouse area, down a road skirting the left-hand side of the fairway.

On the right was Lake Katuma, which is frozen from mid-December until late March. Now, its gently lapping waters were accompanied by birdsong. In the evening? Well, that would be stretching things considering my watch told me it was now 11.50 p.m. By the time I reached the green, it would be the witching hour on Finland's splendid Linna course, about 100 kilometres north of Helsinki.

As Noel Coward might have observed, mad golfers in Finland go out in the midnight sun. This was 12 July, about a month later than the ideal time of year for such an exercise.

As the only Irishman in that group of pioneers, I wasn't surprised to find myself assigned to the Ballybunion Suite in the Linna clubhouse, which also boasts the Oakmont, Muirfield and Carnoustie suites. A sauna attached to the bathroom was a reminder of the local lifestyle.

The course, stretching to a muscular 7,244 yards off the back tees, followed an undulating route through plentiful birch and pine trees. As we set off at 7.00 p.m., Pekka, our Finnish guide, confessed to being apprehensive about the weather, having just endured three days of torrential rain. He needn't have worried. It was a glorious evening, prompting him to conclude that if doctors diagnosed with the same accuracy as meteorologists, half their patients would be dead.

Among his stories was an almost inevitable reference to Finland's most celebrated composer, Sibelius, who apparently lived part of his life in the Linna area and was inspired to compose his best-known opus, Finlandia, while looking over the countryside from a viewing tower in Aulanko, about a 10-minute drive away.

Linna, where Ilonen was the touring professional, represented an overall investment of €14.5 million, which would be considered relatively modest by Irish standards.

Why the interest in Irish tourists? 'If someone had asked me that question a few years ago, I wouldn't have had an answer,' replied Petri Peltoniemi, managing director of Linna Golf. 'But we've since had hundreds of Irish people here. We wouldn't dream of trying to compete with the Algarve or the Costa del Sol in numbers, but a big attraction, as you've discovered, is that you can start golf at 7.00 in the evening and complete your round. And you can still play until 10.00 in the evening in September.'

He went on: 'You get a lot of Finnish visitors to Ireland because we like your people. Our way of living is very close to the Irish. Like you, we have a friendly country. That is also what we're trying to sell.'

Five minutes' walk away was the four-star Vanajanlinna Hotel, a former hunting lodge where golf packages of bed and breakfast and a green fee were a very modest €130. Generally, the price of golf was very competitive by Irish standards, and I was informed that the target months were June, July and August, when the weather was generally at its most appealing.

Of the courses within a 30-minute drive of the hotel, the 36-hole Kytaja development overlooking Lake Kytaja was especially impressive. With a golf season squeezed into six months from May until October, the Finns faced a difficult battle in promoting the game among their own people, much less in attracting tourists. Still, I remember silently admiring the efforts of a country that once had the courage to go to war with its mighty Russian neighbours.

Finally, it would be a serious omission to talk of golf in Finland without mentioning the nine-hole Arctic Club. Though it wasn't on my itinerary, I was assured that it was well worth the trip inside the Arctic Circle, as the name suggests.

7

Palmer

When Arnold Palmer turned 70, his good friend and long-time manager, Mark McCormack, felt it was safe to tell some tales of their school time. Like the bets they had with each other over the previous 39 years, and how none of them was honoured.

McCormack recalled:

> Years ago, when we were flying from Australia to Honolulu, I stopped on the way to the airport and ended up with the scores of all the NFL [American football] games. We were leaving Australia on a Monday which was a Sunday in the US and were going to arrive in Honolulu on Monday morning.
>
> While on the plane, we spent two hours making bets and when we got to Honolulu I told him to get the newspapers and check the scores. Needless to say, I won all the games. And the expression on his face had to be seen to be believed. Ultimately I confessed – and never collected.

In July 2001, two years after these revelations, Palmer was about to hit shots on the practice ground at The K Club, when he felt a twinge in his left shoulder. Apparently, it was an ongoing problem which came as no surprise to a doctor friend who had travelled with him from the US.

On being told that medication would ease the inflammation, Palmer protested: 'I don't like pills.' 'Well then', said the doctor, 'you're gonna have to lay off golf for a month.' After considering this for the briefest of moments, Palmer growled: 'OK. I'll take the pills.'

He looked across at me and grinned. 'There are times when I think that maybe I shouldn't play,' he conceded. 'But I can't stay away. Right now I should be reading a book or having a drink with friends or whatever, but I need to hit a few golf balls.'

So he began to hit some balls. From the two sets of clubs he brought with him to the Senior British Open at Royal County Down the previous week, he settled for the ones with the graphite shafts. He removed a pitching wedge, noticed that the leather grip had come undone and with a well-practised adjustment, rectified the problem.

He hit another ball. 'Hell, let's talk,' he said. It had been a busy morning. In the company of Ed Seay and Harrison Minchew from his design company, he had looked over the new course at The K Club which was started earlier that year, across the Liffey from what are now the 16th, 7th and 8th holes.

Then there was a lightning buggy trip around the existing championship layout in the company of Michael Smurfit and director of golf, Paul Crowe. The objective was to pinpoint areas of improvement for a general update of the course but also in preparation for the Ryder Cup. I joined the entourage.

'The course is going to be in fantastic shape for the Ryder Cup,' Palmer enthused. 'It will be so good, the players will love it. What I think is now a nice golf course will be very competitive for match play. It's going to be very exciting.'

There was also time for reflection on the climactic stages of the Senior British at Royal County Down. 'How did Jack [Nicklaus] do? Did he get close?' I explained how Nicklaus had got within two strokes of the lead before slipping away. He had, however, hit a great drive down the 18th to be within 236 yards to the front of the green. 'Oh! He drove it that far, did he?' said McCormack, the other half of this legendary duo.

Estimates vary, but Palmer was acknowledged as the wealthier of the two, with a fortune of around $400 million. He was then a month from his 72nd birthday and hadn't won a Major championship since 1964, nor any tournament other than the odd seniors title since 1975. Yet he could still command $90,000 for a company day and remained among those featured by *Forbes* magazine among the leading earners in world sport.

Against that background, it seemed odd to hear him talk of his early days of deprivation, accompanied by surprising bitterness while relating one particular instance. He was reminded of it by the fact that his first visit to this country in 1960 was also his first experience of links terrain.

'Sam Snead and I handled it fairly well, as I remember,' he said modestly of their fine Canada Cup victory at Portmarnock. 'But when you love the game as much as I did, it was a new experience which fell right into place.' Then he went on: 'I was devastated in 1954 when, after winning the US Amateur, I found I wouldn't be able to play in the British Amateur or the Walker Cup team.

'I couldn't afford it. I had no money. I had gone to Wake Forest on a full scholarship – my books, tuition and room and board. And there wasn't money for any frills.' Instead of an extended amateur career, he turned professional and joined the PGA Tour the following year.

So was it true that he eloped with his wife, Winnie? With a grin, he admitted:

> I did. I met Winnie when she was a hostess at a tournament I was invited to play in the week after the US Amateur. I met her on Tuesday, took her out Wednesday, Thursday, Friday and asked her to marry me on Saturday. I had a job as a manufacturer's rep, making $500 a month. But in truth, I had no money. Zero.

How did he plan to finance a marriage? 'Well,' came the innocent reply, 'I was bold.' He explained:

> After asking her to marry me, I had to buy her a ring. And not having any money, I had to borrow from my golfing friends who were more than happy to oblige. It cost $4,000 so I was now seriously in debt.

I suggested that that was a considerable amount of money back then. 'It was a nice ring,' he said, with one of those disarming smiles. And was the story about Pine Valley true? 'This is how it happened,' he went on. 'My friends then took me to Pine Valley to play golf and I won enough to pay back the money I'd borrowed. I had never played the course before, but I shot 68 on my first round and that was worth a lot. They were betting me I wouldn't break 100.'

His eyes noticeably misting over, he then talked with moving sensitivity about his relationship with his wife, who had died of cancer two years previously. 'I suppose you could describe Winnie and I as lovebirds – every minute for 45 years. Her death was terrible. She was not just a wife, but she was a friend, a partner.'

Suddenly he changed the topic. 'Do you have a copy of my latest book?' he enquired. 'Then I must get you one. All this stuff is in there. It would save you a lot of notes.' Later, without having given him any name or address details, a remarkable thing happened.

Two weeks after our meeting, a signed copy of *A Golfer's Life* arrived at my home address. Inside was a card from Donald W (Doc) Giffin, with the message:

> Dermot – Happy to fulfil Arnold's promise to send you a copy of his latest book. Glad to hear from you via the Boss. Best regards. [Signed] Doc Giffin.

Back at The K Club, I told Palmer of my trip to the 1994 US Open at Oakmont from where a group of visiting golf writers went to Latrobe on the Saturday of the championship. While playing there, Winnie arranged to have a waiter bring out drinks to the 10th tee. She had said to the waiter, 'Put that on my tab,' and then, almost as an afterthought, added: 'And put my tab on Arnie's tab.'

He laughed heartily, adding, 'She was great.' Referring to her death, he said: 'With Winnie going, I'm a bit lost right now.' But he would readily acknowledge that life goes on, and he was helped enormously by a wonderful relationship with people.

'It started a little differently,' he continued:

> My father, Deke [a professional golfer], was a very tough taskmaster. He was a fighter but also a guy who could be very sentimental. He liked people and he didn't like it when others did things that weren't nice. And he drove that home to me constantly.
>
> Sure, you treat everyone the same as you'd like to be treated, but there was more. You had to play the whole thing out and remember it at all times. It became bred into me to the extent that I didn't have to work on it. Now, people are my life.

He talked of his close friendship with golf writer Pat Ward-Thomas of the *Guardian* and how they and their respective wives played bridge together. And how Ward-Thomas, a wartime pilot in the RAF, had flown one of Palmer's planes.

Flying, incidentally, had been a huge part of the great man's life since 1955. When we met, his craft was a Citation 10 and he was immensely proud of having flown 17,000 hours in total, which was about 70 per cent what the average airline pilot would do over an entire career.

When considering Palmer's incalculable contribution to tournament golf, it seems that his legacy was already determined as far back as a fateful July day at Troon in 1962. That was when his great friend Ward-Thomas paid him this beautiful tribute: 'In technique, attitude and manner, he makes some of his famous rivals seem puny. Palmer's presence has brought greatness once more to the old Championship. It has inspired others to compete and has set a new standard which can only benefit all who follow.'

And as I discovered, he had a wonderful capacity to warm to people, which they happily reciprocated.

TREVINO'S CALL

In response to *Golf Digest*, Lee Trevino listed the best players he had seen in every key department of the game. And it made for fascinating reading, especially his description of the best shot he ever witnessed.

This came from Sam Snead, who, at 66, was playing in the 1978 Inverrary Classic in Florida. He and Trevino were on a long par-four where, from 'a real tight lie', Snead had 220 yards to the hole for his second shot, with the wind against him and slightly from left to right.

From there, he proceeded to hit a high hook with a driver to leave the ball 12 feet from the hole. 'I couldn't believe it,' said Trevino. 'I just stopped walking and stared at the ball up on the green. Now, I saw a lot of great golf in more than 30 years, but I've never seen anything like that shot.'

So to Trevino's list:

- Best shot-maker: Sam Snead
- Best long irons: Jack Nicklaus
- Best driver: Greg Norman
- Best middle irons: Johnny Miller
- Best competitor: Arnold Palmer
- Best sand-player: Gary Player
- Best fairway woods: George Knudson
- Best player in bad weather: Tom Watson
- Best putter: Ben Crenshaw
- Best chipper: Hubert Green
- Best short irons: Chi Chi Rodriguez
- Best trouble-shooter: Seve Ballesteros

****

'I don't trust doctors. They are like golfers. Everyone has a different answer to your problem.' Seve Ballesteros

****

After the Masters in April 1995, I was given the opportunity to retrace the steps of the great Bobby Jones, back beyond the founding of Augusta National to his childhood days at East Lake. It came courtesy of Augusta member Tom Cousins, who flew a small group of us to Atlanta in his private jet.

OB Keeler, Jones's biographer, informed us that 'Bobby was a tiny, spindling figure in rompers ... just past his fifth birthday,' when he first took a club in his hand. And he wasn't much older when his parents placed him under the guidance of Stewart Maiden, a stocky little Scot from Carnoustie, who had just arrived at East Lake to replace his brother, Jimmy, as club professional.

East Lake is also famous because it was there, in 1948, that the onset of serious illness caused 46-year-old Jones to play his last round of golf, shooting birdies at the closing two holes, to finish on level par. For a variety of reasons, the club that played host to the 1963 Ryder Cup and has since become home to the PGA Tour Championship went into serious decline, almost to the point of extinction.

Much of the problem was connected to violence in the local community, making the club a dangerous location for patrons. The solution? Tom Cousins and a group of business colleagues bought the club in December 1994 and, in co-operation with the US government, put together a radical rebuilding scheme to give the locals new pride in their neighbourhood. It meant matching public money, dollar for dollar, to the tune of $32 million.

At the same time, Cousins and his colleagues invested $25 million in restoring the clubhouse and the course designed by Donald Ross to former glory. The club, which was closed in June 1994, was reopened 13 months later. By way of an endorsement of the restoration work, the US

Golf Association committed to staging the US Amateur Championship there in 2001, when Bubba Dickerson captured the title.

'I'm afraid the notion of perfection appeals to me, which probably explains why we're spending enough money here to build five courses, let alone restore one,' said Cousins. Part of the work involved relaying the greens and a major clean-up of the 24-acre lake that dominates the layout. And by stripping ugly additions away, the 40,000-square-foot Tudor-style clubhouse was restored to how its architect had conceived it.

'East Lake was the in-place in Atlanta in the 1920s and we want to make it that way again,' Cousins added. 'We're overwhelmed by the response we've already had from prospective members. With the Olympic Games coming to America next year [1996], the world is going to hear a lot about Bob Jones and the club which nurtured his unique talent.'

****

Finding shamrock in Texas

Leaving behind the lush, windswept plains of Oklahoma, we crossed the state line into the Texas Panhandle. About half an hour later, there was no mistaking our destination when very familiar names came into view on either side of the street.

First there was the Shamrock Inn, followed by the Blarney Inn. And if that wasn't enough, every other lamppost had attached to it a banner with the lettering 'Shamrock Texas', above and below our national emblem.

Indeed when one included the plaster-castings on public buildings, it would have been difficult to find more shamrocks in O'Connell Street, Dublin, on our national feast day. And this was September.

When my son, Mark, and I set off on a recent American road trip from Chicago to Santa Monica on the Pacific coast, this was always going to be a special stop for me, because of the Shamrock Country Club. It would be my one indulgence towards the royal and ancient game.

Lest we enrage the purists in our midst, we're not claiming to have slavishly followed Route 66, much of which, as it happens, lies beneath major interstate roadways. We did, however, manage to make the most of iconic stops, of which Shamrock is a significant one, not least for its status as the 'Crossroads of America.' This stems from the crossing there of Interstate 40 and Highway 83, a unique occurrence in the US road system.

We were both ready for lunch and, after I had assured my son of the renowned hospitality of the golfing community, we decided to eat at the country club, little more than a mile out of town.

Those who have experienced lengthy road trips will know that music is an important part of the enjoyment. To this end, we relied on an eclectic mixture from local radio stations and CDs we had brought from home. It was now time for something with a golfing flavour.

Ever amenable, Mark had no problem with my choice of Kiri Te Kanawa singing Mozart, especially when I explained that she was quite an enthusiast with a club and ball and was, in fact, president of Brocket Hall GC in Hertfordshire 13 years previously, before being succeeded by none other than Nick Faldo.

'I believe that there are only a few women who have been given this role in the golf world, so I am especially proud to be counted amongst them,' was how the New Zealand diva described the distinction.

Anyway, her magnificent voice filled the hot Texas air as our SUV eased into the golf club grounds, where there was not a soul in sight and the only sound was the drone of a mower, somewhere out on the course. A single-storey corrugated-iron structure incorporated the professional's shop, the lounge and, behind that, the grandly titled banqueting room, all of which were closed. At 2.30 in the afternoon.

Located behind the local national guard armoury, the club was launched in 1946 and currently had 120 members enjoying the challenge of its par-36, nine-hole stretch of 3,238 yards, where drives are struck from elevated tees to severely undulating fairways.

It was tempting to draw comparisons with the bleak Texas landscape of the movie *Tin Cup*, with Kevin Costner playing a down-at-heel pro at a down-at-heel driving range. On further inspection, however, this had a lot more to offer. And if Shamrock, with a population of little more than 2,000, could claim to be a city, its local country club was entitled to have similar pretentions.

There are no sand or grass bunkers, but by way of hazards, three ponds have to be negotiated. The signature hole is the fourth, where the ideal tee-shot is a 200-yard drive between water on the left and out-of-bounds down the right. And for $20, you can play all day.

I didn't dare mention the additional hazard of rattlesnakes in those parts, given the enduring shame of my behaviour in the Route 66 museum in Clinton, Oklahoma. In a corner was a wooden barrel on which was written: 'To view baby rattlers, lift the lid.' With considerable trepidation, I eased up the lid, only to see five babies' rattles lying innocently on the bottom of the barrel.

Just as we were about to leave, a tall figure emerged from a pick-up truck and unloaded his golf bag beside a club buggy carrying a four-leafed clover as an emblem. Jim Tindall extended a warm Texas welcome, offering further evidence of the small world that golfers inhabit.

Having introduced myself as a golf writer from Ireland, I mentioned knowing a one-time president of Clontarf GC, Bill Tyndall, who spelt his name with a 'y'. 'There aren't many of us around,' he replied. 'We're of Scottish origin. And I don't know what the connection with the shamrock is all about. But the town has a piece of the Blarney Stone.'

Seemingly unoffended at my scepticism, he insisted: 'Well, it makes a good story, anyway. And the way ours is situated, you don't have to break your back to kiss it.' That was followed by a long, low laugh.

Originally from a local townland called Twitty, from which country and western singer Conway Twitty apparently took his surname, Tindall claimed to be retired, though he looked far too young for such ease. 'Our family did some ranching, and we sold it some time ago,' he explained. How many acres? 'Oh, about 6,000,' came the reply, and the Texas drawl couldn't have been more nonchalant.

'We're a small club, but we enjoy our golf while trying to serve the community,' he went on. 'St Patrick's Day is a great occasion. As you know, it fell on a Monday this year and over the preceding weekend, we had a big 36-hole competition to celebrate the occasion.' When I remarked on the decidedly brisk wind, he said: 'This would be fairly calm by our standards.'

Very much a local man, he took obvious pride in relating how his grandfather was responsible for the Conoco building in the centre of town, where the locally famous 'U Drop Inn' is located. 'The only time I went beyond these shores was to Germany for my national service,' he said.

Remembering a few Fáilte Ireland shamrock badges which I had picked up during Masters week the previous April, I gave him one as a gift. Clearly charmed by the simple image, he asked us to 'hang on a minute.' Whereupon he went to the pro shop with keys at the ready, opened it and emerged with two Shamrock hats, one for me and the other for Mark. 'Now,' he said. 'You've something to remember us by back in Ireland.' Indeed we did.

Originally named Wheeler, the town's change to Shamrock stemmed from the previous local abode of George Nichols, a late 19th century Irish sheep farmer. And at 175 feet, its water tower in the centre of town is the tallest structure of its kind in the State of Texas.

It's the country club, however, that I'll best remember – especially its name, which seemed more than a little incongruous so far from home.

Ben Hogan and Phyllis Wade

Ben Hogan's battle for mobility created a special bond between himself and Phyllis Wade. He knew her pain and she knew his. And she felt he admired her stubborn refusal to think of herself as being handicapped.

'I think that's why he was always checking on me,' she told me when we met at Riviera CC, California, in January 2018. 'He'd smile, and as you know, he didn't smile a lot.'

Then, pointing to the neatly placed railway ties on the steep incline from the 18th green to the elevated clubhouse, she said: 'Those ties weren't there when he walked up that hill on his shattered legs in 1950.

It was just mud. They didn't put the wood down until maybe the sixties. I remember the way he used his clubs as walking sticks.'

Photographs on the clubhouse walls were a shrine to Hogan's triumphs there. There were also shots of Spencer Treacy and Katherine Hepburn from the filming of *Pat and Mike* at Riviera in 1952. Jerry Lewis was remembered from *The Caddy* in 1953, and Gregory Peck as a club member.

Outside, close to the first tee, was a bronze of Hogan, sculpted by Ron Pekar, who, interestingly, had the great man holding a driver reduced to two-thirds its normal length and with his legs cut off at the knees.

Phyllis was 19 when she first worked as a volunteer at the Los Angeles Open in 1948. She was assigned as the walking scorer for the defending champion – who happened to be Hogan.

The experience taught her about sporting greatness from up close when Hogan again became LA Open champion that year at Riviera, where he also won the US Open. It's a small wonder he adopted Phyllis as a lucky omen.

It is generally acknowledged that *Follow the Sun*, from 1951, was the first feature film made about golf. The movie was prompted by the horrific 1949 car crash and subsequent recovery by Hogan. I'm quite proud of my copy of the movie, largely because the actual golf shots were played by leading professionals of the time, including Hogan.

Promoted as the 'real-life love story of two kids from Texas, Ben and Valerie Hogan,' it stretched credibility, not least for the fact that, at 39, Hogan could hardly have been considered a kid. And it wasn't exactly 'real-life'. Also, it was said that Glenn Ford, playing Hogan, waggled the golf club like Errol Flynn preparing for a sword fight, and that he hunched over putts like a man suffering severe stomach cramps. Phyllis remembered it well:

> I grew up knowing Glenn Ford and when I heard he was going to play Ben in the movie I thought he was a bit tall. Glenn was over six feet. Valerie wasn't more than 5ft 2ins. Anyway, Glenn and Ben

were friends and he actually promised me he would do his best in the part.

Mind you, I don't think people were overwhelmed by the outcome, though I thought it turned out OK. Anne Baxter, who played Valerie, was very pretty and I thought she did a very good job. But Glenn was like James Stewart playing Glenn Miller. A foot too tall!

I have some wonderful golfing memories of Hogan, Snead and Arnold Palmer. Winnie Palmer was an absolute doll. She was very shy, unassuming. Very few people really knew her. I knew Bob Hope and William Holden. And Frank Sinatra, who was a nice man, but volatile. And Andy Williams. I don't drink so I never did the party scene. My husband used to call me his cheap date.

Memories remained fresh of Hogan's famous comeback in front of 9,000 dedicated fans, when he tied with Snead after 72 holes at Riviera and was then grateful that the play-off had to be postponed by eight days because of rain. We're told that he limped to the first tee of the play-off and ultimately lost to his old rival by 72–76.

Phyllis was very much a part of this rich period in American golfing history. Apart from meeting at tournaments, she and Hogan contacted each other a few times every year. She also talked about getting very close to his wife, emphasising that her relationship with the great man never extended beyond pure friendship.

'Valerie was an absolute doll,' she recalled of the woman who married 'The Hawk' in 1935:

Very quiet, very sweet. I talked to her about my injuries, and she talked about the severity of Ben's surgeries. She was absolutely devoted to him and was shattered when he died in 1997.

I was invited to attend his funeral, and I was also present when he was the honouree at Muirfield Village in June 1999. Barbara Nicklaus told me it was going to happen and I made a point of being there. I hadn't seen Valerie since Ben's death and we had what proved to be our last lunch together. She died a few weeks later. And I shed tears for Valerie, just as I had shed them for her husband.

In her capacity as a tournament volunteer, Phyllis claimed to have done everything from on-course scoring to babysitting competitors' children. More recently, she had been helping out in the media centre. 'I visited your country [Ireland] some time ago,' she continued. 'My brother, who is a doctor, had a conference some place outside Dublin and he took me along to mind his children.'

Her triumph over cruel physical disabilities can be gauged from a successful return to active golf, which she had first played as a six-year-old. Having become good enough for play off four-handicap, she enjoyed the thrill of a hole-in-one with a five-wood on Riviera's famous short sixth, with its quirky bunker in the middle of the green.

'They would have to drain the blood off my knees when I played, so I eventually decided to stop about 25 years ago,' she said. 'After that, I realised I could still be happy, simply being involved in the game. And I also do volunteer work for the Special Olympics and was PGA Volunteer of the Year in 2007.'

Phyllis was born in Florida in December 1928 of English, Irish and Dutch background, but lived most of her life in Santa Monica. She suffered her injuries when she was 12. 'My mother was involved in a car accident,' she explained. 'A taxi ran into us and both my knees were crushed. I've had 28 operations on my left leg and seven on the other.'

Though she was married, she had no children and her husband died in 1979. 'I worked as a nurse for a doctor who happened to be a golf enthusiast,' she went on. 'When we got the golf schedule each year, we'd mark off a week and we'd all go. Whatever tournament he wanted to attend. I was in my twenties at that time.'

The week of our meeting happened to be the 60th consecutive year she had volunteered at the Tour's stop in Los Angeles, prompting the California Golf Writers Association to honour her with a Waterford crystal bowl for her volunteering spirit and decades of service to professional golf.

She was a spectator at the 1960 US Open at Cherry Hills, following the triumphant Palmer on crutches. 'I couldn't see very much at Cherry Hills but I saw him drive the first green for his closing 65,' she recalled.

Later, she scored for Tiger Woods when he was about 12 and thought he was a very nice, talented kid. Nothing more. She also remembered Phil Mickelson and Craig Stadler as juniors and worked at LPGA tournaments.

'I've made some wonderful friends in golf, just walking the fairways,' she concluded. 'Nowadays, I like to think of myself as a general flunky. With great memories.' Just so.

****

I was fortunate to have covered every Open Championship from 1980 until Shane Lowry's triumph at Royal Portrush in 2019. Predictably, the Irish victories by Pádraig Harrington in 2007 and 2008, followed by Darren Clarke in 2011, Rory McIlroy in 2014 and finally Lowry, had a very special impact.

In terms of pure sporting enjoyment however, the one that stands apart was the victory by Seve Ballesteros at St Andrews in 1984.

It seemed that anything the great Seve was involved in at that time had special appeal, and so it was with the Open. Details remain vivid, especially of Tom Watson's bogey on the 17th where he over-clubbed with a two-iron second shot, which overshot the green and ended by the wall.

I remember afterwards, the acknowledged Open specialist at that time blamed a 'balky putter' for a closing 73, which pushed him into a share of second place with Bernhard Langer, two strokes behind the hugely popular Spaniard.

An analysis of Watson's closing round, however, revealed that his most significant error was a pulled drive into whins on the 12th, running up a five where he would have expected a birdie three. Though Greg

Norman and Nick Faldo made birdies there, Ballesteros and Langer had to settle for pars.

This was the Open which attracted a record aggregate of 187,753, up 45,000 on the previous year at Royal Birkdale. It was also when Ben Crenshaw holed out with a five-iron for an ace on the 178-yard eighth in his final round.

Sometime afterwards, I happened to get Michael Bonallack in a reflective mood and he, too, highlighted 1984 as exceptional in his tenure as secretary of the Royal and Ancient. This is how he remembered it:

> My first Open as R&A secretary was at St Andrews in 1984, which obviously remains special to me. Being at the Home of Golf and with absolutely magnificent weather, a heatwave, added to its appeal. Everything seemed to go like clockwork.
>
> Then we had that wonderful finish with Seve holing the putt on the 18th green and punching the air like a matador. And afterwards, there was the party that went on in the whole of St Andrews that evening, making it probably a bit like Paris must have been like after the World Cup, except on a smaller scale.
>
> Though I had taken over from Keith MacKenzie the previous September, that became a wonderful introduction to my secretaryship of the R&A as far as the Open was concerned. I remember Seve coming up to my office and I still have photographs of him drinking champagne with me.
>
> Obviously, Seve was a very exciting golfer to watch and, of course, he beat Tom Watson who was a very great favourite.
>
> I was apprehensive going into that event, as I would be prior to any championship, wondering how it was going to work out. But we had a very skilled team and I had something of a dry run the previous year, at Royal Birkdale.
>
> On joining the R&A, I went straight there at the end of June 1983, when the final preparations for the Open were in full swing; stayed until the championship was over and then went back to St Andrews.

That was when I was understudy to Keith and I remember he had a new plan for the prize presentation. It involved having a mobile stage made, which could be dismantled in sections. Rising to about two or three feet off the ground, there were steps onto it.

It was an enormous thing, very heavy, and the idea was that it would be erected quickly on the fairway, 50 yards short of the 18th green, after the last putt had dropped. Given its prime position out there on the course, everybody in the stand would be able to see the presentation.

So, four little dots were placed on the fairway to mark exactly where it had got to go. And they had a rehearsal with people rushing out from the side of the stage and putting it up there. Which, of course, was fine when there was nobody else around.

When the big moment arrived, Keith took me out to the back of the 18th green to watch his plan go smoothly into action. But he hadn't bargained for one of the most traditional happenings on the final day of the Open. Horrified, he saw the crowd do their usual breakthrough before coming straight down the middle of the fairway, where the stage was meant to be.

He then grabbed me by the shoulder and said 'They can't do that. Go and stop them.' With that, he turned round and went straight back into his office.

Well, there was clearly nothing that I or any of the marshals could do in the face of a formidable charge of 3,000 people, coming down the middle of the fairway. And the people who were waiting by the sides of the 18th, ready with the sections of Keith's stage, were fully aware of this.

Still, out of a sense of duty I suppose, they eventually struggled out there and assembled it as best they could where it was originally planned to go. With that, a section of the crowd went and stood on it to get a better view.

While all this was going on, the presentation was set up at the back of the green, in front of the clubhouse window. The next day, when we had our usual wind-down press conference, somebody asked Keith what the odd-looking platform erected on the 18th fairway was for. Without batting an eyelid, he said he was concerned that the spectators coming down the final hole didn't really get a proper view of the presentation ceremony.

So, the idea was that with this easily assembled platform, the problem would be overcome. I remember thinking that he got out of it very well. Two months later he had retired, and nobody was any the wiser about his special plans for the Royal Birkdale victory ceremony.

Which, come to think of it, was as it should have been.

Reflections on Seve and Supermex

In the spring of 2010, I was in Savannah, Georgia, for the Legends of Golf on the Champions Tour, which Des Smyth had won in 2005. On this occasion, I made a point of meeting with Lee Trevino because of his friendship with Seve Ballesteros, who was quite ill at the time.

I wondered how he was feeling about the conquistador's battle for survival after surgery to remove a cancerous tumour from his brain. 'I'm very sad for him,' said Trevino:

> I was the last to play with him when he came into the Seniors here in the Regions Charity Classic in Birmingham [Alabama] three years ago. And I have to say he didn't play extremely well. In fact, he played probably as bad as I've ever seen him play. Little did we know he had a brain tumour. That was the reason he was so erratic with his shots.

This was the player of whom Trevino had said two decades earlier:

> Every generation or so there emerges a golfer who is a little bit better than anybody else. I believe Ballesteros is one of them. On a golf course he's got everything. I mean everything: touch, power, know-how, courage and charisma.

Now, Trevino was recalling a very different man:

> When Seve went back home after that Birmingham tournament and there was a tragedy involving his girlfriend, I then heard he had a brain tumour. I lost my mother-in-law with a brain tumour and my wife and I were very concerned because that's the one place where cancer is very difficult to overcome.
>
> But I'll tell you one thing about Seve. He's held on a helluva lot longer than most people with that type of cancer. It tells you what type of a fighter he is. He was always a magician on the golf course. I remember the one-club match I played against him at St Andrews. He grew up like I did with one golf club on the beach at Pedrena. I had a four iron and he had a five iron. And he beat me.
>
> St Andrews is a very easy course if you keep it out of the bunkers. It's a very easy course to play with one club because you can bump and run everywhere. But if you get in a bunker you've got to pretend it's a hand-grenade and you throw it out.
>
> You holler 'fore!' then everyone ducks and you throw it out.

That last remark produced hearty laughter from what by then had become a sizeable audience. Of course, the truth is he and Ballesteros were so skilful that they had no problem in escaping from the deepest bunkers, even with relatively straight-faced clubs.

Then suddenly he exclaimed: 'Gotta run.' And he was gone. But the laughter he had generated lingered.

On the road

Pebble Beach was always an exceptional treat, but I have a very special memory from covering the US Open there in June 1992. On the Thursday, a splendid celebration was arranged at 'Sea Drift' on the 17-mile drive, to honour Joe Carr in his capacity as captain of the Royal and Ancient.

Among those present was David Feherty, who displayed an impressive tenor voice, especially in an excellent rendition of 'Danny Boy', high finale and all. One was forced to conclude that his training as an opera singer had not been a wasted exercise.

Also there was Nick Faldo, delighted at 'being back among the Irish' after his triumph at Killarney at the beginning of that month. Predictably, he was joined by golfing guru David Leadbetter, who had become his shadow at the time. Others among the assembly were Ian Woosnam and Nick Price.

Joe Carr was at Pebble representing the Royal and Ancient at the US Open, so it seemed an ideal opportunity to acknowledge his status at a high-profile American social occasion. He addressed the gathering in his usual polished manner, as did Mayo's Mixie Murphy, a former President of the Golfing Union of Ireland.

Hosts of the party were wealthy American industrialist Bob Fisher and his wife, Marilyn. There was ample room at their 12-bedroom, 18,000-sq-ft residence, which enjoyed the exclusive location of a three-acre site on the Pacific shore.

I learned that the Fishers were going to be at Muirfield as Carr's Open Championship guests the following month, when Faldo would capture the title for a third time. They had also been at Portmarnock the previous September for the first staging of the Walker Cup in the Republic of Ireland.

Then we were informed that a further Irish link was the presence of Tim Kinsella, who was responsible for much of the event's organisation.

As a six-handicap member of the Monterey Peninsula Country Club who claimed to be a cousin of Skerries professional, Jimmy Kinsella, he had been quite successful in public relations in the area.

Sometime later, I discovered that not all matters concerning Tim Kinsella were as he would have us believe.

'He owned a pub in Kildare at one stage and played the game well enough to pass as a pro,' Jimmy Kinsella told me. 'He had no relationship to me, but I understand that at one point he actually called himself Jimmy Kinsella. But I didn't mind. It was all a bit of fun and he seemed to do well out of the deception.'

Meeting the Bear in his lair

In the spring of 1999, Jack Nicklaus and Bobby Ramos crouched together on their knees in the dusty soil of southern Florida. Hip-replacement surgery in January had finally freed Nicklaus from a nagging, arthritic pain. By his side, Bobby Ramos paid rapt attention as miniature shapes were created in the malleable earth.

Not planning to return to competitive action until late May of that year in the Bell Atlantic Classic on what was then the US Seniors' Tour, Nicklaus was caught up in a special personal project. This was the embryonic Bear's Club in West Palm Beach and Ramos was shaping a course which their combined skills would bring to splendid fruition, over two years.

As they embarked on the project, Nicklaus was travelling very little and playing no golf, so he had the rare luxury of being able to go out to the site almost every day. Ramos recalled how, with no plans and only the guidance of a richly experienced mind, hands that had wrought wondrous magic in tournament play were pushing soil to build tiny greens and even tinier bunkers. 'Then Jack would point to his handiwork and say to me: 'That's what I want. Do that.' The two men had never been closer.

This relationship between designer and shaper found splendid expression on the lush pastureland of County Meath, in the creation of Killeen Castle. For Ramos, it became truly a home from his Californian home, when he, his wife, Melissa (Missy), and their two children settled in Dunshaughlin in the spring of 2005.

As with most golfing matters, his arrival in Ireland had a rather intriguing appeal. Responding to a phone call from Seamus Carroll, a key member of the Killeen Castle development staff who informed him that the contractor was on site and that they were 'ready to go', Ramos duly met his future employer for the first time.

Less than a year later, Kathy and I were on our third trip to Hawaii, this time for a three-week stay. That's when Carroll e-mailed a proposal to call at West Palm Beach for a meeting with Nicklaus on our journey home, which we accepted. We stayed in the newly created Bear's Club, in the St Andrews Suite.

Then came the purpose of the trip: to interview the great man for an informative video aimed at Meath County Council. Everything went well and to cap a memorable visit, Jack and Barbara invited Kathy and me to dinner in a local Italian restaurant that evening. This proved to be a delightful occasion, not least for the respect of the restaurant's customers who, though they must have recognised the celebrated diners at the corner table, extended them the courtesy of an uninterrupted meal.

With Jack's daughter, Nan, and her husband joining us, the conversation was warm and convivial, so much so that I ventured to tell Jack a tale he might not have heard before. Incidentally, I was encouraged by sensing that Greg Norman would not have been at the top of the Nicklaus Christmas card list.

The story was connected to Augusta National on the Saturday evening of 13 April 1996, when Norman was leading the Masters by six strokes after 54 holes. And the Shark – as he was called by fellow golfers – had just learned that Nick Faldo would be his playing partner in the final round.

Noting that Norman looked somewhat down at heel, British scribe Peter Dobereiner put a comforting arm around his shoulder and remarked cheerily: 'Don't worry Greg old son. Not even you can fuck this one up.' Which, of course, he sensationally proceeded to do.

Nicklaus loved it. In fact, he was so taken by it that he immediately told Barbara, with one essential difference from my version. Exposing classic Midwestern conservatism, he omitted the four-letter expletive, which I found both surprising and very revealing.

On another note, given the extent to which their careers overlapped, it seems very odd that Peter Thomson never shared a tee with Jack Nicklaus in the Open Championship. Yet the great Australian's respect was undiminished.

The Bear (Nicklaus) was introduced to links golf in the 1959 Walker Cup matches at Muirfield. That was when his father, Charlie, and three of his friends made the journey to play St Andrews. As The Bear recalled:

> When they came back, my dad said you won't believe it. That's the worst golf course I've ever seen.
>
> When I asked why, he said it was so hard and bumpy that things bounced all over the place. And you couldn't make any putts on the greens. I later found out he and his pals three-putted 13 or 14 greens. And, you know, they just had a horrible time. So I wasn't prepared for much when I showed up in '64 [the Open won by Tony Lema].
>
> But when I got there, I looked at it and I immediately liked it for what it was. In fact, I fell in love with it right from the first day. And when I returned in 1970 and won, the galleries basically took me as one of theirs. It was like a Scot winning. That's the way they treated me, both times I won at St Andrews.
>
> I've loved the British Open, the challenge of it; the fun of it. I've always loved going over there to play on the different golf courses, getting a break from the heat of our summer. I loved planning for the different conditions and the type of golf you had to play. Every year would be totally different.
>
> I mean it would be dry some years. Others would be wet. And sometimes it would be windy. There's so much variety, even though the golf courses, to all intents and purposes, have stayed relatively the same throughout most of that time. You knew what was going to be there.

Then, of course, there was a constant awareness of what St Andrews had meant to Bobby Jones. 'Growing up, all I heard was Bobby Jones, Bobby Jones and his 13 major championships. And how he played the Old Course and walked off and tore up his card. But he later said that if you're going to be a player people will remember, you have to win the Open at St Andrews. That thought was always in my mind.'

This would explain why, on a private trip there in May 2005, two months before his final farewell, Nicklaus sat at the 18th while his eyes filled with tears – 'Just because of what it is; what it has meant to the game of golf, and what it's meant to me.'

His emotional declaration illustrated the immediate respect and affection he had for Cecil Whelan and the work the Dubliner did with the Links Society. 'I love the name, which conjures up stirring images of battling nature over classic golfing terrain,' he said.

> For my part, I didn't grow up in wind and had to learn how to play in it. And I know I learned a lot from watching Joe Carr play links golf. Watching him hit an awful lot of two-, three- or four-irons off the tee, I came to realise that this was a pretty good way to play those courses. It was the only way you could be certain of avoiding the bunkers.

Through his involvement with the First Tee charitable organisation, he and his wife, Barbara, were special guests of Whelan's at a Links Society affair at Luttrellstown Castle during Open Championship week in July 2011, when the remarkable sum of €640,000 was raised.

At my suggestion, Cecil arranged a special gift for their celebrated guest. It was a piece of Waterford Crystal on which were etched the clubhouses from St Andrews and Augusta National. Nicklaus had often talked of these as his two favourite places in golf – 'one for where it is and the other for what it is.' And then, as a gesture typical of the host, the Bear was made an honorary life member of the Links.

By way of appreciation, he responded:

> You Irish love your golf and apart from Cecil himself, I understand that the Links Society owes much to the dedication of its first president, Christy O'Connor, whom I first saw in events like the British Open and the World Cup. We also played on opposite sides in three Ryder Cups – 1969, 1971 and 1973 – though never against

each other. I guess Christy was probably nearing the end of his golfing peak at that time.

Christy was always a great competitor and over the years he became a great personality within the game of golf. I always think of him as having been a very, very good player. What is equally important, however, certainly from my viewpoint, is that he has been a good friend and I couldn't have been happier about his induction into the Hall of Fame.

8

Working towards Pinehurst and the Hall of Fame

The notion of a labourer being worthy of his hire has always had a special appeal for Pádraig Harrington. That is why his induction into the World Golf Hall of Fame on meant so much to him, when the honour was bestowed at Pinehurst on 10 June 2004, the Monday of US Open week.

From his earliest days in competitive golf, Harrington admits to having had an insatiable desire to get better. And Pinehurst proved to be a crucial step on that journey, due to Michael Campbell's inspirational victory over Tiger Woods in the 2005 US Open.

'I hope to be remembered as someone who was a competitor who got the most out of his game,' said the Dubliner. And while Joe Carr and Christy O'Connor Snr each took a different route to this particular distinction, Harrington earned it through his three Major triumphs. And that pleased him enormously. 'Emotionally, it brings me a deep sense of satisfaction and validation,' he said in an acceptance speech that was closer in length to fifteen minutes than the eight minutes he was officially allotted.

He spoke after his 20-year-old son, Paddy, had told an audience of millions some home truths about the inductee, notably that 'a tee-time is the only thing Dad isn't late for.' And that he loves to sleep in until 11.00 on mornings he's home from the Tour.

This latest honour came in the wake of honorary fellowships and doctorates that had also been acquired through pure golfing prowess, with the difference that these would have allowed him to place a string of letters after his name. Yet with obvious regret, he admitted: 'I can't use the ones that I actually passed an exam for.' Harrington was 23 when completing the Association of Chartered Certified Accountants (ACCA) finals at Dublin Business College. 'That made me a certified accountant,' he said. 'But I never did my articles and wouldn't be entitled to practise as a fully fledged accountant until I have acquired about three years' work experience.'

The point was brought home to him somewhat forcibly when the advertising authority in the UK received an official complaint regarding a golf-associated advert in which Harrington was described as an accountant.

'I was given to understand that the accountancy body would take a different view if I was prepared to do a talk for them,' he added bitterly.

Prior to Pinehurst, arguably the greatest distinction bestowed on the Dubliner was in September 2020, when he became an honorary member of the Royal and Ancient, along with triumphant Solheim Cup skipper Catriona Matthew OBE, Ernie Els and Nick Price. At the time, they were considered to be among the most successful and influential professional golfers of the modern era and outstanding ambassadors for the sport. As Harrington said:

> I have had a long association with the R&A and was fortunate enough to crown my career by winning The Open in 2007 and 2008. I then became an ambassador for the R&A, so now becoming an Honorary Member brings the relationship full circle. Golf is a huge part of my life and I live by its traditions, rules and etiquette,

> so I am very proud to become a member of this esteemed club and flattered to join the other illustrious names on the list.

Prior to that, Harrington had joined the elite company of Arnold Palmer and Tom Watson as the recipient of an honorary doctor of laws degree from the University of St Andrews. Royal and Ancient professional Jim Farmer and the South African banker Johann Rupert were also honoured that day. Harrington was returning to a St Andrews Open for the first time since 2000, having missed the 2005 staging due to the death of his father, Paddy, on the Monday of that week. Naturally, this poignant link didn't escape him:

> To get the award not only for what I did on the golf course but for my behaviour off it, was a nice remembrance of my dad. That [off-course behaviour] would have come from him and I'm proud that it would have made him happy.'
>
> The whole occasion was very special, because it happened at St Andrews and because of the company I was in. There's no doubt about it. Arnold was obviously before my time, though I soon learned how influential he was in the professional game. In the nicest possible way, I can say that I wouldn't have sat at his table unless I was invited, whereas I would seek out Tom's company whenever the occasion might arise.

I had the honour of writing the Harrington profile for the official programme of the conferment. As it happened, Professor Andrew Mackenzie, School of Physics and Astronomy, included in his citation Harrington's claim that having the discipline to see his accountancy exams through to a satisfactory conclusion 'was one of the most rewarding things I got from the process.' Professor Mackenzie remarked:

> His [Harrington's] comments on the self-discipline and time-management skills that his academic work brought to his life, are

> music to the ears of any university professor like me. I think they should be inscribed in the clubhouse of any students' sports team.

The honours roundabout began seriously for Harrington in November 2006, two days after he had beaten no less a figure than Tiger Woods in a play-off for the Dunlop Phoenix Tournament in Japan. One of the most recent was an honorary degree from Dublin's Irish-American College, conferred by Dr Joe Rooney of the celebrated Pittsburgh sporting clan.

The venue for the 2006 conferment was the RDS in Ballsbridge, where Harrington was attired in a fetching pancake hat and robes in two shades of blue, separated by a narrow green stripe. There, he received an honorary fellowship from the Dublin Business School, in association with Liverpool's John Moore University. As he recalled:

> I started accountancy when I was 18, having had no idea what I wanted to do when I left school. It struck me as a good, general business degree which is essentially how I viewed it. My plan was to get a job in the golf industry via accountancy, but halfway through my exams I decided to become a tournament professional and try my luck on the PGA European Tour.
>
> So from that point onwards, whenever I applied myself to studying I had in the back of my mind that there was always golf. This had the effect of taking the pressure off the exams.
>
> The interesting thing is that when I was competing at golf, I could reassure myself that there was always the accountancy to fall back on if things weren't going as I hoped. So it could be said that my academic pursuit eased the stress on my sporting ambitions, and vice versa.

Following that phase of his life, honours continued to come Harrington's way, some in the most unlikely circumstances. For instance, in the summer of 1999, he was made a freeman of the town of Cromwell (population 14,000), Connecticut. With Jack Charlton's demise fresh in mind, the town got its name from arguably Ireland's least-loved Englishman.

So, did Harrington accept the opportunity to highlight this hate-figure in his native country? 'No, I didn't,' he replied. 'I simply expressed my surprise that the good people of Cromwell had given this Irishman free access to all their fine hostelries.'

Apparently, it's not unusual for local authorities to come up with such a scheme. As Harrington explained:

> There's a quid pro quo to most of these things; they give you something in order that you'll do something for them. Mind you, it's not unknown for some personality, sporting or otherwise, to be conned into providing entertainment, free, as guest of honour at an annual function. But I don't think I've ever fallen for that.

When I suggested that his long-time manager, Adrian Mitchell, would protect him from such pitfalls, he nodded agreement. He then explained that the Cromwell affair had to do with charities associated with the Travelers Championship at nearby River Highlands GC, where he has been a regular competitor over the years.

Interestingly, by way of religious balance, as it were, Cromwell happens to be the location of the Catholic Padre Pio Foundation of America.

When I wondered how many honorary memberships in golf clubs had come the Dubliner's way, he replied matter-of-factly: 'It would be easier to count the ones I don't have in this country. While I rarely use them, it's really nice to be honoured in this way, even though I'm sure they realise I wouldn't have the time to do anything for them.'

As for degrees and fellowships, apart from those already mentioned, these include ones from the Royal College of Surgeons in Ireland and Maynooth University, where he has donated a scholarship.

'Being honoured tends to mean more as you progress in life,' he continued. 'Which makes my induction into the Golf Hall of Fame a greatly prized honour.'

It was through his physical trainer, Dr Liam Hennessy, that he came to fully appreciate the merit of these distinctions. In fact, he tended to view such honours as undeserved, given that they had not been earned academically. The exercise physiologist at Setanta College, however, categorised them as 'awards for a contribution to the lives of others.'

Dr Hennessy explained that while a PhD can be earned through four or five years of study, Harrington has contributed a whole lifetime's experience to the body of knowledge and understanding relating to his chosen pursuit. 'This, quite apart from an ambassadorial role and standards of sportsmanship, is eminently worthy of a PhD in my view,' he claimed.

For his part, Harrington responded: 'By all accounts I've done a good job of what I set out to do, playing some fairly decent golf along the way. That's how Liam made sense of it for me.'

Then he concluded: 'The really nice thing is that ten or twenty years down the road from your competitive peak, awards make you appreciate your career all the more. By reminding you of the good times.'

When considering the enormous contribution Tiger Woods made to tournament golf over the last 30 years, we think of the generosity of his many fans in overlooking some of his less appealing behaviour during that time. And how little that generosity was reciprocated.

Yet it has to be acknowledged that El Tigre made a very notable exception in his public treatment of Pádraig Harrington. In fact, I cannot think of any other leading player who has been so highly regarded by him.

I especially remember the media centre at Hazeltine National on Friday 14 August the second day of the 2009 US PGA Championship. Woods had shot a 70 to lead the field on 137 while Harrington, his playing partner, was four strokes back, in a share of second place on 141.

It was the Dubliner's performance on one particular hole, however, which brought obvious warmth and renewed respect from the championship leader. Woods highlighted a stunning three-wood shot of 301 yards which Harrington hit out of a bunker onto the green at the 640-yard, par-five 15th.

> I was saying to Steve [caddie Steve Williams] that that was one of the best shots I'd ever seen. I don't remember what the number was [meaning distance], but you could hear he didn't mishit it. He hit it flush, out of an uphill lie in a bunker where you can't use your legs to get any power.'
>
> There was always the chance of slipping but he still hit it flush enough to carry it that far. It was a pretty impressive shot; definitely worth the price of admission.

Hearing about it afterwards, Harrington seemed pleased that Woods considered his shot worthy of public acknowledgement. 'Actually, Tiger did say to me at the time that he would have paid to have seen it,' said the Dubliner. Then, as if to make light of the compliment, he added with a grin: 'So I asked him for 50 bucks.'

For Harrington, this unlikely relationship first became meaningful in Japan in November 2006, when he beat Woods on the second hole of a play-off for the Dunlop Phoenix Tournament. Achieved through some extraordinary wedge-play, it ranked as unquestionably the most significant victory of his career up to that point. It meant that unlike most of Woods's rivals, Harrington would hold no fear of going head-to-head with the great one in the years ahead, even with a Major title at stake.

'When it was all over, I found myself remarking that Tiger really wanted to be pushed, no matter what,' Harrington told me:

> After hitting a great chip to save par on the 71st, I could sense his excitement, his focus. Sure, he wanted to win, but he also wanted to be pushed. He wanted the competition.
>
> There is the point that the higher up in the face the ball gets, the fresher and sharper the grooves are. If you saw my chip shot on the 72nd hole in the Dunlop Phoenix, the ball came out very low.

> I hit it with an open-face lob wedge which was in the mid-sixties in terms of loft. And because I slid the ball over the clubface, the more it spun, even at a low trajectory. It's part of a chipping technique I have developed over the last few years.

That was with a new lob wedge, which delivered a spectacular result to set up a birdie four. For another birdie at the first play-off hole, which was again the 18th, he hit a nine-iron to ten feet. But when he and Woods went down the 18th for a third time that afternoon, his approach shot was a 98-yard sand wedge from rough, which spun back to three feet from the pin. Later, he explained that his pitching wedge was about two years old with grooves 'not especially sharp', simply because he didn't want it to deliver too much spin.

His short-game masterclass in this event had much to do with the nature of the course, which is part of a seaside resort in Miyazaki. 'It's important for me to have the right feel for a course, and this layout was very similar to what you'd find in Portugal, seeded with bent grass all the way through,' said Harrington. 'The rough was long and thick, except in shaded areas under pine trees.

> Grass is normally dormant at that particular time of the year but not on this course, which was in lovely condition. And while there was no grain in the superb greens, they were nonetheless challenging, because of some very tricky undulations. This was a major feature of the course, a lot like at Westchester [where Harrington won the Barclays Classic in June 2005].

Digressing, he then went on to relate a highly significant exchange he had with a fellow Irish professional in Malaysia two years previously. 'That was when Gary Murphy gave me a chipping lesson,' he said.

> He normally finds the long game easy and the short game difficult, but on this occasion he gave me a terrific short-game drill. It involved a split-hand grip, with the left hand at the top and the

right hand at the bottom. This has the effect of making you flick at the ball, which is the exact opposite of what you would teach people. By practising this quite a bit, I have acquired a good technique involving a crisp action with a lot of speed going through impact. In fact, in practice, I spend my time trying to hit the ball as hard as I possibly can through impact.'

The most incredible chip shot I've ever hit was in the play-off for the Honda against Vijay [Singh in 2005]. It was from about 30 yards and how it stopped as it did [about five feet from the hole] still baffles me. That was out of dry rough to a dry green and the only way I can explain it is that being hyped up, my hands were even faster than usual.

But nothing comes easily. I spend hours in my garden hitting that shot. I spend all my time with a lob wedge trying to get it to spin back.

Harrington's dedication to becoming even better around the greens was reflected in discussions with his golf-ball supplier, Titleist (he plays their ProV1x). 'I've told their R and D people that it's only when you get the cover of the ball to shear, like the way the old balata did, that you'll get the ultimate grip,' he said. 'You need to at least scuff it. Get into the ball.'

Meanwhile, his objective in tournament action became disarmingly simple: to make it as difficult as possible for an opponent to win. And during the climactic holes in Japan, he was struck by the fact that even Woods, his playing partner, was failing in this. 'It got me thinking that he wasn't closing me out,' said Harrington. 'And I thought I could sneak this. That's when I really began applying myself to winning.'

The decisive shot in Japan would normally have involved a three-quarter sand wedge, given that a full swing would have delivered a distance of 105 yards, which would have been extended to 110 by the gentle breeze. But coming out of wet rough with spin, he calculated that he would lose yardage. And he judged it perfectly.

'I remembered watching Tiger winning the 2005 Masters and how, from the right side of Augusta's 18th green, he hit a 10-yard chip which he flopped up in the air and spun back about an inch after it landed,' recalled the Dubliner:

> There are only two ways you can do that. You've got to have good grooves, and you've got to hit the ball really firmly.
>
> I hit my chip shots about twice as hard as most players. That's how I get the spin. My hands are flying through impact. I do the opposite to the old recommendation of soft hands. I'm unbelievably quick and fast. I used to apply soft hands to chip shots until I played once with Mark McNulty, who hit everything hard with spin. And I got further help from Gary [Murphy].

Tiger's admiration for Harrington was expressed again in the final round of the Bridgestone Invitational in August 2009 and in the opening two rounds at Hazeltine. Though he had been conscious of the Dubliner's talent for some time, he still picked his words carefully in public. For instance, this was his response when asked what he thought of Harrington's first Open win at Carnoustie and his PGA triumph at Oakland Hills 13 months later. 'I was on my way home from Carnoustie where I heard there was quite a bit of water,' he said with a smile. 'As for the PGA, you can't argue with two 66s over the weekend.' A Woods associate told me:

> Tiger has a deep respect for Pádraig and believes he is a really hard-nosed competitor. In fact, he likens him to a pitbull, with that sort of tenacity. Socially, the twosome of them wouldn't have a lot of common, not like established Tiger pals such as Mark O'Meara, John Cook and Mark Calcavecchia, as Isleworth neighbours and practice partners.
>
> But he really likes the way Pádraig plays, respecting the hard work he has done. He sees him as honest, humble and tough. The slap at officialdom which Tiger made over the slow-play

> controversy at Firestone was really an expression of disappointment at being given outside help to win the tournament.

This was a reference to match-referee John Paramor, who was brandishing the latest issue of the American weekly *Golf World*, when I met him at Hazeltine the following Friday. 'I've never made the front page of a magazine before,' he said. 'But I didn't appreciate the headline in this one.' A picture of the European Tour's top referee carried the caption: 'John Paramor: The official who "cost" Harrington is no stranger to tough calls.'

After both players had hit their drives down Firestone's long 16th in the final round the previous Sunday – Woods into the left rough and Harrington into rough on the right – Paramor approached them as they left the tee. 'Gentlemen,' he said, 'I'm afraid you've slipped further behind the time schedule. I'm going to have to individually time you. I'm sorry.' Paramor explained that Woods and Harrington had already been informed on the sixth green by another official that they were out of position and needed to speed up their pace of play.

Reflecting on the dramatic events of the 16th, Paramor told me:

> I feel desperately sorry that Pádraig hit it in the water. He said himself that he let the situation affect him and that is something I hate to see. We're all after a quicker game and I want players to be positive in what they're doing to make up the lost time.
>
> The situation last Sunday was tragic for Pádraig and unfair on Tiger, in that [as I had suggested] he was deprived of a tight battle to the finish. But Slugger White [tournament director] and I spoke at length about the issue of slow play and decided that something had to be done and that it was absolutely vital to treat everybody the same way. If you don't do that, people would be subjected to penalty on a selective basis. Which would be wrong.

But given Harrington's reputation as a stickler for the rules, would he not have suffered more than most in such circumstances? And wasn't the threat of a penalty largely meaningless, given that it had not been enforced on the US PGA Tour since 1992? 'Anytime Pádraig has gone on the clock, he has always reacted positively to it,' replied Paramor. 'In other words, he has always endeavoured to get back into position.'

In his book *Unplayable*, published in 2010, Australian golf-writer Robert Lusetich made quite an issue of that Firestone incident. He wrote:

> In Akron (2009) I asked Woods whether he had more respect for the toiler who worked hard over the dilettante with natural talent. 'Absolutely. I mean I think that they always ask me who are the guys you should go watch play, who are the guys you think you should model yourself after, and I always say Paddy and Jim Furyk and Vijay.
>
> 'Those guys work so hard on their games. A guy like Paddy and a guy like Jim, they don't have the length that Vijay does, but how they manage themselves around the golf course, I think everyone can learn from that, especially kids.
>
> 'And the work ethic for Paddy, you know what he's done and with [coach] Bob [Torrance] over the years, countless hours in the snow, it doesn't matter, he's going to get it done. I've seen him miss cuts and he's out there all weekend long, practising and getting ready for the next week. I admire guys like that because that's how you become better. You have to go earn it. And I think Paddy is a great example of a guy who goes out there and earns it each and every day.'
>
> It was no surprise that Woods found much to admire in Harrington, golf's most blue-collar champion. The Irishman is just as obsessive as Woods, though less talented, which perhaps makes his determination even greater, given his three Major wins. Harrington isn't a natural at the game but he possesses a huge heart and a single-minded desire.
>
> This is the stuff of Woods's dreams. And perhaps only Woods could truly comprehend what Harrington had done after winning

those three Majors: taken apart his golf swing and rebuilt it entirely.

The rebuilding process was a disaster, at least in the short term, as Harrington laboured through the no-man's-land between the old swing and the new. After two rounds at the Bridgestone though, Harrington had the lead on his own at seven-under par. He revealed he'd finally done enough thinking about his swing and began to concentrate on scoring again.

It was interesting that while many of his peers thought Harrington had been out of his mind to change anything after winning those Majors, Woods not only understood, but also applauded him.

'You have to believe what you're doing is right, even though people tell you what you're doing is wrong,' said Woods. 'I've been through that twice and I think I've turned out on the good side, both times. It's just that you're going to get a lot of bombardment, not just from the Media but the fans, from friends, family, whatever it may be: they're going to always doubt and question you.

'But you've got to have the internal resolve to stick with what you believe is going to be right and that you're going to get better. Paddy has always done things according to his own accord. He's worked extremely hard. We've all admired him for that, because I don't know how many second-place finishes he had [33], but he really didn't win that much.

'But then he kept progressing and kept getting better and better and more consistent, and then all of a sudden, boom! He's a three-time Major championship winner. That's the thing you have to admire about some guys, when they are able to do that.'

As to how Paramor put Woods and Harrington on the clock at Akron, Woods said: 'I'm sorry that rules official [Paramor] got in the way of such a great battle for 16 holes and we're going at it head-to-head and unfortunately that happened.'

He later told Lusetich that he was so thoroughly enjoying the heat of battle that he felt cheated. 'I got the impression that Woods was more upset with Paramor for what he'd denied him than for throwing off Harrington who took eight at the long 16th.

After the pair had shaken hands on the final green at Firestone, Lusetich reported that Harrington looked Woods squarely in the eye and promised: 'We'll do battle again.'

Interestingly, the entire episode had a profound impact on the Dubliner.

'He didn't feel very good on Monday night [24 hours later],' said his mind coach, Dr Bob Rotella. 'We were all ready to go to dinner after Pádraig had signed a bunch of autographs when he said: "Holy God! I suddenly don't feel good at all." With that, he got a quick sandwich and went to bed.'

Rotella went on: 'On Tuesday, he talked about you guys [media] asking him how he felt when Tiger caught him after five or six holes at Firestone and how he had been thinking that he loved the way he was playing.'

In the meantime, as an inveterate nit-picker, Harrington continued to look at his game for areas where he could improve. 'If I keep getting better, it pushes Tiger along,' he said. 'Then, if he gets better, well I suppose that's what it's all about. If I can rectify weaknesses in my game, it puts it up to Tiger more and more. And that's got to be the key thing.'

It had been only a matter of weeks since our greatest wish for Harrington was that he might make a few more cuts that season.

By the end of 2009, he had played 16 European events with a best finish of third in the Portugal Masters. In the US, he was tied 2nd at Firestone, tied 10th at Hazeltine (PGA), tied 4th at the Tour Championship, tied 4th at Deutsche Bank and tied 6th at the BMW Championship. His PGA Tour earnings for the year were $2.628m/20th. In Europe, he was 15th on the Road to Dubai. In the process, he was targeting the man at the top.

Interestingly, these and other competitive events caused Jack Nicklaus to revise his views on the playing partners of Tiger Woods.

'Harrington is a very fine player who obviously doesn't back off in Tiger's company,' said the Bear.

Nicklaus had long been critical of what he saw as would-be challengers, consistently crumbling under the pressure of playing alongside the world's top player, or when confronted by his formidable victory charges. '[Lee] Trevino and [Tom] Watson always functioned well in my company, but I don't know if we can say the same about the guys out there with Tiger,' Nicklaus asserted.

A chart in *Golf Digest* involving the world's leading players tended to endorse this view – with one notable exception. Statistical analysis of almost 800 tournament rounds from Woods over a 10-year period separated Harrington from the rest.

Of nineteen players who completed a minimum of five rounds as Woods's partner during that period, the Dubliner emerged as the only one to have outscored him. Additionally, the chart was compiled before Harrington's victory over Woods in the Dunlop Phoenix Tournament.

In six tournament rounds, Harrington outscored Woods by an average of 0.67 strokes per round, whereas the others, including Darren Clarke, all faltered in his wake.

Golf Digest also did a separate analysis of the 'Tiger Effect' in 158 rounds in the Major championships, starting with the 1997 Masters, which Woods won. Though outscored by his partners numerous times in the earlier rounds, it happened on the final day on only eight occasions – Jim Furyk (1997 Open), Lee Westwood (1999 Masters), Bob May (2000 USPGA), JM Olazábal (2003 Masters), Vijay Singh (2003 Open), Tim Herron (2004 US Open), Scott Verplank (2004 Open) and Chris DiMarco (2005 Masters). Harrington (74) was outscored by Woods (69) in the final round of the 2001 US Open and in the third round of the 2002 US Open (73–70).

'I don't know if Tiger thinks about intimidating his opponents, but I know I didn't,' said Nicklaus. 'I assumed it was there, but I never thought about it. I was too busy playing my own game. In the 1978 Open at St Andrews, Simon Owen chipped in on 15 to go a shot ahead of me. All I thought about was that I was one shot behind a guy which meant I had to make a birdie and he had to make a mistake for me to take the lead. Otherwise, I couldn't have got the job done.'

****

Harrington the supreme senior

The Harrington watchers among us saw a certain inevitability about it, yet it was still something of a treat to follow his US Senior Open progress and success at Saucon Valley, Pennsylvania in the summer of 2022. And as a further treat to us homebirds, he was back in Ireland a few days later to compete in the Irish Open at Mount Juliet.

That was when I commandeered the only vacant seat in the interview area, just before the newly crowned champion appeared on the scene. 'Move!' Pádraig Harrington instructed with a smile. 'I'm the senior here.'

Indeed he was – the undisputed king of the hill after his nail-biting triumph the previous weekend. And he looked remarkably fresh and fit, despite the additional stress of transatlantic travel to fill his customary role at Mount Juliet.

Though he expressed the fear that stamina could become a factor, the body was clearly willing as he executed a typically deft up and down on the challenging 18th during Friday's second round. 'Gritty, isn't he?' an enthralled observer remarked to Des Smyth. 'He's the grittiest of them all,' replied Smyth with some emphasis.

From decades observing Harrington, certain situations remain strong in the memory – like the moment behind the 72nd green at Oakland Hills in August 2008 when the PGA Championship had given him his third Major triumph. Talking to his manager, Adrian Mitchell, the only words he could utter were: 'It's hard to believe, Mitch.' Yet nothing needed to be added. The calm, thorough Yorkshireman, who has been handling Harrington's business affairs for 29 years, wasn't in Pennsylvania, but he knew exactly what to do. Describing the experience, he said, 'I waited for about 30 minutes after the winning moment, then I phoned him. Our final words were to make arrangements to meet for breakfast at Mount Juliet this [Wednesday] morning. Which made it very different from Oakland Hills. This time, we just looked at each other, shook hands and smiled.'

Was Mitchell surprised by this latest, significant success? 'I prefer to say that Pádraig never fails to impress me,' he replied. 'Having seen all sides of him over the years, on and off the golf course, I can say that he leaves nothing to chance and will shoot the best score he possibly can on a given day.

'If things go wrong, he will deal with it and come back stronger the next time. That's been especially true of his second places, which number as many as 33, depending on which list you have. He has dealt with all sorts of situations and seems to learn from every one.'

Mitchell suspected something special was happening when he observed the famous staring, scary Harrington eyes over the weekend. 'It was the same look I remembered from Carnoustie [2007 Open Championship] and Oakland Hills,' he said. 'Not so much from Birkdale [2008 Open]. He's always talked about his three Majors being different from each other and this one took him down another different road ... the big lead, then Steve Stricker making a charge.' Finally, Mitchell concluded: 'And there will be more. This won't be the last one.'

They say that the great ones manage to find a way. How else can one explain Harrington's resolve when facing a searching test of his putting on greens running at 13 on the Stimpmeter, while Stricker ate relentlessly into his lead?

Essentially, it became a tale of 30-footers, which were largely the product of indifferent approach play by the leader. Seconds before Stricker birdied the 72nd to set a target of nine-under-par, Harrington holed a 30-footer for birdie on the 15th.

Then came another 30-footer, downhill on the 16th where he did remarkably well to stop the ball beside the hole. An even more serious test came at the 144-yard 17th, where another poor approach meant Harrington faced a six-footer for par.

The pressure was at its most acute down the last hole, where he eased a 25-footer across the green before leaving himself a three-footer, straight uphill, for the title. We will never know the stress of those climactic moments, except that he somehow found the mental strength to cope – as champions do.

The most difficult of those closing putts seemed to be the one on 17th. 'In my preparation, I got down and hit putts there,' said Harrington. 'While it looked like a left-half six-footer, I knew from practice that there was no left-to-right in that section of the green. So, I went straight and when I looked up, it was rolling straight in. I was very pleased with that.'

Among his rewards were $720,000, the Francis D. Ouimet Memorial Trophy for one year, a gold medal, exemptions into the next 10 US Senior Opens and exemption into the 2023 US Open at The Los Angeles CC. His victory also meant it was the first time in 25 years that the US Senior Open, US Open (Matt Fitzpatrick) and US Women's Open (Minjee Lee) were all won by non-Americans. In 1997, the three champions were Ernie Els (US Open), Graham Marsh (US Senior Open) and Alison Nicholas (US Women's Open).

On a local level, Harrington became the first Irish winner of this title. The general standard in the senior Majors, however, was set by Christy O'Connor Jnr, who won the Senior British Open at Royal Portrush in 1999 and went on to retain the title at Royal County Down in 2000, beating South Africa's John Bland into second place on both occasions.

Harrington's great strength at Saucon Valley was an awareness of his weakness:

> I didn't feel great on the greens, especially over those three two-putts on the last three holes. But throughout my career, I've always been excellent when my back's to the wall. When I have to do something, and it's very clear what I have to do, that's when I'm at my best. When there's no alternative.
>
> There comes a point when you just have to get it done. It doesn't matter how; just do it. I believe I become a better player when I get to the point where I've no excuse.

All of the tension inherent in such self-examination seemed to make little impact on Shane Lowry. Did he watch his good friend toiling down the stretch of the US Senior? 'I didn't,' he admitted with remarkable candour. 'I fell asleep. When I woke up, Wendy [Lowry's wife] said he'd won.'

Which was clearly a far less stressful way of seeing things through.

9

From Portrush to Killarney with Ian Bamford

In June 2023, a few months short of his 90th birthday, Ian Bamford made a 600-mile round trip by road from Belfast to Killarney with his wife, Rosemary, to honour a golfing rival from another era. Given the circumstances, I felt the least I could do was drive them from our hotel downtown to Killarney Golf Club.

The Bamfords had made the journey as a gesture to local man Michael Guerin, who had beaten Ian in the final of the 1960 South of Ireland Championship at Lahinch. Guerin's achievement in winning the South successively in 1960, 1961 and 1962 was hailed, quite correctly, as a landmark feat by his local club, where he still plays regularly.

Bamford's confidence in my driving could have been seriously questioned given his experience four years previously at Royal Portrush. The memory of the media outing prior to the 2019 Open Championship still sends shivers down my spine considering how I might have seriously injured or even killed both of us.

Ian thought it would be a splendid idea if we took a club buggy out onto the Dunluce Links to examine the various changes made in preparation for the great event. Behind the wheel, I thought the way to do it would be to travel the course in reverse, so as to study where balls would be landing, rather than the other way around.

All was fine until Ian shouted a sharp warning. From decades of local knowledge, he could see that I was heading up a slope which would have sent us, buggy and all, into a cavernous bunker invisible to me. Just in time, I swerved to safety and avoided what would have been a potentially calamitous crash into sand. On reflection, the retired judge displayed a remarkable sense of calm which must have served him admirably during a career on the bench.

As the crisis passed, composure was restored when we looked down the 574 yards of the second hole on a beautiful, sunny afternoon, smugly accepting the charming weather as almost the norm for Irish golf in those blessed days, now that The Open was set for a return after a lapse of 68 years. We couldn't have imagined the boundless joy that Shane Lowry would bring later in the year to our golfing island, north and south, as a glorious champion. Bamford recalled:

> It wasn't like this back in 1951. In fact, the weather was absolutely foul for the final round on the Friday afternoon. The rough was drenched with rain and Max Faulkner's extrication of a third shot from the right of the 18th was amazing.
>
> I wasn't far away, and could see that the ball was completely buried. He made a scythe-like motion with a full swing and the ball came out as desired. And he managed to make the par putt which secured The Open by two strokes.

Our visit seemed like an ideal way to link the present with the past. Bamford was 17 back then and on the threshold of a fine amateur career which delivered victories in the North of Ireland Championship of 1954 and 1972, on either side of the 1957 Irish Amateur Open, all achieved on his home course of Royal Portrush.

Since then, a move into the game's administration from a home in Belfast culminated in presidency of the GUI in 1993, when his various assignments included a memorable dinner with Gene Sarazen at The K Club. He became captain of Royal Portrush in 2002/2003.

His enthusiasm for the revisionary work of architect Martin Ebert hadn't diminished an enduring admiration for the masterful layout of the great Harry Colt. Bamford was especially conscious of Colt, the Hastings solicitor, turning his back on the law to become one of golf's most celebrated course designers. Sadly, one of the game's finest architects was too frail to attend the 1951 Open and died in November of that year, aged 82.

Next, Bamford pointed out a new bunker on the left of the par-five second, just beyond 300 yards. Then, further on, there was the more significant change of a newly located green, 40 yards further on and back left, where the putting surface replicated Colt's much-admired original contours. Bamford explained:

> I called into Norman Drew the other evening. When I suggested I could get him a ticket for one of the days of The Open, he replied: 'Look Ian, thanks very much but it's not on. I'm just not up to it.'
>
> Norman won the Ulster Boys in 1949 and John Glover won the British Boys the following year and both of them got into The Open. They were golfing colleagues of mine at the time though I wasn't as good as them and I imagine I was a little jealous of the fact that they got in and I didn't.
>
> Stevie [Portrush professional PG Stevenson] was coaching me at the time and by way of having me usefully occupied as a spectator, he told me to go out and watch Jimmy Adams of Wentworth. 'He's the best swinger of them all', was his verdict.

The legal profession seemed well represented at the 1951 Open. Bamford continued:

> We were allowed to walk the fairways behind the players except in certain areas and the whole operation was controlled by a chief marshal. He was Major Robin Wray, a Coleraine solicitor

who served in World War II and used a megaphone to control the growing crowds which still amounted to no more than 8,000 for the third and fourth rounds on the Friday.

By today's standards, the organisation was probably a bit haphazard. There were no changes to the course which was then a par-73, but I seem to remember the clubhouse being touched up a bit, and they opened a mixed bar which was mischievously named the 'Bird Cage'. It had no shortage of customers, including my dad, who was a club member playing off single figures.

Out on the course, our buggy swept us down to the famous fifth hole, appropriately named 'White Rocks', after its stunning backdrop. Then came the short sixth, 'Harry Colt's', from where a pathway to the right took us to the back tee on the magnificent new seventh, a par-five of 592 yards.

Looking down the serpentine fairway, Bamford declared: 'If the wind blows here, not even Dustin Johnson will make it in two.' Down on the right at driving distance a large bunker could be seen as a nod to 'Big Nellie', the original of the species on the old 17th, now departed.

Then we took in the new eighth, a 434-yard dog-leg par-four with a steep dune bank running down the left-hand side, inviting a big hitter to bite off as much as he dares. On the forward tee, a flock of red-beaked oystercatchers had gathered and further into the distance was a delightful view of the Royal Court Hotel. Bamford mused:

> I wonder what Rory will make of these new holes. I can still remember vividly the North of Ireland in 2005 when he did that 61 in qualifying. I was on roving duties for the Ulster Branch and saw every shot of his homeward journey of 28, which was the best nine holes of golf I've ever witnessed.
>
> It started with an eagle three on the 10th, followed by a two at the short 11th. Then came pars at the 12th and 13th before he proceeded to birdie the remaining five holes. Gradually, word got

to the clubhouse about what he was doing and the gallery began to grow with every passing hole.

It had grown to such a size by the 17th that I had to stop the players to allow the crowd to settle. That's where Rory over-hit his pitch a little to leave himself a tricky six-footer, but he managed to hole it. Then came a midiron on the 18th to 30 feet past the pin and again, the putt went down. Amazing.

As we drove over the flattened terrain where the 17th and 18th holes once lay, Bamford recalled some of the remarkable shots the winner, Faulkner, had played. Among them was a glorious escape from a cavernous, greenside bunker on the old 12th – now the 14th – and a third-round recovery from close to the out-of-bounds fence to the left of the old 16th, now the last.

'I remember other shots, like the one the Argentinian genius, Antonio Cerda, hit to two feet on the 10th,' he continued. 'But most of all, I remember the pride we all felt in what had happened in this small town on the Antrim coast.'

Bamford concluded: 'To be honest, I doubted if the Open would ever come back. But here it is, and I can't wait to see the stars of today follow in the footsteps of players who captivated my youth.'

THE CHALLENGE OF ROSSES POINT

RORY MCILROY

When the cheering subsided around Dubai's Earth Course on a memorable Sunday in November 2012, it was a safe bet that very few in the assembled gathering would have heard of Dominic Rooney. Yet in relative terms, the former steward of Co. Sligo Golf Club, who had passed on to kinder fairways early that month, had made as significant a contribution to Rory McIlroy's coffers as the €1.82 million he had just received as winner of the DP World Tour Championship.

Gerry McIlroy, Rory's father, would have remembered him. So, too, the player's mother, Rosie. It must be emphasised, however, that Dominic made the payment unintentionally, though with admirable grace.

This was the same Dominic who, as unofficial bookmaker to the West of Ireland Championship, was not noted as a morning man. In fact, he definitely preferred to do his business at night. So it was that when famously receiving a knock on the back door of his living quarters at Rosses Point at 8.15 one morning, he had to rub sleep from heavy eyes on being confronted by a giant of a stranger.

'Say, guy,' the American visitor boomed, 'I want to pay the green fee.' To which Rooney replied, 'It'll do when you come in.'

'But I am in,' came the retort.

They enjoy telling that story around the 19th at County Sligo almost as much as Dominic's involvement in the West of Ireland Championship of 2005. That was when the talk of the 36-hole qualification revolved around the performance of a remarkable 15-year-old from Holywood, Co. Down. With rounds of 68 and 67 for a seven-under-par total of 135, the debutant had the effrontery to be tied second in a field sprinkled with past, present and future internationals, including Brian McElhinney, who would win the British Amateur title later that year.

By the time the leading 64 qualifiers had advanced to match play, Dominic and his bookmaking colleague, Tom Gavin, decided they needed one more decent bet to be sure of at least balancing the figures when the time came to assess that year's venture. Casually, Gavin enquired if any further bets had been made. 'Yeah,' said Rooney, totally overlooking the form of the previous few days. 'I gave eights on a young fella named McIlroy.'

'Oh sweet Jesus, we're ruined,' exploded Gavin, with the look of a man who had just caught his foot in a rat-trap.

Unlike his colleague, he was acutely aware of the prodigious talent of the young Northern lad whom he had noted from the qualifying stage. Later, Gavin admitted: 'We took a hiding when Rory went on to win.' He further explained that Gerry McIlroy had bet €100 each way at odds of 8/1, which would have covered the family's expenses nicely from a dividend of €1,000. This, of course, was a time when both of Rory's parents gladly worked two jobs so as to give their talented son every chance of furthering what was then a promising golfing career.

As it happened, McIlroy won his quarter-final match by 3 and 2; went on to beat former Ireland Boy and Youth international, Rory Leonard, by one hole in the semi-finals and then captured the title in the final that afternoon, by a 2 and 1 margin over David Finn of Mallow.

Some years later, as one of the world's leading tournament professionals, Rory smiled at the memory:

> I can certainly recall the bet, but Dad only told me about it after I'd won. He wouldn't have wanted to put pressure on me beforehand. Whatever about the money involved, I'm sure the bet added to the fun and excitement both for my Dad and the bookie as events unfolded over the following few days.
>
> I know any amount of money would have come in handy at that time, because when I'd reached 15, my equipment, clothing, travel and accommodation had become very costly, especially during the months of spring and summer.

The player retains a vivid recollection of the remarkable happenings of those early months in 2005:

> Long before I was 15, I had become aware of the West as a very significant event in the amateur calendar. It stood apart for me, even from the North and the Close, as an almost mythical challenge which was certainly the one to win. And when I became it's youngest-ever winner, I'm not sure the significance of what I had achieved actually sank in, but I certainly saw it as something of a psychological stepping-stone in my amateur career.
>
> Then, to go on and retain the title in 2006 was massive for me; another enormous boost to my confidence. Without wishing to give the impression of being overly confident back then, I had very high expectations of myself going to Rosses Point that year,

while being aware that match play can involve a bit of luck and no small amount of risk.

By then, I had also shown a lot of form in other national amateur events, especially when winning the 2005 Close. Then there were my performances in the Faldo Series, playing against some of the world's best amateurs and learning new skills that were giving me a more complete game, both physically and psychologically. So, while I didn't kid myself that retaining the title was guaranteed, I felt really good about what I had already achieved and about what I had done in terms of practice and preparation.

To what extent did he feel that the testing conditions in the West actually shaped his development as a player? He replied:

Handling the weather was definitely a factor. A windswept links really does demand great ball-control and creative shot-making, not to mention concentration and patience. I think I learned to hone many of my skills in that environment. At the end of the day, however, I'd like to be remembered for having had the adaptability to transfer those skills, along with my knowledge and creativity, to any serious test of golf.

As to the fact that Co. Sligo was designed by Harry Colt, who was also responsible for Royal Portrush, Rory said:

I've always thought of Rosses Point as an iconic Irish links, very playable on benign days but an absolute handful when a touch of weather blows in from the Atlantic, which in truth, happened more than not. But after all, it is one of the beauties of links golf when a relatively easy nine-iron approach one day can be a firm six the next. And Colt's design really has stood the test of time.

Co. Sligo boasts a lot of great, thought-provoking holes. While the better part of the course is played along the shoreline, the elevated third and fifth are excellent driving holes. If I was to pick

> one above all the others, however, the 17th most stands out for me. It represents everything you don't need after being seriously challenged over the previous 16! It's long, uphill, dogleg-left and simply demands nothing less than a solid, accurate drive. A par there is always a great result; a birdie usually the stuff of fantasy.

Rory concluded his reflections on Co. Sligo by speaking of the club itself. 'Oh, I have very happy memories of the times I spent there,' he enthused.

> The hospitality we received as a family during the West was beyond generous and from a competitive standpoint, the atmosphere at the club was nothing short of electric. The place was rammed with young and sometimes not-so-young golfers, all attempting to carve a name for themselves on the Irish scene.
>
> Families, friends and whatever followers individual golfers could muster were welcomed year after year to one of the most prestigious amateur events in Europe. The entire membership of the club really embraced the event, making it feel like something special. Which for me, it always was.

Pádraig Harrington

When Rory McIlroy shocked the golfing world with his Rosses Point heroics in 2005, Pádraig Harrington took a rather detached view. 'I know nothing about him except that he still looks like a kid,' he said. 'He will get taller and stronger and can only improve. It's great to see.'

After he had become the winner of three professional Major titles, Harrington could see the significance of the West of Ireland challenge in shaping his own destiny as one of the finest players of recent decades. 'It instilled a determination to simply get on with it when things looked especially bleak,' he said. 'Finding a way to cope with the demands of a professional career is what the West did for me. And I imagine it would have had a similar impact on Shane Lowry and Rory.'

Harrington gained the distinction of capturing the West in 1994, the Club's centenary year. And having led the qualifiers, he did it in remarkable style, coming from four down after nine to beat the formidable 1992 champion, Ken Kearney, by two holes in a thrilling final.

Crucial to the Dubliner's success were typical Harrington birdies at the 12th and 15th where he holed from six and eighteen feet. 'With my Dad looking on and my brother Tadhg caddying, I looked destined to lose,' he recalled. 'But in the end, beating the home-town favourite became a really nice exception to some serious disappointments I had during my amateur career.'

He went on:

> The West was special, a little bit like watching the US Masters on TV. It meant a new golf year had begun. And the really interesting thing was that you went to Rosses Point not knowing what to expect. It could be really intimidating to watch the weather building in the Atlantic, knowing there was no place to hide, except perhaps in a dip in the dunes.
>
> I remember shooting 90 in my opening qualifying round in 1989 and still getting through. Nowhere in the world have I played in wind as strong or temperatures so cold, and while it wasn't good for your golf swing, it really tested you as a competitor.
>
> Yet the impact of what could be a brutal challenge, was that I developed a great affection for the place. I was too young back then to get involved in the social scene, but I always liked the cosy feel of Rosses Point – the village atmosphere, especially in the little pubs. The idea of spending a wet, cold wintry day sitting in a pub beside an open fire and having a few quiet drinks always appealed to me. For a lot of players, the West was a social thing. Much of that may have gone now, because the game is so competitive. Either way for me, the golf was the thing.

He went on to recall hitting shots on the practice ground that would come back over his head. 'You'd be doing it on purpose, probably with a nine iron,' he said. 'Messing. But it still illustrated the difficulty of the conditions, which made a big difference to me as a player.'

By way of contrast to his following the sun for games these days, he explained:

> I'll put it like this: I've never played golf in conditions that matched those at Rosses Point. And that's a fact. Nowhere in the world have I played in wind as strong, weather as cold, or such generally hostile conditions. To be honest, I could no longer do the scores I used to do in those circumstances back then. They were pretty decent match play scores. You simply found a way of getting it up and down and holing putts. And, of course, links golf courses are designed to cater for that.
>
> I can imagine a lot of people writing me off in the 1994 final. But I turned things around, which went on to become a crucial part of my golfing make-up. With my short-game, I always viewed the 17th as a special hole for me, despite the birdie Kearney hit me with on that occasion. Four was always good up there, and I felt I generally had a better chance of getting a four than the other guy.

Inevitably, thoughts of the West are prompted for Harrington on the occasions when it clashes with the Masters at Augusta National in the first full week in April. 'In my early years as a pro, before I had the opportunity of playing the Masters for the first time in 2000, I would always be conscious of the West,' he said. 'And later on, thoughts of Rosses Point would never be far from my mind around Easter time.'

Shane Lowry

History was on Shane Lowry's side when he competed in the West of Ireland for the first time in 2006 – but not in the way he would have wanted. Instead of the spectacular debut his friend Rory McIlroy had achieved the previous year, Lowry found himself being compared with Philip Walton's ill-fated experience back in the early eighties.

With Cecil Whelan, secretary of the Links Society, at one of his splendid functions.

Among the annual award winners at the Irish Youth Foundation Dinner 2005.

On 20 May 2009, three days after he had won the Irish Open, Shane Lowry informed Golfing Union of Ireland General Secretary, Seamus Smith, that he was turning professional.

With Padraig Harrington and the Claret Jug in 2008.

Dining out in West Palm Springs in 2006; Kathy and I with Barbara and Jack Nicklaus.

'ormer *Sunday Independent* sports editor Adhamhnan O'Sullivan, myself, Paul Kimmage
:nd a mutual friend, Aidan O'Mara.

ı the background for a memorable six-ball at Old Head in July 1999. From left, Mark
'Meara, Tiger Woods, David Duval and Lee Janzen. The other two were Payne Stewart
nd Stuart Appleby.

/ith John Redmond, interviewing Tom Watson at Portmarnock, July 1981.

O'CONNOR'S WONDER 63 WON THE £1,000

MASTER GOLFER, CHRISTY O'CONNOR (ROYAL DUBLIN) LANDED THE TOP PRIZE OF £1,000 WHEN HE DEFEATED KEN BOUSFIELD (COOMBE HILL) BY 8 STROKES IN THE 18 HOLE PLAY OFF AT WOODBROOK THIS MORNING. NOT ALONE DID CHRISTY TAKE THE GOLD BOWL BACK TO IRELAND, BUT HE DID SO IN A MAGNIFICENT RECORD BREAKING ROUND OF 63.

This beats last year's winner, Max Faulkner's round by two strokes, and improves on Christy's day old record of 64 by a stroke. As usual it was O'Connor's magnificent iron play that won him the spoils. Except for a few occasions he never failed to get chips within a few feet of the pin.

Ken Bousfield was indeed a very game loser. He played consistent golf for the first nine holes but on the return journey struck patches of bad luck which added to the awe inspiring display of his opponent, cost him the return of a more respectable score.

Needed birdie

Deadly accurate

CHRISTY O'CONNOR

To-day's Racing

Folkestone

Samoan Sun in July

Rest of Killarney runners

First Day Card at Killarney

'Sandy' can take the first race

Results in brief

...eir goalkeeper Terry Moloney ...aterford at Limerick yesterday.

A face in the crowd … Walking up the ninth fairway, Darren's final hole, in the second round of the Smurfit European Open in 1999. Needing a birdie for a 59, Clarke carded a par for a 60.

My first golf report in the *Evening Press*, 1960.

Vith golf course architect Robert Trent Jones Jnr.

)inner at The K Club in 1993 with guest of honour Gene Sarazen; Tánaiste Dick Spring;)onald Panoz; GUI President Ian Bamford; K Club managing director Ray Carroll; and nyself.

With golfing friends Joe Richardson, Donal O'Brien and Michael Duffy.

Warm greetings from Arnold Palmer at The K Club.

Top: Marking my retirement from the *Irish Times* in 2002 at Sawgrass, with a presentation from the chairman of the Association of Golf Writers, John Hopkins.

Middle: Checking a handout in the media centre.

Bottom: With Allan Walton in front of the motel we shared in Carmel during the Walker Cup at Cypress Point in 1981 when his brother, Philip, was a member of the British and Irish team.

Indicating the plaque erected by the third green at Royal Dublin to the centenary of Michael Moran's death in 2018.

Arnold Palmer armed with designer drawings at The K Club.

Retirement photograph from the *Sunday Independent* of Kathy and I, by Mark Condren.

Cartoon by the inimitable Martyn Turner to mark my round at Augusta National in April 1993.

With Joe Carr, who became a dear friend when we collaborated on his biography in 2002.

Irrepressible Ryder Cup partners, on the occasion of a visit by Peter Alliss to see Himself at Royal Dublin.

Interviewing Nick Faldo.

On a pilgrimage to the home of Seve Ballesteros in Pedrena after his third Open triumph in 1988.

Top: Kathy joins Christy O'Connor for a family celebration in City West.

Bottom: Meeting Jim Tindall on a visit to Shamrock Golf Club, Texas.

Sept 6-1993

GENE SARAZEN

P.O. BOX 667
MARCO ISLAND, FLORIDA 33937

Dear Dermot

Received your letter along with your Story, You sure recorded the Conversation right from the mouth, Its a Very good Story I am forwarded on to Mr Paroz.

We had a delightful trip back, But two Days later I came down with Bronsitis, Was sick for over two weeks, I stayd at My Daughter's house for over three weeks, But it left me in a weaker condition, now I am back home, Its Very warm hear

Top: The second handwritten letter I received from Gene Sarazen.
Bottom: In his nineties, Gene Sarazen still handled his own correspondence, even down to addressing envelopes.

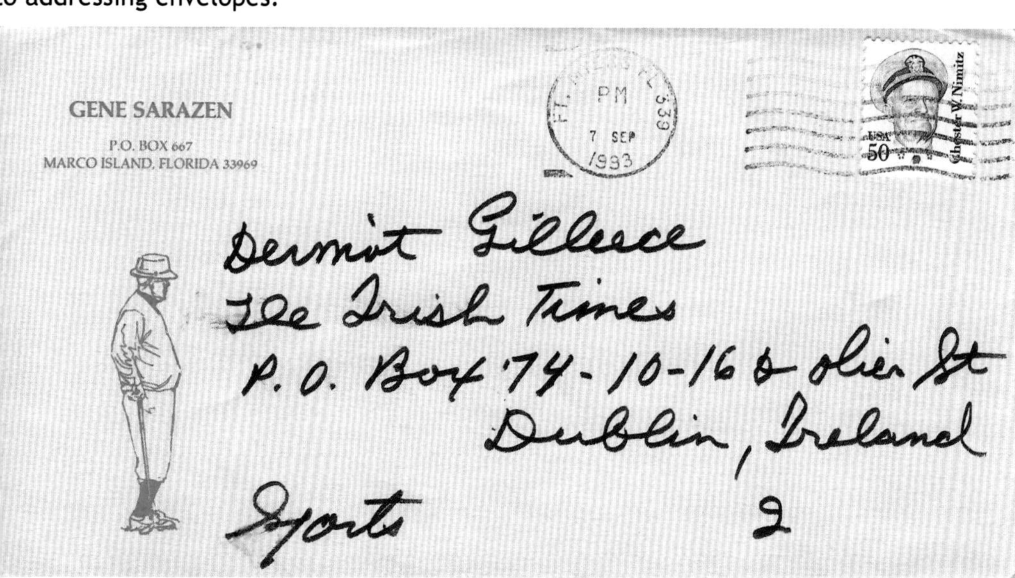

Top: Myself, Claire Dowling and Shane Lowry at the Irish Golf Writers' dinner.

Bottom: A charming drawing as a surprise gift from Val Doonican, whose artistry extended to sketching and watercolours.

Left: A Christmas card from Gene Sarazen.

Top: Trying the other side of journalism.

Bottom: Long before LIV … a chat with course designer Greg Norman, during the media day at Doonbeg, 2002.

Top: A spirited exchange with Des Smyth.

Bottom left: An alternative to the midnight oil …

Bottom right: Enjoying the company of Kitty MacCann on the 50th anniversary of her British Women's triumph.

That was when Walton, as a highly fancied challenger, was disqualified for failing to sign his card in qualifying. In Lowry's case disqualification came for signing for wrong scores on two successive holes. 'I remember being pleased with myself after an opening 73, even though it was six strokes behind a remarkable 67 by England's David Horsey,' Lowry recalled.

> As it turned out, I was set to lead the qualifiers until it was discovered that I had signed for wrong figures in a second-round 66. While the total was correct, it included an eagle on the long fifth and a par on the sixth, whereas I had actually birdied both holes. I had turned 19 less than two weeks previously, and though it wasn't to be an ideal memory of my first West, it proved to be a very valuable lesson.
>
> Even then, there would be tremendous excitement about the West coming around and it seemed to build with every year. As I progressed onto the international panel, I found myself being away quite a bit, playing in overseas amateur events, which made returning to the West all the more special.
>
> Myself and Rory loved everything about the week, staying in a B&B with one of our friends. At the time, you felt life couldn't get any better. Even when I was beaten, there would be the involvement of caddying for a friend. So, winning it in 2008 was a huge deal.

When Lowry returned to Rosses Point for the 2008 Championship, he did so as one of the more popular contenders. 'I remember there used to be a book down in Austies' pub and the guy who was caddying for me backed me to win,' he recalled. 'I think I was 8/1 that week. By then, Rory had turned pro and was actually playing his first full year on the European Tour and I was conscious of having climbed the pecking order. In fact, I can remember thinking that I was going there to win.'

Though he had a few close calls, notably when taken to the 20th by Ryan Boal of Castle GC in the quarterfinals, he won his remaining two matches inside the distance. In the final against Mullingar's Desmond Morgan, Lowry secured the title on the 17th by a margin of 2 and 1. He recalled:

> I always felt that to win at Rosses Point, you had to play certain holes well. Getting an edge on tough holes like the 6th, 7th, 8th, 11th, possibly the 14th and certainly the 17th, was the key to winning a match or shooting a qualifying score there. In fact, the first is not an easy proposition either, with the bunkers and that bush on the left. And I remember days when I might be hitting a nine-iron into the fourth and other days when it could be a two iron.
>
> I always felt confident about qualifying and if I didn't give away those hard holes, the chances were I'd win my matches. And there was huge excitement when I made the breakthrough. The crowds were huge and it seemed like half of Sligo had backed to win.
>
> For me, winning the West back then felt the same as it would be to win a Major nowadays as a professional. Little did I realise that I would outdo myself the following year in the Irish Open at Baltray.
>
> During my amateur days, the Irish Open always seemed to clash with the Brabazon Trophy which carried additional importance in 2009, it being a Walker Cup year. But as the country's number one amateur, I had my heart set on the Irish Open, even though the GUI would often decline invitations because of the Brabazon.
>
> Kevin Flanagan was the international captain and I remember telling him what I was thinking. Though it would mean missing the Brabazon, he assured me he'd see what he could do. And he got me into Baltray. I'll be forever grateful to him for what became a huge stepping-stone in my career. God knows where I'd be if Kevin hadn't been so supportive.

And the Flanagan connection remains strong in the life of the Lowrys. Shane's brother, Alan, a regular competitor in the West, happened to work for Deloitte where his boss was Alan Flanagan, Kevin's brother.

'In fact, Alan is very friendly with Kevin's son and he stays with them,' said Shane. 'So my feelings about the West of Ireland remain very much caught up with the Flanagans.'

Lowry concluded:

> When I think of Rosses Point as a golfing challenge, I picture a really tough test, especially if the wind gets up. I would rank it up there with the most difficult links courses we play. I suppose any course where you do well tends to become a favourite, but for everything that it represents in the shaping of my career, I will always think of Co. Sligo as a very special place.

Paul McGinley

> When I think of Co. Sligo, images come to mind of a great golf course, a brilliant links which I always enjoyed. I've so many happy memories of going there as a youngster when I caddied for my Dad in the West of Ireland. Then, later on, there was the thrill of winning the Irish Close there in 1989, which was obviously a big deal for me.
>
> From my caddying days, it's a golf course I got to know really well. I came to appreciate the wide range of different shots you needed to play if you have success there. Like some well-hit long irons, which I can still recall with a great deal of satisfaction.

He also remembers Co. Sligo for his first sight of Rory McIlroy hitting a golf shot. The Dubliner had gone there with his father to watch brother Michael Jnr attempting to qualify for the West. 'I remember saying to my Dad that I'd heard a lot about this McIlroy guy,' recalled McGinley who, seven years later, would captain a victorious Ryder Cup team at Gleneagles where McIlroy was a key member of the European side.

McGinley went on:

> On the short ninth, with his playing partners both in the left-hand bunker, Rory was last to hit, probably having bogeyed the eighth. Into a stiff 25mph wind off the right and hitting maybe a five iron, he produced this stunning, knock-down cut which held its line beautifully to finish comfortably on the green. The ball control he displayed was way beyond his years, while executing an amazing shot that I can remember clearly to this day.

Regarding the course, McGinley continued:

> My appreciation of its challenge was heightened on learning it was designed by Harry Colt, whose work I have since become familiar with as a member of Sunningdale. And, of course, he designed the West Course at Wentworth too, and Portrush. I've great admiration for his work, which seems to fit my eye. And when I think of Co. Sligo, I picture a lovely flow to some stunning golf holes. Beautiful holes offering a varied challenge in a great setting.
>
> I remember the friendliness of the clubhouse, especially the atmosphere when I won the Close, which effectively set up my career as a tournament golfer.

His victory came in August 1989, when he was joint third leading qualifier (75 and 68 = 143) behind Darren Clarke, Francis Howley and Paddy O'Looney on 141. As it happened, the only time he was taken beyond the 16th in six rounds of match play was in a one-hole over Jim Carvill in the third round. He eventually beat a prospective Co. Sligo specialist, Niall Goulding of Portmarnock, by 3 and 2 in the final.

Fred Perry

Golf officials fall largely into two contrasting groups. There are those motivated by a genuine desire to serve, and those ego-trippers seduced by a blazer and the prospect of a full Irish in a quality hotel, preferably beyond these shores.

Born in 1933, Fred Perry belongs unquestionably to the former group. And by way of emphasising his status as Connacht's longest-serving delegate, he completed 40 years on the West of Ireland Championship in 2017. As it happened, he died on Saturday, 3 March 2018, four days before Co. Sligo's annual press conference for the West.

'I enjoyed every bit of it,' Perry had said, having gone through the period up to his retirement without ever skipping a year. 'In fact, I never missed a meeting of committee.'

In filling the roles of starter, referee and any other administrative function that arose, he was invariably out on the course, whatever the weather. 'And despite the bar talk about slow play, I can tell you that the championship always went smoothly,' he added with typical bluffness.

As it happens, 1977 was his first year involved with the West and five years later, he was president of the GUI. Countless youngsters passed through his hands as West of Ireland challengers, from Philip Walton, Ronan Rafferty, Garth McGimpsey and Pádraig Harrington on to Rory McIlroy and Shane Lowry. Which made him a sort of golfing equivalent of the beloved Brookfield schoolmaster in *Goodbye Mr Chips*. Ironically, a favourite memory of those players was away from Rosses Point, when he refereed the final of the Irish Close Championship captured by McIlroy at Westport in 2005.

10

Old Head

2018

Record business for the 2018 season gave cause for a coming-of-age celebration at the Old Head Links in Kinsale. It had been 21 years since the spectacular development was launched in June 1997.

This emphasised the wisdom of a crucial decision taken by the owners back in 2004 when Donald Trump attempted to buy their precious property. The future president of the United States was told bluntly that the property was beyond his means.

Back then, the facility was battling to rebuild American business which had been rocked to its roots by the devastating effects of 9/11. Faith in the future, however, has been rewarded with green-fee traffic up 10 per cent on the previous year, which had also been a record.

'With more than 20,000 rounds, we will have to limit numbers in 2019, so as to protect the quality of the product,' was the end-of-season prediction by club president Patrick O'Connor.

On the other side of the Atlantic, August 2004 marked the launch onto the international scene of a very different venue. Whistling Straits was designed by Pete Dye on the shores of Lake Michigan and was scheduled to stage the Ryder Cup in 2020, with Pádraig Harrington as the likely European captain. On this occasion, as host to the PGA Championship, it delivered a fine winner in Vijay Singh while Paul McGinley finished sixth, only to secure Ryder Cup selection for Oakland Hills a month later. As things turned out, Covid caused the Ryder Cup to be held back a year until 2021.

Meanwhile, among those officiating at the PGA was MG Orender, the 33rd President of the PGA of America. He also happened to be co-founder of Hampton Golf Inc, specialists in all facets of golf-course development and management. This role had brought him into contact with the owners of the Old Head and caused him to lend an ear to golf devotee Trump, who was attending the championship.

Back here, Patrick O'Connor was involved in the more gentle pursuit of fishing at Boulakeel, close by his brother John's home in south Kerry. However, his fishing idyll was interrupted by a phone call from Whistling Straits where his friend Orender had an interesting request.

'Donald Trump wants a word with you,' he said to Patrick, who agreed to take the call. Though he knew Trump and had played the American's Mar-a-Lago Resort in Florida, their relationship was essentially a casual, golfing one. The conversation went something like this.

'What do you want, Donald?'

'I want to buy the Old Head.'

'You can't afford it.'

'What do you mean I can't afford it?'

'It's not for sale, therefore you can't afford it.'

O'Connor has since added: 'He then threw a ridiculous figure at me, but I insisted it wasn't for sale, to which he acknowledged: "OK, that's fine."'

The established position of himself and his brother John as co-owners of the property, until John's death in 2013, was that the Old Head would not be sold, no matter who came calling. And that included the man who would become America's 45th president.

Trump had never been to the West Cork promontory and the fact that the offer was made, sight unseen, lent telling emphasis to the international reputation of the development, simply through word of mouth. But that wasn't the end of the story.

In the winter of 2004, Patrick O'Connor happened to be shooting on the Menie Estate, owned by Tom Griffen, five miles north of Aberdeen in Scotland. An American lawyer, Griffen had been in the area for 20 years, working in the offshore oil industry.

Aware of O'Connor's involvement in the Old Head, Griffen talked of being constantly pestered by people wanting to buy or lease the linksland on the coastal side of his property. While expressing the view that the site would make a magnificent links, O'Connor spoke of his exchange with Trump only a few months previously.

In addition, Brian Morgan, the noted Scottish golf-course photographer who has done considerable work in this country, found himself involved in an invitation extended by O'Connor for Griffen to visit the Old Head. He explained:

> It transpired that Patrick was otherwise engaged on the agreed date and it fell to me to show Griffen around, given that I happened to be there at the time.
>
> I eventually went to see the site in Aberdeen and did a helicopter photo-shoot of it. I then sent copies of the images to a number of leading golf architects. Eventually, a set of images were passed from Tom Fazio to his nephew Tommy, who had been doing design work for Trump at the time.
>
> The upshot was that Trump sent his representative to look the place over and within a few months a deal was struck.

So it was that a deal reportedly valued at £7m stemmed from Trump's rejected overtures for the Old Head and culminated in the official launch of Trump Aberdeen in 2012.

Two years later, Trump spectacularly extended his portfolio of Scottish golf terrain through the purchase of Turnberry, the scene of Tom Watson's celebrated 'Duel in the Sun' with Jack Nicklaus in the Open Championship of 1977 and a crushing near-miss in 2009, when

Stewart Cink triumphed after a play-off. It was considered a snip at a reported £35.7m. Mind you, there is no sign of The Open returning there in the immediate future, which must be a concern for Donald.

On a related note, the official launch of Doonbeg in June 2002 represented an estimated investment of $25m by Landmark, an American development company which owned Kiawah Island and had US Senator George Mitchell as a board member. The site's potential was originally noted by Shannon Development, which bought 377 acres from four farmers for a reported €6m before they, in turn, sold the property on to the newly formed Irish National Golf Club, a subsidiary of Landmark.

Two months before buying Turnberry, Trump had turned his attention once more to Ireland in February 2014. In the aftermath of the economic collapse, he bought Doonbeg out of receivership for only €8.7m. When set against the figure Shannon Development had paid for the land alone, this meant he had acquired the design skills of Greg Norman, a five-star hotel lodge and seven unsold suites all for €2.7m.

Those sorts of figures would have worked admirably at the Old Head – 30 years previously. Michael Roche, owner of the 216-acre promontory at that time, had decided to put it on the market in 1984, but nobody seemed interested.

It remained for sale until 1989, when the O'Connor brothers paid £300,000 for it, simply as an investment. The notion of building a golf course there wouldn't germinate for another two years.

When the brothers eventually turned to golf at the end of the 1990s, costs had risen to about £10m, during which time the Old Head had gained the distinction of becoming the last golf course development in this country not to have required planning permission. Apparently, a change in the legislation was a direct consequence of the extended legal wrangling associated with its development.

So, what's its current value? A leading figure in the Irish golf industry suggested: 'When you factor in the vanity value attaching to such a unique site, it could be worth €50m.' Which would be an unlikely fit among Trump's bargain buys.

Sidenote: In 1998, the Old Head Links had been in existence for a year and so much controversy surrounded it that the *Irish Times* thought it appropriate that I should travel there and establish what all the fuss was about. This is the piece I wrote arising from that trip. As a reward (not that I expected one for simply writing the truth), they made me an honorary life member, which is a distinction I value to this day.

> *Certain elements of golf are not only regrettable, but impossible to defend, even by someone like myself who makes a living from writing about the game. Stubborn elitism and discrimination against women immediately spring to mind, as does a sometimes cavalier attitude towards the environment.*
>
> *Against that background, some perfectly reasonable golfing people are made to feel so vulnerable that they decline to defend themselves. So it is that I wish to defend the right of Old Head Golf Links not only to exist, but to prosper as the most spectacular course in Europe, when it officially opens on June 1st.*
>
> *Since work began about seven years ago (1991) on building a golf course on Kinsale's celebrated peninsula, it seems that every environmental crank has made it a target for ill-informed comment.*
>
> *Accusations have piled up remorselessly. How is it that the public have been suddenly denied free access to this national treasure?*
>
> *Why weren't those with an appreciation of the environmental value of the site allowed to take it over?*
>
> *How dare these golfing types actually charge the public admission to the site? How dare they destroy such a wonderful wild-life preserve, for the sake of a stupid old game? And if they are to be allowed [to] build this wretched course, how can they be permitted to ban Irish people from playing there?*

The accusatory list prompted a wry smile from John O'Connor, the Kerry-born owner with his brother Patrick, of the Old Head. However, he thought it rather refreshing that, unlike his journalistic critics, I should have taken the trouble to visit the site and observe for myself what he was attempting to achieve there.

'The notion has been put about that the Old Head is the Phoenix Park of Cork,' he said, when I journeyed there to meet him. 'A national treasure it is; a national park it most certainly is not.'

But we're getting ahead of ourselves. We haven't explained what the status of the Old Head was before O'Connor arrived on the scene. Well, it had been the home of the De Courcy chiefs who, until their fall from power in the 16th century, occupied the castle whose ruins still dominate the neck of the headland.

By the 20th century, it had become farmland through which the Commissioner of Irish Lights was granted an official right of way, down to the lighthouse: there are no other rights of way on the deed. Under the ownership of Michael Roche, however, people took to wandering all over the Old Head in increasing numbers, free of charge.

Though gates and fences were knocked down, Roche took no action against these trespassers. Eventually, in 1984 (as mentioned), he decided to put the site up for sale. The auctioneer was Dominic Daly, who would later become a director of Ashbourne Holdings, the company responsible for the golf course development.

'The property was on the market for five years, during which time the State could obviously have bought it,' he said. 'I find it quite revealing that none of the environmental bodies expressed any interest in it at that time.'

Eventually, the O'Connors bought the Old Head in 1989 for the relatively modest sum of around £300,000 (punts). 'That was when people were made aware they could no longer trespass for free,' he said. 'I could have closed off the site completely, allowing nobody in there, but instead, I permitted access at £1.50 per person or £3 for two people in a car.'

Why charge? O'Connor replied:

> Because as owner, I have certain responsibilities to discharge, such as public liability insurance. Quite apart from that, I am spending about £1 million in developing the site for the public's enjoyment,

> through the construction of walkways and access to a jetty at the second hole.
>
> I also have in mind to construct a spectator platform which can be suspended down the cliff-face at the 12th, where people can view the birds flying into the caves. Our intention is that these wonderful amenities should be shared in a controlled manner. Don't you think it reasonable that people should be charged for that privilege?

And what of membership? Recent newspaper reports suggest that no Irish citizen need apply for club membership when it's open for business. 'This is patent nonsense,' responded Daly.

> As a marketing strategy aimed at promoting the venue internationally, we decided that to qualify for our categories of Founder and International Membership, applicants should be resident outside the state for nine months each year.
>
> But Irish people can avail of our corporate membership, while our intention is to have a local membership by invitation. Other than that, as a pay-and-play facility, our main target will be the Irish market.

Meanwhile, with the help of ecologist Tom O'Byrne, another goal is to achieve an environment in which the immensely varied flora and fauna can prosper. Significant headway has already been made by forbidding a local coursing club to trap hares on the site.

Then there is the work of consultant agronomist Brian Robinson, who has been involved in such high-profile projects as the soccer pitches at Anfield, Goodison Park and Ibrox. 'The wind-chill factor and the remarkable fluctuations in temperature from October to March presented a major challenge in getting grass to thrive here,' he said.

'After extensive trials, we came up with hybrid, salt-tolerant grasses, mainly fescue and bent. And the unique nature of the environment meant that we were forced to throw the rule book out the window, in terms of maintenance procedures.'

All this could hardly be described as the work of a man hell-bent on destroying a precious amenity. Essentially, O'Connor's ambition is to have golf and nature living in harmony. And if he and his fellow directors had been seeking a quick return on an estimated investment of £10 million, they could have found countless more attractive projects.

The Old Head Links deserves to succeed, which is not to say that environmentalists won't continue to have problems with the project. One would hope, however, that the next time their voices are raised in protest, it will be with the benefit of first-hand experience of the subject.

A Royal Visitor

Instructions were that he be referred to only as 'Your supreme Majesty' and that he should not be touched physically under any circumstances. So, you could imagine the consternation when the leading local caddie Tom Griffin wrapped his arms around the esteemed guest, addressed him as 'King' and then saluted him with high-fives.

This is how Jim O'Brien recalled a visit by the King of Malaysia to the Old Head Links. It became a treasured memory at the time of his retirement after 25 years as general manager of a stretch widely acknowledged as the most spectacular in the world.

His appearance there was linked to conferring with the degree of Doctor of Laws, honoris causa, of His Majesty at University College Cork on 18 June 2003. Apparently, a condition of agreeing to the ceremony was that His Majesty, as a keen golfer, could play the Old Head as part of the Cork visit, which is what happened. His Majesty's full title is the Yang di-Pertuan Agong XII Tuanku Syed Sirajuddin Ibni Al-Marhum Tuanku Syed Putra Jamalullail, King of Malaysia.

Among this and other notable happenings, O'Brien's tenure led to an enduring partnership with the late Florida-based architect, Ron Kirby, who provided some brilliant design refinements under the official's guidance. These have been greatly appreciated by overseas members who, at the beginning of a new season, would inquire: 'Well, what have you got for us this year, Jim?'

Kirby's attachment to the Co. Cork promontory was such that he travelled there in 2020 to fulfil his late wife Sally's wish that her ashes be placed there, in a special location beside the sixth green. And his own remains went there too, when his time came in 2023 to join her in the great beyond.

Some splendid work by Kirby in this country dates back to his involvement with the Jack Nicklaus design team at Mount Juliet. Most notable have been Dromoland Castle, Castlemartyr and, of course, Old Head, where he had the distinction of finding the final routing on a seriously challenging site.

Kirby also left a significant stamp internationally, which was recounted in his book, quaintly titled *We Spent Half Our Lives on the Wrong Side of the Road*. Projects included one in the Philippines, which involved a phone call in 1977 from Imelda Marcos.

The conversation, we're told, went something like this:

Mrs Marcos: 'The president [her husband] turns 60 in September this year.'

Ron Kirby: 'Very nice.'

Mrs M: 'We want to build him a golf course in his hometown of Laoag.'

RK: 'Very nice.'

Mrs M: 'Can you build 18 holes by September?'

RK: 'No. It's now June.'

Mrs M: 'Can you build nine holes by September?'

RK: 'No. It's not possible.'

Mrs M: 'Can you build one hole by September?'

Kirby: 'Yes.'

Mrs M: 'Great! We will get nine contractors to each build one hole. When can you start?'

So it was that for his 60th birthday, Ferdinand Marcos played nine holes at the Poway Course in Laoag on 11 September 1977.

Kirby's ongoing involvement at Old Head included significant changes to the third, sixth, eighth, tenth, twelfth and thirteenth holes.

'I came up with the ideas, ran them past John O'Connor [joint owner] and, with his approval, Ron and I got the work done,' said O'Brien.

When Kinsale native Noel Hurley was entrusted with assembling a group of caddies at the resort prior to its official opening on 1 June 1997, Tom Griffin emerged as the leading bagman. Since retired, he was known only as Big Tom due to a generous girth, created by his capacity to shift serious quantities of stout.

Another distinctive feature was his pronounced Cork accent, which was often difficult to decipher. In fact, there was an occasion when he and another caddie, Doc, were toting for four Japanese visitors. Afterwards, in reporting to Hurley, Doc remarked: 'I was out there on the course with four Japanese and Big Tom and I was the only one speaking English.'

Returning to the event of the King of Malaysia's visit in 2003, O'Brien rejected any suggestion that he was taking a risk by sending out the indecipherable Big Tom with the King who, as I've indicated, had his heart set on playing the Old Head. 'During the previous week, his Minister for Protocol contacted me with instructions as to how the King should be treated,' said O'Brien. 'And on the day itself, he and I kept tabs on things from an accompanying buggy.'

It seems to have been quite a round. The first thing was the King's vain attempt at lighting a cigarette on the exposed headland. That was when Big Tom, with outstretched arms, shielded His Majesty from the wind, an action which left the minister ashen faced.

When the bagman was asked the line of a putt on the fifth green, he replied: 'Two balls, left edge.'

The King proceeded to miss on the right, whereupon he gave Tom an angry look – but Tom was having none of it. 'I told you it was two fucking balls on the left,' Big Tom barked, articulating every word.

'After that, they appeared to get on famously,' added O'Brien, 'even to the point of high-fiving each other while Tom shouted "Well done, King", after every good shot. Meanwhile, the minister beside me simply closed his eyes, hoping, no doubt, that none of these proceedings made it back to Malaysia.'

Interestingly, it was only when he re-entered the clubhouse that His Majesty resumed his regal demeanour.

Some of O'Brien's early activities reflected the challenge ahead as he and his staff worked out of portacabins. Then came an unexpected break.

As part of a programme they were doing on Irish golf, the Golf Channel in the US paid an impromptu visit on a stunning Sunday in June. By way of preparing for their arrival, O'Brien was out on the course the previous evening, putting cosmetic touches to unfinished tees, like cutting lines into rough terrain to make them look presentable from the air.

In the event, the TV crew were so impressed by the stunning nature of the site that they decided to make it a standalone programme, which prompted a remarkable public reaction starting in September of that year. O'Brien recalled: 'We were inundated with green-fee bookings.'

There could be no question of memberships, however, until the Supreme Court reached their verdict.

'That was when we discovered we had very good friends in influential places, where publicity was concerned,' the general manager went on. 'At around the same time, *Links* magazine in the US put us on their cover as the world's most dramatic golf course. This and the Golf Channel's programme did wonders. If we had a million to spend on marketing, we couldn't have done a better job.'

Still, it was only in May 2003 that the threat of litigation was finally removed. In a unanimous, 54-page judgment, the Supreme Court dismissed in its entirety an appeal by An Bord Pleanála against a High Court decision affirming that no public right of access existed on the promontory.

In a damning indictment of the board, the Supreme Court accused it of over-reaching itself so as to achieve goals foreign to its statutory purpose. The judges further ruled that Cork County Council and An Bord Pleanála had acted in a 'manifestly unreasonable' manner in attempting to impose such conditions. As a public criticism of a statutory authority, the judgement could hardly have been more explicit.

All this effectively gave O'Brien his raison d'être. As he said: 'I'm just so proud of the place. Even with the number of difficulties we encountered along the way, it's the best thing that's happened to me.'

Guiding the fortunes of the world's most spectacular golf course has been, by his own admission, a privilege. In a collection of wonderful memories, there have been meetings with some of the game's great exponents such as Arnold Palmer, Nick Faldo and Rory McIlroy. Also, world number one and future Ryder Cup captain Luke Donald equalled the course record of 68 as another satisfied customer.

Accompanied by his second wife in a buggy, Palmer played a few holes and was 'very gracious'. When cancellations became necessary because of Covid, payments were refunded just as they had been for 9/11, though a lot of travel agents wanted to leave the bookings in place.

When John O'Connor died in 2013, the main speaker at his month's mind was O'Brien, who captured the essence of the man in a few simple sentences:

> When somebody dies, it is customary to use the Gaelic phrase, 'Ní fheicimid a leithéid arís' [We won't see their like again]. In John's case, however, nothing could have been more appropriate or apt. During 30 years in the bank [ultimately as a manager], I met a lot of people, many of them fascinating characters. But John stood apart as a truly unique individual.

The two men enjoyed a remarkable relationship which encompassed the crucial, formative years of the Old Head Links. And whatever the circumstances and differences of opinion, they almost invariably succeeded in furthering their common objective of delivering one of the greatest destinations in world golf.

As a keen golfer who found his true working vocation late in life, O'Brien delighted in sharing this fascinating journey with O'Connor. He remembers being told, on numerous occasions, 'Remember Jim, we are merely guardians of the headland for future generations. Everything we do must be in harmony with nature and our surroundings.'

And both men were as good as their word.

11

A Charming Imprint in West Clare

What you're achieving in Ireland now is a mixture of different courses which offer a wide appeal to the travelling golfer. And the great advantage you have is that they're all accessible. We have some new seaside courses in the States, but they're out in places like Oregon. How the hell do you get there? You can't even find them on the map. On the other hand, my sons Steve and Jack came here to Ireland in September [2003] and they played Portmarnock, Co. Down, Mount Juliet, Ballybunion, Waterville, the Old Head and Lahinch. Now there's a great mixture. Jackie really likes Lahinch. Last year they went to Scotland and played Loch Lomond, St Andrews, Carnoustie and Turnberry. That's the sort of selection the discerning golfer wants.

Jack Nicklaus, during an Irish visit in December 2003.

On the Friday of Irish Open week in 2019, Pádraig Slattery headed back into Lahinch village from a special event organised by the sponsors,

Dubai Duty Free. It was twenty minutes past twelve and Slattery expected the traffic restrictions, in place until midnight, to have been lifted.

Instead, a local Garda on duty on the corner into Main Street, indicated they were still very much in place. About 8,000 revellers remained in full voice. And with a Garda blessing, they could continue their noisy enjoyment until some time past 2.00 a.m. 'That's when I realised that Lahinch had finally come of age as the international golf venue my father had envisaged,' said the proud local who had been born in this village on the Atlantic coast of West Clare 63 years previously. 'And when I spoke to the Garda superintendent the following morning, he explained that extending the traffic restrictions wasn't a difficult decision to make, with so many people in a party mood.'

I had enjoyed the same experience the previous night, when it was a treat to see the place dressed in its absolute Sunday finery. As far as the eye could see, residential properties and business premises were freshly painted, courtesy of a scheme initiated by the council. Locals joked: 'You daren't stand still for fear of being macadamised.' And there were flower displays at every turn.

With hordes of visitors thronging the streets, it could hardly have been more different to visits I remembered from years covering the South of Ireland Championship. The mood created by glorious Irish Open weather certainly contrasted starkly with memories of poker sessions in the back room of Kenny's pub on wet, hostile afternoons.

One local newspaper was predicting a commercial jackpot of €5 million for a weekend when up to 100,000 visitors had passed through the village. 'That might be overstating things a bit, but I would still expect about three times the normal take for the first week in July,' said businessman Alan Logue.

He was responsible for floral displays in the form of charming baskets on up to 70 premises. 'We put a proper irrigation system in place, whereby the baskets are watered at 5.00 every morning,' said Logue. This was achieved through a one-off payment of €180 for each premises, accompanied by an annual contribution of €90.

It was all part of the festival atmosphere promised by the championship host, Paul McGinley. Locals and visitors had enthusiastically bought into the notion when I rambled the streets around midnight. 'I'll tell you what this bar is about, it's about everybody being treated equal,' proclaimed Conor Flanagan, security man at the famous 19th, once owned by the Lions and Ireland prop Gordon Wood. 'They may not be equal when they're leaving, but they're equal coming in.'

With that, a familiar face appeared. 'Conor,' I said, 'say hello to a decent Yorkshireman.' With that, Pádraig Harrington's manager, Adrian Mitchell, extended his hand as if to a long-lost friend.

In the Claremont bar and nightclub, a singer with guitar was beating out the old Cat Stevens number 'Father and Son.' And Kenny's, now with its roofless beer garden at the back, looked very different from how I remembered it.

McGinley's caddie, known as 'Edinburgh Jimmy', was among the patrons. I suggested that with a name like his, he should be across the road in the Aberdeen bar. His reply could not be repeated. Further down the street, I stopped to admire a motorcycle with gleaming chrome. 'It's a Harley Davidson 1600 Softail Custom,' said the proud owner, Gerry O'Connor from Miltown Malbay. Then, looking me up and down, he offered: 'Would you like to come for a spin?' Somewhat taken aback, I gently declined.

Golfing people were everywhere, many of them wearing Lahinch GC apparel. Among them was Raymond Burns, the resident professional at Lisheen Springs GC in Brittas and a former semi-finalist in the South of Ireland. 'I brought my assistant, Conor Coyne from Youghal along, to show him what the Irish Open is all about on a great course,' said the one-time tour player.

'Isn't Harrington phenomenal,' Burns went on. 'He hit a shot today to the second hole which people said was lucky but for me it was just class. From the left-hand rough, he hits it to 15 feet and holes the putt.'

He concluded: 'This place has everything anybody would want. There's even a road beside the 18th hole. Just like St Andrews.' Golfing praise doesn't come any higher.

Among other things, the success of the Irish Open left Lahinch all set for the staging of the elite amateur event, the Palmer Cup, in July 2024. After this, there will be the ultimate team event, the Walker Cup, in 2026. 'We took these on board for prestige reasons, to enhance our international standing,' Slattery explained.

The challenge of staging the Irish Open was to make the event work in a novel, village environment. 'It completely changed the thinking about Lahinch as a truly international venue,' Slattery went on. 'We were blessed in so many ways, including the quality of the winner, Jon Rahm. And it was the first time I could fully appreciate the notion of our course running into the village. All of Lahinch was involved.'

Reflections on what was once called the St Andrews of Ireland would be impossible without remembering its beloved secretary, Brud Slattery, who was 80 when he died in 1997. And here I was, chatting to his son, Pádraig, whose golfing distinctions include winning Brud's prize – a beautiful silver salver – when he was centenary captain of Lahinch in 1992. One could imagine it, in Brud's youth, as a quiet village, a long way removed from the horrors of World War II, devastating mainland Europe, areas of Britain and even the east coast of Ireland.

From a golfing perspective, it was a time of almost total dominance of the South of Ireland Championship by the great John Burke, who was attempting to win the title for a seventh successive time, when he met Brud in the final of 1947. That was when Brud had his greatest competitive triumph, with a 6 and 5 win in the final, after Burke had been stunned by six successive threes, from the eighth to the 13th.

'It was a pleasure to beat him and pay for the party, even though it cost me 14 guineas, which was two weeks' wages at the time,' Brud later recalled.

As it happened, the last of Burke's run of victories had been against a richly promising Dubliner in 1946. On his competitive debut at Lahinch, Joe Carr had a hole-in-one at the famous short sixth, The Dell. By his own admission, however, he was outsmarted by Burke at the third tie-hole of a thrilling final. Against the master of all he surveyed at Lahinch and further afield, we're told that Joe, the younger man by 22 years and with an equally youthful Paddy Skerritt caddying for him, was smashing the ball as far as 30 yards beyond the local hero. Yet a typical piece of Burke roguery brought him victory on the 39th.

The crowd was one of the biggest ever to watch an amateur final in this country and according to Joe, Burke used the spectators to his advantage at the old short third, which has since disappeared in the course reconstruction by Martin Hawtree. 'He hit it towards the back of the green knowing his supporters would stop the ball, which they did,' he recalled. 'And I made the mistake of coming up short in the bunker.'

Meanwhile, Brud was elected to the committee of Lahinch in 1948 and became club secretary in 1954, a position he held until his retirement in 1984. His distinguished service was acknowledged four years later when he was honoured as president of the club before he went on to be captain in 1992, its centenary year.

I first met him more than 50 years ago during trips to Lahinch when covering the South of Ireland for the *Daily Mail*. At that stage, press facilities were Spartan in the extreme, with 'wind-up' telephones and a tiny tent in which it often became necessary to strike matches to have enough light to type and then phone copy late in gathering dusk.

Brud's commitment to promoting Lahinch and the 'South' gave him a great understanding of newspapers, which led to a marked improvement in our lot before his retirement.

As a product of this environment, Pádraig went on to claim the remarkable distinction of becoming captain of Portmarnock in 2005, of Mount Juliet in 2009 and of Lahinch in 2017, all of which could be attributed to an idyllic childhood.

When I talked about the remoteness of his home place, he was happy to acknowledge as much, though not as any sort of a hindrance. 'I remember our phone number was Lahinch 3, which also happened to be the number of the golf club,' he said. 'By that stage, Brud, who was a career schoolteacher, was teaching in Furglan National School outside Ennistymon. Not a million miles away.' He went on:

My first trip to Dublin, when I was about five, was a considerable undertaking. My mother, sister and I were driven by my father to Limerick from where we took the train to Dublin. I remember one of the main reasons for the trip was that my mother wanted to see the film *My Fair Lady* and we stayed in a hotel in Mountjoy Square.

That would have been the early sixties. The film was in the Ambassador Cinema, which was fine. But I also have a distinct recollection of a lengthy wait in the hotel while my mother went shopping. She had a habit of saying 'I'll be back in half an hour', which could mean anything.

I imagine the only reason we had a phone was to do with Brud's position at the golf club. There were three phones in Lahinch, number one was the guard's barracks and number two was Dr Bill O'Brien, the local GP. It was a party line, which meant that it rang once for the guards, twice for the doctor and three times for the club.

Growing up, I remember always being aware that I lived in a village, especially during my early years at Lahinch Primary School. Later, I went to Furglan where Brud could give me a lift every day. We were told that the population of Lahinch was 313. Which meant something of a kerfuffle when somebody died or when a baby was born. The population went up and down accordingly.

But for us, the figure seemed to remain constant. A small village. And most people were connected in some way with the golf club, whether they worked on the course, in the bar or as members.

From his early years, Pádraig was aware of the importance of the golf club as the local industry fuelling Lahinch. Such thinking explained why his father had insisted that the clubhouse bar should be closed every evening between 7.30 and 8.00 p.m., so that local hostelries could get their share of the drinking custom.

Brud became aware of future business possibilities from further afield when the noted American golf scribe Herbert Warren Wind visited in 1967 for articles in the *New Yorker* magazine. Though he visited Lahinch and chatted to Brud on that particular trip, his main focus was on Ballybunion, which received a huge boost from Wind's description of it as the best golf course in the world.

In the process, he had ignited in Brud an awareness of the possibilities associated with American golf tourism. In fact, afterwards, Brud never missed an opportunity to promote Lahinch. As, for instance, with the goats. Since the 1920s, a local named Tommy Walsh had established grazing rights for his goats on the links. So it was that they gained a reputation as wonderfully accurate weather forecasters. If they were seen close to the clubhouse, it was a sign of impending rain, or possibly worse.

Was the notion well-founded? 'Not at all,' replied Pádraig with a laugh. 'In fact, members would shoo them away for defecating on the greens.'

As it happened, they gave Brud a brilliant idea. When the club barometer broke, he took it home to try and repair it. When his efforts failed, he hit on the idea of handwriting a notice which he placed inside the frame: 'See Goats', it proclaimed. Paddy Hillery, later president of Ireland and a long-time member of the club, saw the goats as potentially unique to Lahinch and that they should be promoted. So it was that they were honoured with the club crest, much to the delight of American visitors, who loved the novelty of it. 'I had the idea that the damn goats ran for the shelter of the clubhouse in bad weather,' Brud later explained. 'People's imaginations did the rest. Indeed I came to believe it myself!'

When Pádraig Slattery took up the game during the 1960s, Shell's Wonderful World of Golf had become a highly popular show on television. And the involvement of Sam Snead caused one of the American commentators, Bob Crosby, to coin the phrase 'Big Ball Sam', when Snead would unleash a particularly impressive drive. As youngsters do, Slattery picked it up. So it was while observing adults driving off the first tee, he was likely to greet a particularly good effort with 'Big Ball Sam'.

Ever since, friends and associates at Portmarnock Golf Club, where he is a prominent member, refer to him as Sam Slattery. Many, I'm sure, do so without actually knowing why.

Not even the player himself knows why he plays the game left-handed. 'I remember my first golf club was an old wood that our pro, Bill McCavery, cut the back of. I have no idea why I began playing the game left-handed, other than it may have been influenced by a mirror-image of Brud, going through the regular routine of fiddling with his swing while looking at his reflection in the glass of the club foyer.'

Though it took several years for Herb Wind's writings to have the desired impact on tourism, Brud Slattery's own plans for Lahinch were already taking shape. Noted for a phenomenal ability to remember people's names, he would amaze Americans by greeting them personally on their return to the club. As far back as Pádraig could remember, Lahinch and its promotion were what Brud was about, but he had no interest in going to the US to do so, as Ballybunion did under the stewardship of Sean Walsh.

As part of the club's development, a second course would be crucial. Utterly obsessed with the game, Brud had a significant advantage in bringing on board the Castle Course on the other side of Liscannor Road, given that he owned the land, which he leased to the club.

His anticipation was that by creating greater scope for the championship course, it would become 'an extra lung for the club.' As a facility for youngsters, it would attract more families on holiday to Lahinch.

Nine holes of the Castle development were opened in 1966 to a design by Commander John Harris. But Brud continued to push hard for 18, which were eventually completed in 1975. Meanwhile, green fees began to increase, which was critical towards meeting top-level standards that wouldn't have been attainable through members' subscriptions alone. Indeed, the completion of the Castle course was done at a considerable cost to the Slattery family in that it meant the loss of an estimated ten potential sites for housing developments.

Meanwhile, green-fee revenue grew towards £50,000 a year which, though modest compared to current figures, was significant at the time.

A supreme communicator, Brud would promote stories about Lahinch and its local characters and their interaction with American visitors. Particularly, tales about Mick O'Loughlin, the golfing butcher (Mickey the Meat, pronounced 'mate') from Ennistymon, loomed large. Twice a winner of the South of Ireland in 1937 and 1938, O'Loughlin was clearly a gifted player. Equally important, however, was his friendship with Brud.

Their closeness can be gleaned from Brud's decision to promptly send a messenger for O'Loughlin after two American visitors, proud of their golfing skills, suggested they might have a match with a club pairing. On being informed that the butcher would close his shop for the afternoon to accommodate the golf match, one of the Americans concluded: 'He can't make much money doing that.' To which Slattery famously replied: 'No, but think of all the friends he makes.'

It was a time when Portmarnock always seemed to be rated ahead of the rest, having been the venue for the 1960 Canada Cup. Among the remaining locations, Rosses Point, Lahinch, Ballybunion, Royal Portrush, Royal County Down and Co. Louth at Baltray took pride in hosting the various championships. In a decidedly quaint setup, everyone seemed to know everyone else involved in the game's administration.

The arrival of the Americans had the effect of gradually putting these courses beyond the reach of the average Irish enthusiast, due to the significant increase in the cost of green fees. 'By comparison, I can remember as a student at UCD in the 1970s, I played most of the courses in the Greater Dublin area,' said Slattery. 'If someone wanted to play Lahinch, however, their only chance for a green fee of around £50 would be to do so with a member. And Open weeks, which once attracted significant visitors during the first week in August and the first week in September, became club weeks, for members only.'

Nor were the laws of supply and demand helped by the fact that during this period, Slattery could remember only one new course in the Munster area coming on stream, which was Waterville, developed by John A. Mulcahy and the architect Eddie Hackett.

Meanwhile, a major demographic change was the closing down of the West Clare Railway in February 1961. From 1955, it had been the only diesel-run, narrow-gauge railway in Britain and Ireland. Among other things, this had been the reason the Limerick-based Black Watch Regiment chose Lahinch rather than Doonbeg to build their Co. Clare links in 1882.

Slattery reflected:

> I remember going down on a weekend to Doonbeg at a time when it was rumoured they had discovered oil there. And there was a guy setting up a derrick, an oil rig. In fact, know if it was a half-baked effort but it looked real enough to me. I later learned that the reason the Black Watch didn't go there was because it was too far from the train, maybe four miles from the closest point on the West Clare Railway. Lahinch was far more appealing, for an original 18 on either side of the Liscannor Road.

As a reflection of increasing business, the 1970s saw the introduction of time sheets. The members remained admirably active in the various club competitions, which would have put comparable establishments to shame by their sheer number. All this caused Brud to become increasingly involved in financial matters. At the same time, he was conscious that the club's growing benefactors shouldn't be exploited, notably by clever caddies who would regularly 'arrange' holes-in-one on 'The Dell', which wasn't difficult through the use of fore-caddies.

Aware that each ace was going to bring a handsome tip for the caddie, Brud instructed that their frequency had to stop. So it was that things gradually returned to normal, and there was no doubting American satisfaction with the overall quality of the product. The fact was that they loved its quirky uniqueness. Nothing comparable could be experienced in the US, especially features such as the Klondyke and The Dell.

This posed potential problems when the decision was made to upgrade the links to an acceptable, modern standard, for which it was crucial that the club pick the right architect.

As it happened, Brud had been dead for two years when work began on major course reconstruction to a design by Martin Hawtree. It was difficult to imagine Lahinch without him. He loved the club and had a great affection for those who graced its ancient terrain, whether they happened to be rivals from his competitive days or products of its more recent development as a major tourist amenity. But Pádraig believed his father would have approved of Hawtree's finished product, which went on display in March 2003. Most significantly, the Klondyke and The Dell visibly remained intact. Where club policy was concerned, it was simply unthinkable to change the sixth as their signature hole and Hawtree was clearly sensitive to the original design work by the great Alister MacKenzie.

In the event, the decision makers were confident they had made the correct choice, if only based on the evidence of proposed changes by Peter Thomson, the five-time Open champion, who submitted a redesign. Not only did he want to remove the two controversial holes, but he also planned to effectively level the first hole by removing the elevation to the opening green.

When Nicklaus played Royal County Down in the 2001 Senior British Open, he talked candidly about design problems created by the degree of blindness on the renowned links. He even went so far as to suggest that the threat of litigation would make it impractical to have such a design in regular play nowadays. One could imagine a similar view being taken of Lahinch.

In the event, Hawtree's handiwork met with almost universal approval, including a totally new par-four seventh and a new short eighth, along with changes to 14 of the existing 18 greens.

So it is that the club has progressed comfortably into the 21st century, with a current green-fee income of €3 million per year. But there is no question of complacency in what they accept as a seriously competitive international market. 'There are plans for a new clubhouse costing in the region of €4.5 million,' said Slattery. 'We're also conscious of the need for upgrading the Castle Course. And who knows when we may be hit by the next Coronavirus? The importance of the club to the local community forces you to think progressively.'

JB AND A FEATHERY BUTCHER

Considering his future competitive commitments after capturing a third South of Ireland Championship in 1969, Joe Carr was unusually candid. By that stage, the irrepressible champion had 40 titles to his credit and could feel his appetite for the game beginning to wane. In fact, by 1971, he felt moved to remark: 'I'm in my 50th year and there comes a time when you have to decide that you have had enough. I have lost my enthusiasm for practice. I still go out and hit a few shots in the mornings and will play competitive golf for a while yet, but business has taken over. You know the feeling, having been at the top and then knowing that from there on, you can only go downhill.'

Still, golf remained a hugely important part of his life. And in the company of friends, he would recall some wonderful stories of Lahinch and the South of Ireland – like his particular tale about Mickey the Meat.

'My tale about him concerned a good friend of mine, Joe O'Reilly, who was a Dublin bus conductor and a member of Newlands,' said Carr:

> At the time he came up against O'Loughlin in the South, Joe was a bloody good player, off scratch.
>
> Anyway, when they were playing the old 12th hole, O'Loughlin hooked his tee-shot onto the beach and with the green hidden from view, he walked up to have a look at its location before walking back along the sand to his ball. He then played a wonderful recovery onto the green and holed it for a three.
>
> There was consternation, however, when O'Reilly promptly claimed the hole on the grounds that O'Loughlin had employed an outside agency, by using his own footprints in the sand as a line for his second shot to the green. But O'Loughlin insisted he had done nothing wrong and with the argument raging between them, they were brought in before the championship committee.

These wise men carefully considered the situation. Remember, Mick was a great favourite around Lahinch and the committee wanted to ensure that he wouldn't be the victim of an injustice. And when they gently asked him if he had played over his own footprints when executing his second shot to the 12th, O'Loughlin admitted that he had. In that case, they said, he would have to be disqualified.

Whereupon the outraged butcher retorted: 'Does he [O'Reilly] expect me to stick some seagull feathers up my arse and fly back to my fucking ball?' Needless to remark, after a little further consideration, the committee found in O'Loughlin's favour.

Carr went on:

We had some wonderful fun at Lahinch. I knocked around with my usual pals, Kevin Hogan, John Deegan, Billy McMullan and John Cullen, but as a teetotaller, there were no late nights and no hangovers for me. And I soon realised the tremendous edge this gave me. I could imagine how a fellow must have been feeling on the first tee after a rough night. He certainly wouldn't be as alert as I was and if the weather was rough, he was going to suffer, especially over the finishing holes.

I didn't play Lahinch as often as I did the West or East [each of which he won on 12 occasions]. In fact, my success rate of three wins in the South was quite good for the number of appearances I made there, probably no more than eight in all. I loved the course, with its high dunes and wide-open space, where you could hit the ball almost anywhere.

As for my many friends in Northern Ireland, I can assure them there was nothing political about my decision regarding their championship. In fact, I received a number of death threats for playing Walker Cup golf under the red lion of the R&A. Rather unpleasant terms like 'turncoat rat' were used, but they were wasting their time. I was never politically minded. I'm proud to be

Irish but the notion of being part of a so-called British Isles team was never a problem for me.

Of three South victories in 1948, 1966 and 1969, the most memorable was unquestionably the last, if only for a fascinating exchange which Joe had with his son, Roddy. As it happened, Roddy failed to get through the qualifying stage that year whereas Joe was exempted, by way of acknowledging his status in the game.

So, he decided to ask Roddy to caddie for him instead of his regular caddie, Big Tom. Before teeing off in the final against Noel Fogarty, Joe turned to his son and said: 'I'll show you how to win a championship. I'll illustrate how important it is to win from the front. You don't win from behind. Noel is a good player and only once in a blue moon will you get a good player from behind.'

In the event, Carr's grand plan to win from the front looked rather skewed when he lost the third, fourth and fifth holes to be three down at that stage. 'I remember Roddy looking at me as if I had two fecking heads,' the dad recalled. 'All I could think of saying to him was "Look Roddy, the one thing about this situation is that I can't get them all back to level the match at one hole. Get one and he'll give you one; that's how it's done."'

Such confidence was the product of priceless past experiences in the heat of championship battle. Like the time at Lahinch when, in a match against the brilliant Waterford player, Joe Brown, Carr was one down with one to play. With the wind howling from the right, he proceeded to smash a huge drive down the 18th. Fearing the worst, Brown felt obliged to go for the par-five in two, only to witness the horrific sight of his fairway-wood shot sailing into the army camp on the far side of the Liscannor road, comfortably out of bounds. Predictably, he went on to lose on the 19th.

Going back to 1969, Roddy Carr took up the story:

In a way, JB's greatness was that he didn't think or know what he was doing. Man-to-man combat was entirely instinctive to him, just as it was to Seve Ballesteros, when he was at the peak of his powers.

From my experience as Seve's manager for some years, I could see that he and JB shared the basic match play objective of mentally breaking their opponent. If you analyse this, it's impossible to do while one is concentrating on playing golf. Yet it became possible for them because it was instinctive. They simply stood on the first tee, looked their opponent in the eyes and straightaway thought of ways of seeking out his weakness.

For instance, JB always said to me that matches were won in the first three holes. And he always believed himself to be two up on the first tee. Always. So, by his own reasoning, he was stone-cold dead when he stood three down after five to Noel in the 1969 final. I saw a special significance to that three-hole deficit because it had always been an understanding between JB and his mother that when he was three-up in a match, she would quietly slip out of the gallery to prepare sandwiches for his afternoon match.

Yet, totally unruffled, he turned to me and said, 'If I don't lose another hole I'll win by 2 and 1.' To make a statement like that, in such a matter-of-fact way, staggered me. No need to panic. He wouldn't go chasing his opponent. He'd just hang around and wait his chance.

As it happened, he won the ninth to be two down at the turn. Then he won the 10th. And though he made a half at the 13th, he was clearly disgusted at having three-putted when he could have drawn level. That lone flash of anger carried to the next tee where he snatched the driver out of my hand and smashed two shots to the front edge of the green at the long 14th to square the match with a birdie four.

We were still level going to the short 16th. Now, he had trained me to work to yardages, something he never did himself. He always played totally by instinct. He wanted to hit a raking hook with an eight iron from 178 yards but I insisted there was a one-club wind against him. This is the stuff he had taught me, but he wasn't in the mood to listen.

So he hit this hook which plugged in the face of the bunker. He then lifted a lump out of the face out of the trap with the power of his recovery, and when the ball emerged from the debris, he was about three feet inside Fogarty.

Still, the notion of a grand plan eluded me, and when Noel putted up five feet past, the Angelus bell rang. In the eerie silence after a quiet prayer, JB proceeded to sink a 30-foot raker which slammed against the back of the cup. And, of course, the shock to Fogo's system was such that he proceeded to miss his five-footer. Then, at the next, JB two-putted from off the front of the green for a winning par after Fogo had pitched short. Match over.

Speaking separately about the match after the passage of more than 30 years, father and son had contrasting memories. Roddy talked of the drive back to Dublin and of asking his father: 'How did you know?' The reply came: 'Sure, he left the door open.' The fact that Fogarty had charged his putt on the 16th five feet past the hole seemed to convince Joe that his own effort was holeable, even from 30 feet.

For his part, JB recalled: 'When it was over, I turned and said: "Now Roddy. That's the way not to win a championship."' And at the thought of it, he gave a quiet laugh.

12

A Sporting Life Begins at Joeys

For a teenager interested in Gaelic Games, there could hardly have been a more exciting environment. My secondary-school days at St Joseph's Fairview happened to coincide with a tremendous upsurge in Dublin's footballing fortunes, in the wake of a bitter All-Ireland defeat to Kerry in 1955.

Later on, Joeys celebrated the significant achievement of becoming the first day-school and the first of any establishment in Dublin to capture the Hogan Cup. Sadly for me, that precious breakthrough came in 1959, the year after I had left.

A measure of the remarkable contribution the school made to those heady days for Gaelic football in the capital can be gauged from Dublin's 1958 All-Ireland triumph over Derry. No fewer than ten past pupils were involved in that particular campaign, in which the redoubtable Kevin Heffernan was captain. They included Des Ferguson, Cathal O'Leary, Lar Foley, Mark Wilson, Jock Haughey, Paddy Farnan, Johnny Joyce and Christy 'Buster' Leaney. And as a bonus, the school had contributed Joe Young to Galway's All-Ireland triumph two years previously.

Arguably the greatest player of them all, however, had yet to progress to senior ranks. Des Foley, who was a class behind me, captained Dublin's minors to success in 1958, marking a notable double both for the county and its most productive nursery.

I was to discover St Vincents GAA Club and Clontarf Golf Club as very much a part of North Dublin sport when school days were left behind. In fact, the two clubs combined splendidly about 30 years ago around Clontarf's notoriously tight fairways. That was when a four-member St Vincents team event was won by a quartet comprising Kevin 'Heffo' Heffernan, Des Foley, Tony Flood and George Hurley (Heffernan's nephew) with an outrageous score of 108 points. 'As I remember it, we had 13 birdies and Kevin knocked great fun out of ribbing the also-rans about it afterwards,' recalled Flood.

By that stage, Heffo had already left an indelible mark at Clontarf, where he was honoured with the club presidency. More of that presently.

Back at Joeys, inspiration for the school's glory days in sport could be attributed largely to the arrival as headmaster of Brother Michael Geraghty, a native of Mullingar, in 1956. As it happened, Joeys won the Leinster Colleges senior football title that year, while supplying five players to the Leinster squad which captured the colleges interprovincial title.

Buster Leaney and Noel Fox were subs, but the team included Des Cashel and Lar Foley and a strong, blond 15-year-old corner forward who captured everybody's attention. Des Foley had arrived, and by the following year he had become the rock in a group defeated by Ballyfin in the Leinster final. He was there again in 1958 when Joeys lost in the provincial semi-finals to Franciscan College Gormanston.

Some time before Simon Behan died unexpectedly in January 2009, he had outlined the gradual progress towards the 1959 triumph. The son of a Laois father and a Donegal mother, he would joke that his dad had shown admirable astuteness in deciding to settle in Marino, from where Simon and his five brothers went to Scoil Mhuire and later to Joeys.

'We were very fortunate to be part of all that the school represented,' he said, 'especially the tremendous will to win instilled in us by the teachers.' He was in fifth year, a class behind me in 1958, and could recall the significant physical development in players when reaching 17 and 18 years. And by 1959, their Leaving Cert year, he felt sure that he and his colleagues had come of age in a footballing sense.

Brother Geraghty, who taught me honours maths at Leaving Cert level, doubled up as trainer of the senior team in 1959. His preparation included a trip with Des Foley and Simon in a car provided by Foley's father, Paddy, to watch Gormanston in the semi-finals of the Leinster campaign.

As it happened, Gormanston were crushed by Joeys in the 1959 Leinster decider in Navan. A hardly credible scoreline of 9–9 to 1–7 contained an equally stunning 3–3 from a tightly marked Foley in midfield. Mind you, he had already gained Railway Cup honours with Leinster by that stage.

As Simon Behan recalled: 'No one would dispute that Des was the best player of his age in the country at that time. He was such a figure-head for us that we knew we had to be in with a great chance of going all the way at colleges level.'

In the event, the all-Ireland semi-final victory by 1–7 to 0–7 over St Flannan's Ennis on 22 March in Roscrea unexpectedly proved to be the toughest of the series, against a college noted more for its hurling prowess. Foley contributed three points and Behan got two.

St Nathy's Ballaghadereen, the Hogan Cup winners of 1957, were Joeys' opponents in the final, which was refereed by Mick Higgins of Cavan at Croke Park on Sunday, 19 April 1959. Given the venue, our school had understandably strong support, though one suspects there weren't quite as many as have proudly boasted their presence over pints in pubs on the north side of Dublin in the last 50-odd years.

Predictably, Foley played a captain's role, exerting a huge influence on the Joeys' effort. He covered an enormous amount of ground while moving from defence into attack, especially in heightened tension during the second half. 'Two if not three Nathy's players were jumping with Des for every ball,' said Behan. 'I think they made a mistake by concentrating too much on him.'

One of the beneficiaries in a 3–9 to 2–8 triumph was Behan himself, who scored 2–1. The other leading Joeys scorer was Foley, with 0–5.

More than half a century had passed when Heffo sat with me to recall that historic occasion and he did so largely to honour his great friend, who was only 54 when he died suddenly in February 1995. For those who didn't know him, Foley was a marvellous physical specimen, standing 6ft 2ins, broad-shouldered and with a shock of blond, wavy hair. Heffo recalled:

> I remember the 1959 Hogan Cup final as a classic exhibition of all the qualities that characterised Des as a sportsman. The use of his God-given gifts of size and athleticism; his sportsmanship and the fact that he possessed an extraordinary Rolls Royce engine that enabled him to travel with ease from a defensive role on our goal-line, to create havoc in the opponent's square.
>
> His presence was like a reservoir of confidence to the guys who played with him. And that applied to all stages of his career. My lasting memory of that final is of him, travelling the length of the field, exhorting everyone to effort ... and finally succeeding.'
>
> Des Foley was a huge presence in any company. And when you put these attributes alongside his superb athleticism, his very keen eye and his indomitable will to win, you had a sporting colossus. I was fortunate enough to have had Des as a lifelong friend and I've never stopped missing him.

As might be expected, all of the Joeys players were Dubliners, but interestingly, the Nathy's side was drawn from two counties – eight from Sligo and seven from Mayo.

Simon Behan had already won an All-Ireland minor medal as a sub with Dublin in 1958 and went on to win another when the title was retained in 1959, under the captaincy of Mick Kissane, a classmate of mine. In fact, six players started both the Hogan Cup and Minor All-Ireland finals that year, though Foley was notably absent in September, being three months overage for the minors.

It became a marvellous journey for a closely-knit group of players, who had shared many moments of joy, along with some sadness, in competition through their teenage years. And as a fascinating aside to the All-Ireland Minor final of 1959, the trainer of the defeated Cavan team was none other than Mick Higgins, who had refereed the Hogan Cup final five months previously.

For Heffo, a distinguished sporting career found unique expression on a July Sunday in 1974. It involved his considerable prowess as a golfer along with management skills which were to have an enduring impact on the fortunes of the Dublin football team. And from Clontarf's standpoint, the manner of his triumph in PJ Smyth's Captain's Prize made it one of the most memorable in the club's history.

Typically, Heffo declined to talk about the achievement when I sought to interview him as a fellow club member who also happened to be a golf scribe. So, I turned to the first-hand memories of another member, Cyril Meehan, his successor as President of Clontarf in 2003/04. As Meehan recalled:

> By arrangement, Kevin, another member named Sean Brennan and myself were first off the tee at 6.30 a.m. on Captain's Day in '74. This had to do with the fact that Kevin had a rather special assignment that afternoon. And as things turned out, he played really well.
>
> My recollection is that he birdied the last two holes to finish with 42 Stableford points. Though we didn't dare mention his score to anyone when we finished at around 10.00, my feeling was that Kevin had a great chance of winning.
>
> While I changed and headed home for lunch, Kevin put on his other hat as manager of Dublin and set off for Croke Park and a Leinster semi-final assignment against the favourites, Offaly, who had been All-Ireland champions a few years previously. Dublin, incidentally, had started that particular campaign as no-hopers, but were now about to upset the odds in spectacular fashion. I

> remember Leslie Deegan scoring a crucial goal that day, and he also got the last, winning point.

As it happened, this Dublin performance led to the most improbable outcome of an All-Ireland triumph that year, culminating in victory over Galway in the final.

Meehan dared not consider such thoughts, however, even with Heffo at the helm:

> I remember getting a phone call at home that evening telling me that Kevin had won the Captain's Prize. To be honest, the Dublin win was far more of a surprise. Anyway, a group of us and our wives headed down to the club for the presentation. John Behan and Pauline [Kevin's sister, who was married to Behan] were there, along with Kevin and his wife, Mary, and my wife, Lynn. And we celebrated a truly memorable double at Clontarf and Croke Park.

Heffo was about eight when he and Meehan crossed paths for the first time, and they went on to appear frequently together in St Vincents and Dublin inter-county teams. 'Kevin was a very determined golfer,' said his friend. 'He got down to single figures and competed in the Lord Mayor's Cup. But I suppose that Captain's Prize was his finest golfing achievement.'

Further eyebrows were raised at Clontarf in 2001 when Heffernan, as Club President, took charge of the Best Cup campaign for players of 19 handicap and over. The campaign was characterised by serious attention to detail, along with a demand for 100 per cent commitment from the players. Even with Heffo in charge and Meehan as his right-hand man, however, the team failed to repeat the club's triumphant Best Cup side of 1983, though participants remembered it as a very interesting experience.

Though there were many who would have claimed friendship with Heffernan, he was essentially a very private person. 'When we talked about such matters, he told me he had made only a few friends in his life and that I was one of them,' said Jimmy Gray, a fellow Clontarf member:

> Yet I never really got to know him. I always found him to be a deep fellow who didn't suffer fools gladly.
>
> When I was chairman and he was Dublin manager, all we ever discussed were matters relating to the team. He talked about having three basic requirements of a player: brains, courage and skill, in that order. He never deviated from this, though I'm sure he had to make compromise choices along the way.
>
> Such were Heffo's skills that he could have managed Manchester United, comfortably. The fact that Dublin were relegated in the National League in 1973 indicates the extent to which he transformed the county's fortunes.

Like most youngsters living on the north side of Dublin, I was completely in awe of Heffo as a dual player of rare quality. As I have indicated, however, his own, ultimate advocate of such versatility was Des Foley, whom he described to me as 'a very interesting sportsman; extraordinarily gifted.'

Another player he admired was Paddy Harrington, Pádraig's father. I remember his kind sentiments when I told him in the early summer of 2005 that Paddy was dying. And when Paddy was informed of Heffernan's good wishes, the former Cork half-back said: 'Kevin was a fine sportsman. You know I once marked him in a Railway Cup match when I played full-back for Munster which, of course, wasn't my position. He was quite a handful but I think we both enjoyed the challenge.'

When word filtered through to members of Clontarf around Christmastime in 2012 that Heffo had been removed to the hospice in Raheny, inquiries about him adopted a more anxious edge. 'Any word on Heffo?', or 'What's the latest on Kevin?', his many admirers wondered.

This was a man who had been their long-time golfing colleague, away from his activities in the GAA as a distinguished player and later an iconic manager of the Dubs.

And there were former teammates who, like him, found competitive expression in the Royal and Ancient game when their playing days with Dublin had ended. Men like Norman Allen, who was reduced to tears by the ultimate plight of his friend; Gray, who was County Board chairman during the unforgettable 1970s, brother-in-law, Jimmy O'Neill, and Cyril Meehan, who had shared his passion for our national games.

Heffo's later visits to Clontarf GC were somewhat removed from sporting endeavour. His familiar black Toyota Camry could be seen facing the first tee, usually in the space reserved for the club professional. If the windows were opaque from cigarette smoke, its owner was sitting inside. If they were clear, he was in the clubhouse lounge, probably perusing the *Racing Post* over a cup of tea.

The palpable void he left was to be experienced morning and afternoon at two sporting venues in North Dublin, 50 years ago.

A letter from Augusta National

A rather special letter awaited me when I arrived home in April 2013 from an extended stay in the US, starting with the Masters. It carried the sender's familiar address of 'Augusta, Georgia 30903.'

The brief message from Billy Payne, chairman of Augusta National, read: 'Dear Dermot: We are so glad to hear you are doing well and thank you so much for taking the time to write such kind words about our staff. We will definitely pass them on. Best regards ...'

He was referring to a momentous occasion in my golf-writing career. On getting to the media centre on the eve of the tournament, I was hit by familiar heart symptoms. Among other things, they later caused me to recall words made famous by Richard Boxall, the former European Tour player who moved on to golf commentary with Sky. Reflecting on an unfortunate appearance in the 1991 Open Championship at Royal Birkdale, where he broke his left leg in a freak fall off the ninth-tee, Boxall memorably observed: 'I went out in 34 and back in an ambulance.'

In my case, the ambulance took me from Augusta National's medical facility to the local Georgia Regents University Medical Centre, where

I had two stents inserted. In the process, I was given celebrity status simply by being the hospital's annual Masters heart patient.

After just over two days there, I was discharged at around 5.00 on Friday afternoon. The following morning, I contacted the *Sunday Independent*'s office, where sports editor, John Greene, was horrified by the notion that I wanted to resume my duties. He eventually agreed to take a piece outlining my travails.

That's also when I wrote to Payne, complimenting his establishment on the exemplary reaction of the media-centre staff, who couldn't have been more thoughtful and supportive.

One of them was Mary Sullivan, who has since left their employ. When I reminded her recently that it had been more than 10 years since my experience of April 2013, she sent a typically caring reply. 'You were a sight for sore eyes when we saw you at the PGA party on the Friday night before you returned to the press centre,' she wrote. 'And we were all, yourself included, back at tournament business the following day, settled into our various activities in the press centre. If the front desk had to vote though, the tournament winner came in second to the news of your good health!'

The winner she was referring to was Adam Scott, the first Australian to secure the coveted green jacket. And when I travelled on to Harbour Town to see Graeme McDowell become the first Irish winner of the Heritage Tournament a week later, the Portrush native had a particularly interesting observation about Scott.

'I happened to have been his playing partner at Royal Lytham nine months ago [July 2012],' he said. "As he walked in a shocked daze away from the final green having gifted the Open to Ernie Els [by finishing with four bogeys], I felt moved to say to him: "You're a great champion and your time will come, sooner than you think." The fact that I really meant it made his Masters win so pleasing to me.'

McDowell, who had been tied second behind Scott after 54 holes at Lytham, eventually shared fifth on a quality leaderboard, which meant that his triumph at Harbour Town was no great surprise.

Mind you, completing a double with the 2010 US Open didn't come easily, though Matt Fitzpatrick made it appear so on the magnificent Pete Dye creation in 2023, having triumphed at Brookline the previous June. He did so on the third hole of a sudden-death play-off with Jordan Spieth.

Back in 2013, when languishing on seven-under-par, four strokes off the Harbour Town lead entering the final round, McDowell set himself the seemingly modest winning target of nine under. And with 30 mph winds swirling through the serpentine fairways, it was enough to get him into a playoff in which he beat reigning US Open champion Webb Simpson.

At that stage, his win was only the 15th by an Irishman in official US tournaments spanning 91 years, though additional successes were achieved by Christy O'Connor Jnr (2), Des Smyth (2) and Christy O'Connor Snr (1) at senior level.

A measure of the extent to which Rory McIlroy has transformed our fortunes, however, is that the last 10 years have produced no fewer than 24 Irish victories, with Shane Lowry and Seamus Power joining them. Then there was last year's LPGA triumph by Leona Maguire and at amateur level, Belfast's Matthew McClean had a breakthrough win in the US Mid-Amateur Championship in Chicago last autumn.

With so much money to be had, there is always the danger that a newcomer to the American scene will view events as convenient ATM machines. Smyth's experience at senior level, however, told him a very different truth. 'You get the respect of your peers only if you're a winner,' he said. 'It's the American way of assessing a fellow's mettle. It certainly made a huge difference to how I was perceived.'

Smyth takes the view that Irish aspirants arrive in the US with a considerable advantage:

> Growing up on quality courses gives us a great head start. If you can regularly fire 68 or 69 in tough, Irish conditions, you're not going to be scared on any American golf course.

> Doing it off the blue tees at Portmarnock, Co. Louth or Royal Portrush, gets embedded in your head. Deep down, it gives you the confidence of knowing that if you play your game, the others will find it very hard to beat you. That's what I keep telling young players: play your game and you've no reason to be afraid of anybody on any course.

This is emphasised by the Irish experiences of youngsters from continental Europe, especially Scandinavians, in recent decades. Notable among those who came here to refine their craft was the gifted Finn, Mikko Ilonen, who proceeded to win the West of Ireland at Enniscrone GC in 1999 and then returned as a professional to capture the Irish Open on the parkland of Fota Island in 2014.

Harbour Town marked a notable coast-to-coast achievement by McDowell. In landing the US Open, he conquered Pacific winds at Pebble Beach and then mastered the Atlantic shores of Hilton Head Island on the eastern side of a vast continent.

Meanwhile, you can imagine the extent to which Shane Lowry drew on his amateur experiences when making an American breakthrough in the Bridgestone Invitational at Firestone in August 2015. As a shot-making challenge, there was nothing the renowned Ohio stretch could throw at him that he hadn't experienced on Irish terrain.

And though Lowry doesn't win that often, quality was also a significant element of his Open triumph at Royal Portrush in 2019 – which, as Smyth suggested, was the precious product of an Irish competitive background.

As for McIlroy, ongoing examinations of his repeated failures at Augusta National can diminish the overall quality of US achievements since his breakthrough victory at Quail Hollow in May 2010. That was when he blitzed a quality field with a closing 62 to beat no other than Phil Mickelson by four strokes.

Fourteen months earlier, an opening 64 had pointed McIlroy towards a debut professional success in the 2009 Desert Classic in Dubai. Since then, and up to the middle of June 2024, the Holywood star has amassed a total of 40 career victories, comprising four Major titles, 22 PGA Tour successes, 10 on the DP World Tour, one on the PGA Tour of Australasia and three other global victories. He has had 31 tournament wins on both sides of the Atlantic – which leaves much to be pleased about.

More American mail

Unexpected mail can be a real treat. This was certainly true of a letter to my home address on which the sender was identified as an attorney from West Bloomfield in Michigan, USA. This particular letter from the States concerned a project I had done with Harry Bradshaw 35 years previously.

Dan Bagdade wanted to know if I could help him locate a book of mine, which had been accompanied by audio tapes back in 1988. As it happened, the launch of *The Brad* during Irish Open week at Portmarnock in August of that year had brought back many warm memories.

The gathering included representatives from various strands of Irish golf, and I imagine it was a particular delight for the eponymous hero to have his old pal, Fred Daly, among the guests.

Completed two years before The Brad's death, the project was acknowledged generally as no more than a greatly loved Irish sportsman was due, and owed much to the enthusiastic support of Portmarnock members Peter Webster and the late Paddy Wright, who sponsored it under the Smurfit banner. It comprised two audio tapes and a little book, presented in a specially designed plastic folder.

This had been something that his daughter, Breda, was especially anxious to have done. And I was fortunate enough to be the one to put it together. We decided on the dual production of book and tapes, largely because of Harry's great gift as a storyteller.

So it was that in an effort to create the environment of a fireside chat, three special friends of his – Portmarnock's centenary captain Eddie Butler, Irish amateur international Bryan Malone and businessman Vincent Nolan – were invited to participate in the role of prompters.

Where the tapes were concerned, we had the good fortune of having Niall Tóibín, a great admirer of Harry's, to tie it all together. Working with Harry involved visits to Portmarnock GC and his home in Raheny in North Dublin. It also afforded me the good fortune of receiving a golf lesson from someone regarded to be of genius standard when it came to the putter and the short irons. The advice I especially remember from his extensive instruction was: 'Whatever the club, take her back, low and slow.'

We were fortunate to have Harry Junior, a highly regarded sound recordist in RTE, set up the actual taping process at his dad's home. And I remember we were all a little surprised at how reticent the great storyteller became when confronted by microphones rather than friendly faces around the bar at Portmarnock. Yet he coped admirably, as those who have heard the tapes will testify.

When it was all done, there was the challenge of selling the product. This was a lot more difficult than we had imagined, largely due to the fact that while the little book was exempt from VAT, the same did not apply to the tapes. So, as representatives of Eason made clear to me, it was a complicated creation. In fact, they initially declined to stock it, which was a serious blow.

Then came a breakthrough. Though I had personally approached Gay Byrne, I must acknowledge that the real work was done 'in-house', as it were, by Harry Junior. The upshot was that when I was at home one morning listening to *The Gay Byrne Hour* (which, incidentally, ran for two hours), The Brad's voice suddenly came across the airwaves loud and clear, regaling the nation with some of his wonderful stories.

About 20 minutes later, my home phone rang. It was Easons, wondering how many copies I could get to them, post-haste. Their van called within the hour. We were on our way.

Harry was such a marvellous storyteller that it seemed a pity to have facts interfere with his captivating flow. His great gift of communication, however, created problems for me when information I had established as fact for the book was given decidedly imaginative treatment for the tapes. An example: the 1958 Canada Cup in Mexico City, where he made a remarkable bogey at a par-three on the second day by playing what became acknowledged as the shot of the tournament.

This was a short-iron from a shallow, fast-running stream below the green. One could picture The Brad, surrounded by a rapt audience at Portmarnock, describing how, with water lapping around his ankles, he faced a daunting recovery when, as he claimed, 'this Mexican opened a sluice gate at the top of the hill, and I had to hit the ball before this huge flood came splashing down on me.'

Though it made for a dramatic yarn, the notion of such a happening in the middle of a tournament round seemed decidedly far-fetched. But when I suggested as much to Harry, he was clearly hurt by my scepticism. 'Ask Christy,' he said eventually.

So I talked to his Canada Cup partner, Christy O'Connor Snr, who smiled and replied gently: 'I think Harry's memory is playing tricks on him.' In other chats with O'Connor, it became clear that he had enormous respect for the older man.

As he recalled:

> Myself and The Brad were great pals. They talk about modern players with great short games: I'll tell you Harry used to pitch the ball into the hole three or four times a round. On a regular basis. When I'd tell him he was lucky, he'd go and do it again.
>
> From our four times together in the Canada Cup, Mexico City was obviously a particular thrill. But it was only when we arrived back at Shannon that we realised the impact of our performance in this country. We discovered we had done something very special.

Meanwhile, The Brad bowed to O'Connor's recollection of Mexico City's formidable fifth. As a consequence, the amended version of the story that went on the tapes was:

> In the second round, I hit trouble at the fifth hole, just like at Sandwich in the 1949 British Open. This time it was a par-three of about 215 yards. I played a four-wood and though it wasn't a bad

shot, the ball missed the green by six feet on the left, hit a slope and went down into this water.

After myself and Christy had eyed up the situation, I said, 'Christy, I'm going to play it.' There were trees on the top of the hill between me and the green, but I saw an opening of about four or five feet. As I'm playing it, Christy turns his back and walks away as much as to say, 'The best of luck to you.'

Water splashed everywhere but the ball went through the opening and when I got up there, it was only four feet from the hole. And you know, I was so excited I didn't even try for the putt. It could have cost me anything.

On their arrival into Shannon, O'Connor travelled south to Killarney, where he was employed as professional only until the following April, when he took up an occupation at Royal Dublin. For his part, The Brad travelled on to Dublin Airport where another large crowd was waiting. Amid shouts of 'Good old Harry!', the hero's wife, Elizabeth, claimed she had never been so excited.

In a later e-mail, my American correspondent recalled an Irish pen-pal named James Nolan, to whom he had first written as a teenager. Bagdade eventually got to meet Nolan during the 1972 Open at Muirfield, when he was on honeymoon. 'We continued corresponding until his death about 25 years later,' he told me.

I later sent him *The Brad*, wondering what he'd make of it after all the years that had passed.

13

Tales from the Ryder Cup

My plan for September 2001 was to head to St Louis for the American Express Championship after a holiday in the US with my wife, cruising down the Ohio River. But things turned out quite differently – there would be no trip to Bellerive. Instead, I am now left with vivid recollections of the catastrophic events which caused the tournament's cancellation, and the way Tiger Woods, with all flights cancelled, made the journey from St Louis back to his home in Orlando, Florida, by road.

He later described it as the longest drive of his life, which he embarked on alone. 'Some people might think I'm nuts for driving halfway across the country by myself, but it seemed like the thing to do,' said the world's most valuable sportsman. 'Besides, negotiating 1,000 miles would require concentration, something I welcomed after the events of the day before.'

Woods prepared for the trip by stocking up on protein bars and bottled water. He also relied on music from the car's radio/CD player and on mobile phone calls to friends in his native California. Though he didn't eat dinner, he had four stops for petrol, when he also went to the toilet and, remarkably, was never recognised during the 13-and-a-½-hour trip.

'I learned a long time ago how to limit pit-stops on long trips,' he added. 'The key is not to overload with liquids. I sipped just enough water to keep the protein bars from tearing up my stomach. Averaging 75 mph, I eventually pulled into my driveway at the Isleworth resort at 6.00 a.m. Home never looked so good.'

Ben Crenshaw, the triumphant US Ryder Cup captain at Brookline in 1999, faced similar problems with the same equilibrium. 'I was stranded like everybody else, just me in my car, listening to the radio,' he said. 'Those were some of the happiest and most uplifting moments I've ever spent. The way this country responded was just magnificent.'

Even now, I find the horror of 9 September 2001, or 9/11 as it has come to be known to Americans, difficult to comprehend, possibly because my particular experience of it seemed to border on the bizarre.

On the shimmering, wide waters of the Ohio, the steam-driven paddle wheel of the *Delta Queen* was turning lazily under a burning sun. Tree-lined banks were broken only at lengthy intervals by a riverside town or the sight of barges close by an industrial plant. We were among 170 passengers, cruising the 470 miles from Pittsburgh to Cincinnati in the sort of classic, 19th-century luxury immortalised by Mark Twain. Without phones, newspapers, radio or television, it seemed that nothing could intrude on the idyll. Until Tuesday morning.

The *Delta Queen* had berthed at the town of Marietta, Ohio, when an announcement came at 9.15 a.m. on the boat's public address system. At first, the information was extremely sketchy. Something about New York's World Trade Center being hit by an aeroplane. An unfortunate accident.

It was only while walking through Marietta, in the heart of America's conservative Midwest, that we gained any real sense of the enormity of what had happened. In shops, schools and other workplaces, locals huddled in groups, listening intently as the news unfolded on radio and television. Some people sobbed quietly. The entire town seemed to come to a standstill.

Returning to the boat a few hours later, we noted that a television had been installed on the main deck for the benefit of the passengers.

Mobile phones, which had been inconspicuous since the start of the cruise, were now being used openly. Individuals found a quiet place and wept. In a women's toilet, my wife comforted two passengers who were physically ill because of what they had heard and seen.

Yet, as the only non-Americans in the group, we felt very much at a loss as to how to respond to the devastating developments. What could we say or do by way of comfort? What would happen to the daily entertainment schedule? The following 48 hours provided a fascinating insight into the American psyche.

First, it was decided at the cruise company's headquarters in New Orleans that everything should continue as normal. So it was that once we had all held hands and observed a minute's silence after dinner on the evening of 11 September, the resident band struck up and couples took to the floor and danced.

Initially, the spectacle prompted decidedly uncomfortable feelings. Gradually, however, such reservations were replaced by admiration for the irrepressible optimism that seems to characterise Americans, whatever the circumstances. In the darkest hour these people had ever known collectively, here they were, determined to get on with living, in the frontier spirit that shaped their great nation.

Meanwhile, there was conflicting news from St Louis. Initially, it seemed that the event might go on, but as the full extent of the events unfolded, it became clear that tournament golf would be unthinkable. And what would happen to the Ryder Cup, which was scheduled for The Belfry later in the month?

When the boat eventually berthed in Cincinnati at lunchtime on Thursday, people who view travel as a right rather than a privilege began the great scramble for onward connections. My wife and I stayed until Saturday, when we were fortunate to get a flight back to London.

On 13 September, Jim Autrey, Chief Executive Officer of the PGA of America, issued this statement: 'Like the rest of America, we are deeply mourning the tragic loss of life and the series of events that will change the way we live ... It is our desire for the Ryder Cup Matches to go forward. ...'

On the same day, the Ryder Cup spokesman, Mitchell Platts, issued this statement on behalf of the PGA European Tour: 'We continue to discuss and review the situation regarding the Ryder Cup ... the tragic events of the last 48 hours are without precedent and quite obviously we are currently reviewing all of our plans in the light of the current situation ....'

On Saturday the 15th, Ken Schofield, executive director of the European Tour, eventually arrived back in London after an unfortunate attempt at flying to St Louis for the American Express Championship. He and four European Tour colleagues – Keith Waters, Peter Adams, Gordon Simpson and Ben Watson – had taken off from Heathrow on that fateful Tuesday morning.

They were on a direct flight bound for St Louis, but never arrived. In fact, they never even set foot on American soil. As Schofield recalled:

> The way things panned out, the transatlantic flight was a lot shorter than it should have been, which suggested to us that we weren't anywhere near St Louis. Yet there was no mention of any change in the flight plan.
>
> From my seat next to Keith Waters, I saw through the window that we were landing in someplace strange. Still, there was nothing over the intercom. Not a word. It was only when we had touched down and the plane was taxiing to a halt that we began to suspect something was seriously wrong. That came from overhearing Americans on the plane making mobile phone calls to their home, business, friends or loved ones.

They had landed in the Canadian airport of Moncton, New Brunswick, the next stopping-off point beyond Newfoundland, travelling west. They had been in the air for about five hours which meant it was around midday local time, three hours after the World Trade Center had been hit.

According to the City of Moncton Annual Report 2001, at approximately 11.00 a.m. local time, public emergency vehicles were alerted that due to 'these acts of terrorism upon the United States', and the uncertainty of further attacks, all international flights destined for North America and domestic flights in North American air space were ordered down to the closest airport on their flight paths.

So it was that in the 90 minutes between 11.30 a.m. and 1.00 p.m., 12 planes and more than 2,200 passengers were diverted to the Greater Moncton Airport. The report also informs us that over the next few days, Monctonians and all people of Greater Moncton showed an overwhelmingly warm and caring response to this unprecedented occurrence by opening their hearts and homes to citizens from France, Holland, Germany, the UK and the US, as well as to fellow Canadians, whose flights were ordered down due to what were now confirmed acts of terrorism.

Schofield continued his story:

> Gradually, we began to piece things together. I'll never forget arriving there. We were taken into what could best be described as an aeroplane hangar – pretty basic. There, a Canadian Mountie named Joe Gallagher – for obvious reasons, his name will always stay with me – spoke to us. By this stage, up to 11 or 12 planes were grounded [at Moncton] and we were one of three planeloads of passengers in the hangar at this time.
>
> In addressing us all, Mountie Gallagher spoke of his sadness in attempting to convey some desperate news. He went on to tell us to watch a television set where CNN would inform us in words and pictures, better than he could, what had happened and why we were there. Then the Red Cross arrived on the scene.
>
> Soon we were looking at horrific images on CNN of planes diving into the Twin Towers. Later, when the extent of the devastation had begun to sink in, we were informed that due to the lack of hotel space, we were being assigned accommodation in a certain house which happened to be owned by a local firefighter.

Given the heroism of his counterparts in New York, Schofield and his wife, a qualified nurse, had good reason to respond to an appeal from the efficient Red Cross Response Team. Reportedly, local businesses demonstrated immense generosity in donating food, toys and personal items.

Assuming that the five of them would be split up, Schofield and his colleagues were surprised that they were all housed together under the roof of a normal family home. 'In we trooped in our blazers and European Tour ties,' he recalled. Two of them had to sleep in the same bed and Simpson was assigned a child's bed. But they had no complaints.

In fact, they had begun to feel quite at home when, on rising for breakfast on the Wednesday morning, they looked out of the window to discover that their lodgings were located opposite the corner of streets named Muirfield and Oak Hill.

Telephone communications were difficult for a while, to the extent that there was a virtual blackout for about 24 hours. From a golfing standpoint, Schofield's first concern was to contact his PGA Tour counterpart, Tim Finchem. Discussions with the PGA of America regarding the Ryder Cup would take place a few days later.

'It was probably Wednesday night before we learned that the tournament had been cancelled,' he said. 'In the meantime, we passed the time with a variety of activities, including five-a-side soccer games with other passengers in the car park outside the ice hockey arena. There were Italians and Germans along with us Britons. Looking back on it now, there was a surreal quality to the entire experience.'

When officials were finally in a position to address the mammoth task of getting stranded passengers to their destinations, or back to the airport they had landed at, the quintet from the European Tour travelled by taxi from Moncton to Halifax, Nova Scotia.

They then flew from Halifax to Reykjavik, and from there back to London. 'That was when Jim Awtrey contacted me,' said Schofield.

It happened to be the seventh birthday of Hills's daughter, Fionnuala, and by way of celebration, father and daughter were spending the day at the ski run at Aldershot. 'That was where I received a phone call to the effect that Mr Awtrey needed to talk with Ken and Sandy [Jones, executive director of the British PGA]. A postponement of the Ryder Cup was now very much on the cards,' Hills recalled.

Via a series of transatlantic phone calls, the European Tour were informed by the PGA of America that 'the scope of last Tuesday's tragedy is so overwhelming that it would be impossible for the United States Ryder Cup team and officials to attend the matches this month.' This led to a crisis meeting of the top European Tour officials, which took place at 7.30 on the morning of Sunday the 16th. By 5 o'clock that afternoon, they were ready to announce officially that the Ryder Cup 2001 was being postponed.

Subsequently, there was a proposal that the 34th and 35th Ryder Cup Matches be staged in successive years, 2002 and 2003. On 19 September, the European Ryder Cup Board issued this statement: 'The 34th Ryder Cup matches, which were postponed out of necessity following the enormity of the tragedy in the United States on Tuesday, 11 September, have been rescheduled for The De Vere Hotel, Sutton Coldfield, England from 27 to 29 September 2002 ....'

Arrangements for subsequent matches were also made. 'Consequently,' the statement continued, 'the Ryder Cup Matches will be played at Oakland Hills CC, Bloomfield Hills, Michigan USA in September 2004; at The K Club, Straffan, Ireland in September 2006 and at Valhalla GC, Louisville, Kentucky USA in September 2008.'

On Sunday the 16th, lawyers, insurers and the European Tour themselves began to assess the implications of a postponement. 'There were some very difficult phone calls to be made,' Hills recalled. 'On the Monday morning, I had my first encounter with our loss adjuster. This was Shaun Coyne, who happens to be a very nice chap from Cavan.

'Our first formal meeting with the loss adjusters was on Thursday, 20 September. The insurers behaved impeccably, but it was still 10 months later before the claim was settled for a figure of £17.5 million.'

Fáilte Ireland received compensation of £178,000 as part of the overall package.

As the prospective host for 2005, Dr Michael Smurfit took a positive, pragmatic view of the one-year postponement. 'The reality of the situation was that the organisers had no choice,' he said, reflecting on the phone call he had received from Schofield.

'On balance, I believe the right decision was taken in the circumstances and the important thing was that golf's premier event was still coming to Ireland: it was just going to be one year later than we thought.'

For once, money didn't matter, not even to the British PGA and the PGA European Tour, which had stood to share £10 million from the 2001 staging.

Now, their thoughts were dominated by a profound awareness of America's tragedy and of golfing people everywhere pulling together. Of wanting to do the right thing.

HE'S BLIND BUT HE'S A GOLFER: 9/11'S IMPACT ON ONE MAN

In January 2002, a Scottish 14-handicapper named Ron Conway gained the distinction of out-playing some of the world's top professionals. It involved the simple challenge of hitting the green at a 130-yard par-three in a charity event preceding the Johnnie Walker Classic in Perth, Australia.

But of course, there was a catch. Conway happened to be a three-time winner of the World Blind Championship and his challengers, who included Ernie Els, Sergio Garcia, Nick Faldo, Colin Montgomerie and Lee Westwood, were obliged to wear blindfolds.

In the event, the professionals had the humbling experience of missing the target with a mixture of shanks, pulls, hooks and slices, whereas Conway, who had taken up golf only after being blinded by meningitis, hit it every time, mostly in the middle.

When I related this tale to Paul McCormack, he wasn't at all surprised. 'Professionals like to talk about trusting their swing,' he said. 'But if you're standing over the ball with a blindfold on, all of a sudden the most important sense you have, an asset you take completely for granted, is gone. Trust becomes a far more serious issue when you're blind.'

McCormack knows about these things. As a blind golfer, he outscored fully sighted opponents in September 2019 to win the President's Prize at Portmarnock Links, with the splendid score of 41 points. Playing off 23, he carded six gross pars and a gross birdie on the 10th, for a winning margin of four strokes.

Since then, he has had further successes, most notably in late June 2024, in the British Blind Open at Massereene GC in Antrim. In 36 holes over two days, he carded rounds of 82 and 80 to win it for a third time, adding to his successes in 2016 and 2021. Even more impressive is a reduction in his handicap to 17 since his triumph at Portmarnock Links.

All of which inevitably led to team honours. 'I'm representing North America's Ryder Cup line-up in Austria in a few weeks,' he said. 'It's played every two years and involves the visually impaired against the rest of the world. The match was at Sawgrass two years ago and even at 55, I'm managing to head in the right direction.' In fact, he was back in the States in early July, to compete in the USGA's Adaptive Open for golfers of all disabilities. And as usual, his guide, Luke Waters, travelled with him.

We met at McCormack's home in Sutton in north Dublin, where he lives with his wife, Nicola, and their five children. It was a strange experience for me, in that McCormack looked perfectly normal; there wasn't even the addition of eye shades, let alone a white stick or seeing-eye dog. And he appeared admirably fit for his age.

He went on to explain the three categories of blindness in golf, starting with B1, people without any vision at all. 'B2 is me, pretty badly visually impaired,' he said. 'Those in B3 would have much better vision but are still visually impaired.'

How he lost his sight – most notably his central vision, though some peripheral vision remains – is still a painful issue for him. He declined to describe it in specific detail, other than recounting his role as an inspector with the New York Police Department in the aftermath of 9/11.

McCormack was born in Philadelphia in 1968 to Donegal parents and was a child when the decision was made to return home, where the family settled in Ballybofey. After his Leaving Certificate in 1986, he sought employment here without success. Disappointments included being ineligible for An Garda Síochána, for which he wasn't tall enough at 5ft 7ins.

So he headed for New York where, after working in construction for about four years, he joined the NYPD in 1990. 'It became a very fulfilling career,' he said. 'Having attained the rank of captain, I was promoted to inspector, which meant commanding two precincts.'

He went on:

> It also gave me the opportunity to become involved in golf. The thing about New York's police officers was that we kind of worked the same hours as its Irish bartenders. And the best time to go golfing on the better courses in the Tri-State area is early in the morning.
>
> For a good few years, I was working from nine at night until five or six in the morning. With the bartenders finishing work around that time, we would arrange a few fourballs, three or four times a week. We played top courses like Bethpage Black and it wasn't long before I had a fairly decent game off 15 handicap, even though I never had lessons.

At the time of 9/11, Nicola was a photographer with *Irish Voice* and McCormack was commander of the 41st Precinct, which was immortalised in the Paul Newman movie *Fort Apache*. He explains:

> That was when I became involved in the largest mobilisation in the history of the NYPD. I had 250 to 300 cops working for me, including sergeants and lieutenants and I sent a sergeant and a vanload of cops to assist in getting the crowds out of the buildings.
>
> Everything changed when the towers fell. The most vivid memory I have of 9/11 is of a female officer calling for help over the radio when the first tower collapsed. It was very faint, but as a trained police officer, your ears were tuned into stuff like that. It brings a very sick feeling, especially so when it's a female officer calling for help.

The officer involved happened to be the only female NYPD officer killed in the outrage. She was Moira Smith, a New Yorker whose father was born in Dublin's Coombe Hospital. 'During competitive golf, the ball marker I used was a Moira Smith commemorative coin, with the American flag on one side and Moira's police picture on the other,' said McCormack. 'It means having Moira looking up at me every time I mark my ball.'

Back at 9/11, when it was McCormack's time to head for the disaster area, he had a strange experience. 'I couldn't get my bearings because the towers were no longer there,' he recalled. 'Eventually, I was confronted by a breathtaking mountain of rubble. It took us a while to know what to do. There were no police guidelines for something of this magnitude.'

After four or five days, McCormack and his colleagues had reduced the exclusion zone around the scene of devastation to a large, fenced area of a 10-block radius. 'That became the frozen area around Ground Zero,' he said.

When I returned to the issue of his blindness, he said: 'All these years later, there are a lot of people who are dying right now, people I worked with in the police and fire departments. People are dying of cancer, respiratory diseases. My situation? It is what it is. Fortunately, my condition hasn't worsened in the last few years.'

He began to lose his sight between six months and a year after 9/11. Gradually his central vision deteriorated to the extent that he could no longer see a golf ball. Conscious of slowing down the other players, he decided to quit the game.

Added to that, his work was being affected by his worsening condition and, eventually, he was forced to accept a stark reality. 'If you can't shoot and you can't drive, you can't be a cop,' he accepted bluntly. This meant retiring from the force in 2010 after being 'injured in the line of duty.'

He had settled in retirement in Sutton when he returned to golf. Towards the end of 2015, by which stage he had been away from the game for 13 years, he was coaxed into a charity fourball at Howth GC.

'When I protested that I couldn't see, my playing partners assured me they'd be my eyes,' he said.

> The game worked out fine and at the end, it was suggested I should join Blind Golf in Ireland. I wasn't aware such an organisation existed. Then the following summer, I played in my first event, the US Blind Golf Open at Torres Blancas in Green Valley, Tucson, Arizona. And I won it by four strokes. I had always been competitive, back to playing with the Donegal minors, and this was a wonderful new experience.

He then joined Portmarnock Links where he was warmly welcomed by the members, and acquired the help of Karl Herbert, a teaching professional based in Kinsealy. Still, there was the challenge of putting a ball in play. 'I have guys who act as my guides,' he explained.

> Gerry McCormack and Jim Kavanagh do it regularly and for my biggest successes, my guide was Luke Waters. He lines you up for each shot: we're not allowed to use binoculars or any such visual aid in blind golf. And depending on the speed of a putt, he might tell you that you have to hit a 30-footer say 18 feet, and with a four-foot break from the left.
>
> I don't want to know anything about bunkers, water or out of bounds. I just want to be pointed down the middle of the fairway, which can be tricky enough on the dog legs at the Links.

His birdie came on the treacherously shallow 10th green of the Links, which he managed to hold shot for the first time. And in a splendid finish, he had gross pars at the difficult 16th and 17th before completing the round with a creditable bogey on the last.

When not involved with helping youngsters at Beann Eadair GFC, McCormack and his wife have a 9/11 exhibition that they have brought all over Ireland and the US, as a tribute to the victims and their families. The display includes Moira Smith's NYPD hat and her radio.

All this has become part of a remarkable journey by a player who is relishing the caring side of a notoriously demanding game.

The Brad

Harry Bradshaw was not considered by the British PGA for the matches at Ganton in 1949, despite having forced a play-off with Bobby Locke for the Open Championship at Royal St George's in September of that year. Nor was he a candidate for the team that travelled to Pinehurst in November 1951.

The magazine *Irish Golf* reported in August 1949:

> The [British] PGA have laid down clearly that they consider professionals from the 26 counties as being overseas members of their Association. It is as overseas players that they take part in the Open itself, and in such tournaments as the *Daily Mail*, they had to qualify in the section allocated to overseas players.
>
> We have no wish ever to introduce politics into golf but the time does seem rife when the whole matter of the Ryder Cup was clarified. The Royal and Ancient have ruled that 'Éireanns' as they are termed in England, are eligible for the Walker Cup team.

The magazine's view became all the more reasonable considering that Bradshaw was deemed eligible to travel to South Africa in the winter of 1950–51 as a member of a four-man British PGA line-up invited by that country's PGA. Perhaps this could be explained by the unavailability of Dai Rees and Charlie Ward for the trip. Either way, The Brad completed a quartet which also included Daly, Ken Bousfield and John Panton.

'During four months in South Africa, Fred and me were never beaten as a partnership, and that included some money matches,' recalled The Brad when I was writing his biography in 1988, two years before he died.

By the time officials sat down to pick the 1953 Ryder Cup line-up, however, there had been a change of heart. So it was that the side that had done battle with the US at Wentworth on 2 and 3 October of that year became the first British and Irish Ryder Cup team.

It remains curious that the team was titled 'Great Britain', even when Christy O'Connor Snr became a leading member in 1955. It was only in 1973 at Muirfield that it was renamed 'Great Britain and Ireland.' Ironically, that happened to be the last of ten successive appearances by O'Connor.

Peter Alliss and O'Connor came together for the first time as Ryder Cup foursomes partners for the 1959 matches against Eldorado, and last played together at Royal Birkdale in 1969 when they halved a foursomes match with Billy Casper and Frank Beard. As a verdict on their time together, Alliss famously remarked: 'The day I discovered Christy O'Connor as a partner was one of the happiest of my golfing life.'

EUROPE CHANGES THE RYDER CUP ODDS

Though American players could be somewhat indifferent to Ryder Cup honours because of the one-sided nature of the matches, the event always held enormous appeal to their British and Irish counterparts. And their European peers became similarly excited, especially after a marvellous victory at The Belfry in 1985. Claiming a place in the Ryder Cup had become something really special.

Against this background, Eamonn Darcy struggled tenaciously for automatic selection in 1987, when the trophy was going to be defended at Muirfield Village. By winning a rain-restricted Belgian Open at Royal Waterloo, he moved into ninth position in the qualifying table, where he clung on for the following nine weeks.

'The big pay-off,' reflected Darcy, 'is that I can now look back on it as unquestionably the highlight of my professional career.' The adventure culminated in a typically generous Jack Nicklaus, as the defeated US captain, being moved to talk of 'a great effort by a man who had not won a Ryder Cup point in nine previous matches.' And by way of emphasis, the defeated Bear suggested that 'the putt he holed on the 18th will probably become the most important he will ever hole in his career.'

This, my first Ryder Cup, was staged on what was affectionately known as the 'Course that Jack Built'. And Nicklaus was right about Darcy: for the remainder of his European Tour career, the Delgany man didn't hole a putt to compare with the one that made such a vital contribution to Europe's first triumph on American soil. It surpassed even a glorious Dunhill Cup triumph at St Andrews a year later, when he captained the Irish trio. 'That Ryder Cup stands apart, because of what it meant to European golf,' he explained.

This success also completed a fascinating historical link for the Irish player, dating back to 1953. Darcy was only a one-year-old baby when The Brad was guest of honour at a special function in the Horse and Hound Hotel in Delgany. Now, he stood alongside his celebrated predecessor as a Ryder Cup hero.

Muirfield Village was also where Seve Ballesteros, on hearing that his prospective partner, José María Olazábal, wanted to stand down because of poor form in practice, had assured skipper Tony Jacklin: 'Don't worry. I play good enough for both of us.' And it was the memorable occasion when Sam Torrance announced his engagement to actress Suzanne Danielle while crossing the Atlantic on Concorde. Consequently, on arrival in the US, in announcing his pairings for the opening foursomes on Friday morning, Jacklin said to the Scot: 'Sam, I'm resting you; you're playing.'

While predicting heart-stopping Stimpmeter speeds of up to 13 for the Muirfield Village greens, Nicklaus insisted: 'I have deliberately removed myself from anything to do with the preparation of the course. Our greens are essentially flat and the idea of making them firm and fast is to place a premium on approach shots.'

He then added the telling comment: 'This is the way you separate good players from journeymen, and I believe Muirfield Village is essentially a second-shot course.'

As the week progressed, it became clear that Darcy didn't figure in skipper Tony Jacklin's plans for the early foursomes and fourball matches. Yet the player insisted: 'It is important for me to think of myself simply as a member of the European team; I cannot afford to indulge in personal feelings.'

Meanwhile, with Ballesteros revelling in his regal status in European golf, Jacklin applauded him: 'Seve's contribution has been incalculable. He is simply a wonderful, wonderful player.' Even Nicklaus was moved to comment: 'I don't have a Seve on my team at the present time. I think that he and Greg Norman are head and shoulders over the rest of the world right now.'

Facing a five-point deficit on the final day's singles, Nicklaus took the remarkable decision to leave perceived big guns such as Larry Nelson, Curtis Strange, Lanny Wadkins and Hal Sutton at the bottom of the order. Ironically, that's where the American collapse occurred, with Europe claiming three out of five points, including a precious win by Darcy at number eight in the order.

He faced Ben Crenshaw, the 1984 Masters champion who was so disgusted at three-putting the sixth green, that in an extraordinary act of self-destruction, he smashed the errant club into the ground while walking to the seventh tee. It is now part of Ryder Cup lore how, in the process, the world's finest putter broke the shaft of his beloved 'Little Ben' and was forced to putt with a one-iron, or the leading edge of a sand wedge, for the remainder of the match.

When I reminded him of it during a chat at Oakland Hills in 2004, Crenshaw broke into a warm smile:

> Oh Gosh! Muirfield Village ... Eamonn and I have had so many chuckles over that match. It was one of the most remarkable things that's ever happened to me in golf. Though I had hit my approach shot very wide of the target, I was still angry not to get down in two.
>
> As I walked off the green I just ... you know there were times when I hit my implements much harder, but on this occasion it just happened to snap.

Which, of course, didn't delight his captain. Crenshaw continued to chuckle:

> I'll never forget it. A couple of holes later (with Darcy 2 up), we went to a par-three, and I walked up the steps to the tee, only to be confronted by Jack, who enquired 'How is it going?' And I said quietly, almost under my breath, 'Not so good.'
>
> 'What do you mean?' said Jack. And I somehow managed to tell him, 'I broke my putter back there on ...'
>
> Before I could finish the sentence, Jack said 'You did what?'
>
> 'I broke my putter, back on number six.'
>
> 'Well the way things are going for us,' he said, 'I might be tempted to break a few clubs myself.'

Crenshaw continued:

> Eamonn played so well that day. And he killed me off at the end by making a beautiful birdie at 17. Then he got what he needed on 18, getting up and down from a greenside bunker for a winning par after I had driven into water.

I suggested that he scored a very good bogey on the last. 'I did,' he replied. 'It was all I could do. Eamonn deserved it. He made a beautiful putt coming down the hill. But I'll always remember that match for the way the Europeans, Ian Woosnam, Sandy Lyle, all of them, handled the course so beautifully. They played as if they'd known it all their lives.'

For Darcy, its significance found expression in his feelings on the 18th tee. Looking at Crenshaw he had thought: 'Your Masters and all your other titles are no good to you now. Your insides are churning just like mine. It's man to man and I'm going to win.'

Darcy seemed to take an age over his five-and-a-half footer, downhill and breaking left to right. Having finally decided that it would break from the left lip, he stood over it and hit the putt almost straight away.

Twenty thousand star-spangled banners had been handed to American supporters coming through the gates that morning. Not one was visible as Darcy's putt ran perfectly into the middle of the 18th cup.

'When old Darce sank that putt ... well, what can you say?' was all Jacklin could muster before being overcome by emotion. And after the winning point had been secured by Ballesteros – who else! – the skipper added: 'This is a dream come true for us – a victory that could change the entire course of world golf.'

Darcy had never been happier. 'I was nervous playing the bunker shot at 18, but my hands were rock steady,' he said. 'I kept telling myself I could get the ball close to the pin. Mind you, that was the toughest putt I've ever faced.' It was some time before he revealed what was really racing through his mind as he stood over that fateful putt. 'Don't fucking miss,' he had thought. And he didn't.

A year later, as a postscript to Darcy's achievement, a venerable fellow county man visited Muirfield Village, which is located in Dublin, Ohio, as the envoy of the Lord Mayor of Dublin, Ireland. Remarkably, it was the first time that Harry Bradshaw had met Jack Nicklaus. As The Brad recalled:

> I met him on the steps of the clubhouse and told him, 'I never shook your hand before.' And Nicklaus looked at me and replied, 'Surely not, Harry,' and I said, 'Yes, it's true.'
>
> When I said I wanted to see where Eamonn Darcy had holed that famous putt, two committee men brought me to the 18th. This putt he holed was some putt. Television didn't give you a true picture of the slope. The green was so fast that had he missed that putt, he'd went [sic] eight or nine feet past. But he didn't. It must have been the best putt of his lifetime.

At the annual dance of the Delgany Artisans' Golfing Society in 1953, The Brad was congratulated by the Society's secretary, Charles Byrne, on his victories in the Ryder Cup matches and the Dunlop Masters that year. Replying to the toast, he said: 'I look forward to the time when some other Delgany golfer will bring much greater honours to this area than I ever could.'

Listed among the organising committee for the memorable function was the name C. Darcy. Thirty-four years later, on 31 October 1987, Christy Darcy's son, Eamonn, was honoured with life membership by Delgany GC for the distinction he had brought to his former club and his country at Muirfield Village the previous month.

Harry, too, was honoured with life membership at the same function, in recognition of his past achievements. Delgany is that sort of place.

Jacklin's reaction was to set his sights on a third successive European triumph at The Belfry in 1989. And in the wake of the actual matches, when a tie meant that the trophy was retained, the European skipper was particularly pleased that a much-publicised rift with Christy O'Connor Jnr, going back to 1985, had been healed.

He also took obvious pleasure in his memorable singles victory over Fred Couples. 'I know that many Irish people, especially Christy, were hurt and angry by the fact that I left him out of the 1985 team,' said Jacklin. 'But I remain convinced that I did the right thing at the time, just as I believed that he was the correct choice this time around.'

He went on: 'When I considered players for the Ryder Cup team, I wasn't concerned with nationalities. Professional golfers are essentially the same the world over and the unifying factor which I attempted to instil into my teams was simply an overriding desire to beat the Americans.' He went on: 'I am absolutely delighted for Christy's sake that he played so well.'

Another win on US soil

On the forbidding walk towards the 18th tee at Oak Hill, Philip Walton was pondering a missed four-footer that had caused the torment he was now facing. That's when teammate Sam Torrance administered what Walton recalls as 'the hardest smack on the arse I've ever had.'

As we have seen, Irish players have made memorable contributions to climactic moments of Ryder Cup encounters. Walton, however, was the first to deliver the winning point, which Graeme McDowell emulated in 2010.

Memories remain vivid of 24 September 1995 in upstate New York, where the sylvan setting on a crisp, overcast day could have been borrowed from autumn at Wentworth. Walton remembers being introduced on the first tee to the great Byron Nelson, 50 years after his astonishing 11 wins in a row on the PGA Tour in 1945.

Regarding the match itself, Walton said, 'I knew Bernard Gallacher was under serious pressure having been twice a losing European captain.' As Gallacher's wife, Lesley, admitted afterwards: 'It had been a tough few years and I prepared myself for failure so that I could cope if it happened again.' She added: 'Now we can get on with the rest of our lives with a certain contentment.'

Succumbing to an old weakness by pulling a straight putt on the 17th left of the target, Walton soon realised the worst. Word came back that Nick Faldo had triumphed on the last hole, having been one down with three to play against Curtis Strange. 'Oh Jaysus,' Walton thought. 'I can't believe this. Everything is down to me.'

On that fateful finishing hole, his opponent, Jay Haas, pulled his drive behind a tree and Walton pushed his own drive into semi-rough. Facing a shot of 195 yards to an elevated target, the Dubliner's five-wood came up short, into the grassy bank fronting the green. With the American making a complete mess of the hole, a sand wedge pitch and an approach putt dead were enough to seal victory.

'By that stage, I had already played my most important shot of the match,' said Walton in hindsight. 'It was a six-iron to the short 15th [184 yards] where I was the only one who attempted to take on a nasty pin, back left.'

Bravery and skill were rewarded when the ball finished about five feet right of the hole. When the putt went down for a stunning birdie, he was dormie three and guaranteed a halved match. Which, as he later discovered, still wouldn't have been enough.

Walton was only two feet from the pin in three on the par-four 16th, when an overzealous bunker recovery from Haas clattered against the flag and dropped into the hole for a most improbable birdie. Then came Walton's error to lose the 17th.

The Americans held a commanding 9–7 lead when the singles pairings were announced on the Saturday evening. Walton saw himself facing the experienced Haas at number 11 in the order, while the key pairing appeared to be Faldo's meeting at number eight with Strange, his conqueror in a play-off for the 1988 US Open.

This confrontation was memorably described by commentator Johnny Miller as 'watching two glaciers at work.' It seemed strangely low in the order for competitors of such quality, but Gallacher claimed afterwards: 'I saw the players from three to eight [Mark James, Ian Woosnam, Costantino Rocca, David Gilford, Colin Montgomerie and Faldo] as the main part of the team. I had every confidence it wouldn't get down to Philip – and I was nearly right.'

For his part, Walton liked the singles draw, so much so that he walked over to a blackboard in the team room on Saturday and wrote: 'We will win.'

And they did, by the narrowest of margins. The joy of the occasion, from my perspective, was being able to mix afterwards with the players in wonderful exchanges on and around the 18th green. Seve Ballesteros was in tears as he said to me: 'You must be very proud of Philip. The whole of Ireland must be proud of Philip.'

For his part, the Malahide man appeared stunned, shaking his head as if by doing this, enlightenment would come. 'Strange memories, like looking at the empty stands behind the 18th, where the American fans had been,' he mused.

Per-Ulrik Johansson, who had relinquished an early lead to lose on the 17th to Phil Mickelson in the anchor position, joined in the revelry. Moments earlier, his caddie, Tim King, had talked about 'the image that will stay with me for the rest of my life.'

He explained: 'It was Per-Ulrik's reaction when word got back to us on the 17th that Philip had won the Ryder Cup. I never saw that look before on anybody's face. It was like every possible emotion rolled into one.'

Though Walton can now reflect happily on his most memorable golfing day in the sun, it wasn't always that way. 'For years afterwards, I was scared of being reminded of what might have happened,' he confessed. 'Any time it came into my mind, I got this shiver down my spine, imagining myself having a seven instead of a five at the last hole.'

Carried shoulder-high by Ballesteros and Rocca, he waved the famous trophy aloft after emerging from Concorde at Dublin Airport en route to the Smurfit European Open the following day. Being ushered into the North Terminal, which was used at the time mainly for pilgrimages to Lourdes, appealed to local wits.

Hadn't Walton applied the finishing touch to something akin to a golfing miracle?

Belfry 2002 and Remembering the Peacock's Ruffled Feathers

In December 2002, at a sports function in the Burlington Hotel in Dublin, a legendary figure of American golf turned to a player much wealthier than himself, though almost half his age. There wasn't the slightest hint of bitterness in the soft, southern drawl of Doug Sanders as he said with a warm smile to Paul McGinley: 'I've been famous all my life for missing a putt; you're going to be famous for holing one.'

When the 69-year-old met Ireland's latest Ryder Cup hero, whose singles half with Jim Furyk ensured a European victory, it was almost inevitable that a gaping wound would be probed once more. Nothing in sport is more painful than failure at the last gasp, yet Sanders stubbornly refused to be crushed by his pain. Nor did he think of inventing a noise from the gallery or the click of a camera as an excuse for missing a three-foot putt, which would have given him the 1970 Open Championship at St Andrews.

Instead, he bared his soul to the world and let us all make of it what we would. 'I made a mistake by not letting Trevino [Lee Trevino, his playing partner] putt first,' he admitted. 'I made the mistake of thinking which section of the crowd I was going to bow to. It was all my fault. There was only one person to blame – Doug Sanders.'

McGinley saw the video of the incident when it was rerun for the umpteenth time by the Golf Channel in the US. He observed how, after bending down to pick up an imagined speck on the line of the putt, Sanders made the fatal error of failing to mark the ball so that he could step away from it and compose himself.

The Dubliner then noted how, in his anxiety to finish, the so-called Peacock of the Fairways opened the blade disastrously to send the left-to-right breaking three-footer slipping past the right lip, just like Rory McIlroy did to lose the 2024 US Open. And the eerie silence was broken by the immortal words of the commentator, Henry Longhurst, as he said: 'Oh dear! There but for the grace of God ...'

Such images provided a stark contrast to the glory of The Belfry in late September 2002. McGinley's challenge in attempting to achieve a trophy-winning half also involved a left-to-right breaking putt on the final green, though his effort was from the considerably longer distance of nine feet. And rather than strictly personal gain, he was carrying the hopes of an entire Continent.

Yet the player later argued that his most valuable contribution that weekend was not made on Sunday afternoon, but 24 hours previously. The scene was the final fourball in which he and Darren Clarke were one down to Scott Hoch and Furyk playing the 18th. From the four drives, McGinley was the longest and should have been last to hit, whereas Clarke, in a bunker, should have been first.

But Bernhard Langer saw things differently. He urged European skipper Sam Torrance to instruct McGinley to hit first, to pressurise the Americans. The Scot agreed and an exemplary four iron of 211 yards from the Dubliner achieved the objective. The hole was won for a halved match, leaving the teams dead level going into Sunday's singles. McGinley explained:

> Though you will often see players hit fairway shots out of turn in amateur fourballs, it very rarely happens in the Ryder Cup. On the

> green, yes. But not from the fairway. That four-iron shot was huge, probably bigger than Sunday's putt. And Langer read the situation perfectly. That's one of the things which convinced me he would be an outstanding captain at Oakland Hills.
>
> Nowadays, it is vital that a captain treats the 12 players differently rather than all the same. Standing at the head of a room with a 'Now listen here lads ...' kind of speech, won't work. They're all at the peak of their profession with big egos that require being treated in different ways. Managers must be part-psychologists. There is no longer any room for dictators.

Recalling how his one-time captain, Ben Hogan, had made it clear to each individual player that he didn't want to be associated with failure, Sanders described:

> Standing there, tapping the ash off a cigarette and with those cold, grey eyes boring into me, he said: 'Doug, you will win today, won't you?' I took it as an order. There wasn't a mention of country allegiance: I was playing for Hogan.

As the witching-hour slipped past at that Dublin function, Sanders once more pondered the miss that cost him a fortune. 'I was ready, but I missed it,' he said. For McGinley, however, the chance of a lifetime didn't slip away. Under the most extreme pressure a professional golfer could face, he found a way of getting the job done.

Sanders was honest enough to admit that he hadn't watched that particular Ryder Cup. 'I can't watch those things anymore,' he said. And who could blame him.

THE K CLUB, 2006

A child's red jacket and a saturated baseball cap lay in the mud behind the 18th green. Broken umbrellas, plastic bags and empty beer bottles littered the once lush grass that thousands of feet and several inches of rain had turned into a quagmire. A security guard humorously compared the clinging mud to the World War II battle scene at Arnhem.

It was around 6.00 on the evening of Sunday, 24 September and this was where, a short time earlier, the triumphant Europeans had celebrated with an orgy of splashed champagne, to the unfettered delight of ecstatic home supporters. Now, there was an eerie emptiness about the place. The Ryder Cup was over for another two years.

Surveying the scene, it wasn't difficult to understand the grim assessment of the joint owner, Dr Michael Smurfit, who estimated that it could be 24 months before the course had fully recovered.

Though Wentworth's course superintendent Chris Kennedy was there along with his Celtic Manor counterpart, Jim MacKenzie, they settled for the role of observers. As it was, resident course superintendent Gerry Byrne had a staff of 83 to handle the huge demands imposed by a rain-soaked weekend. 'There was no shortage of willing hands,' he said. 'Starting about 18 months ago, about 200 volunteers applied by e-mail and we narrowed them down to 40 in March 2006, by lottery.'

They included greens superintendents such as Joe Bedford (Hollystown), Dermot Saunders (Luttrellstown Castle), Gerry Collins (Charlesland) and John and Brendan Harmon from Elm Park, along with volunteers from Iceland, Sweden, Portugal, Germany, Holland, Britain and the US.

The Byrne family were also there in strength, including Gerry's uncle John, formerly of Killiney GC, and his brothers Frank and Declan. All arrived on the Saturday prior to the Ryder Cup and stayed to the end. 'I had always planned for a wet week – and, unfortunately, I was right,' said Gerry Byrne.

Though there had been the usual sprinkling of predictable Irish begrudgery in the build-up to the event, ordinary golf fans were now happily celebrating a great sporting occasion that had done the country proud. In the absence of the Olympic Games or a soccer World Cup, they knew this was as good as it got, in terms of playing host to a major sporting event.

While European skipper Ian Woosnam celebrated perhaps excessively in the full-blooded manner we had come to expect of him, Tom Lehman, the American captain, remained admirably dignified in defeat. It would be some time before he publicly admitted what everybody already knew: that he and American colleagues had broken every rule of etiquette by invading the 17th green at Brookline in 1999, with play still in progress.

When I wrote the book *Ryder Cup 2006* in anticipation of The K Club staging, I thought it might be appropriate to give Lehman an advance copy in his capacity as the US skipper. I did this on a trip to Hawaii in January 2006. His wife, Melissa, happened to get her hands on it and proceeded to lacerate me for what she claimed was a perpetuation of the lie about the 17th green.

The truth is that in anticipation of such flak, I did my homework months in advance of committing words to paper. The late Renton Laidlaw, a long-time colleague in the Association of Golf Writers, responded to my request by setting up a private viewing of the 1999 Ryder Cup climax with European Tour Productions in one of their vans.

The evidence was there for all to see and, eventually, Lehman recognised this truth, but not before his wife wrongly attacked me in Hawaii.

At The K Club, the American skipper was admirably candid about the match itself, when asked to explain the beating administered by Europe over the weekend. 'I guess the European team made more putts,' he said. Phil Mickelson reached the same conclusion, remarking: 'We would have putts from closer range and would miss after they [Europe] had already made theirs. It seemed to happen a lot. It came down to the greens.'

Those comments, though expressed honestly at the time, reminded me of how Nicklaus had famously claimed: 'I never missed a putt before I hit it.' It's not unlikely that many American putts were missed before contact was made with the ball, during three days of being subjected to relentless pressure.

Eddie Jordan, former owner of the Jordan Formula One team, was among the leading Irish sports people seriously impressed with the entire enterprise. If he had one criticism, it was that Woosnam, Clarke et al might have learned from Michael Schumacher how to spray champagne 'more elegantly.' Indeed.

Then, Jordan, who had hosted Tiger Woods at his Wentworth home during the HSBC World Matchplay the week before, said:

> Great credit is due to the government for their investment and belief in the project, and to Michael Smurfit for giving us such a great venue. You cannot come to Ireland and expect seven days of sunshine. But the welcome was stunning. We were in Dublin on the Saturday night of Ryder Cup weekend and the place was wild. By comparison, Valderrama in 1997 was decidedly muted.
>
> When we think of major sporting events here, they can't get any better than this. There has been talk of staging a Grand Prix, but with the current safety requirements for cars doing over 200 mph, you would need about €150 million, for starters. And how would you get your money back? You could only do that by erecting permanent grandstands. Either way, I wouldn't advise it.

He concluded: 'I've seen some big shows, but this one matched the best of them.'

Gleneagles, where they hung a great player out to dry

The compelling drama unfolding at the top table of the media centre at Gleneagles on 28 September 2014, evoked the chilling words of Shakespeare's Richard III: 'Why, I can smile and murder while I smile ...' Rarely could a public execution have been carried out with such decorum.

Phil Mickelson was very wrong to slay his captain the way he did. Yet Tom Watson's reaction suggested he had been half-expecting the onslaught.

This lends credence to reports of a blazing row in the American team room the previous night, provoked by Mickelson over Watson's absence from Saturday's US pairings, morning and afternoon, and to the fact that it culminated in Watson angrily departing the scene.

The contrast to the bonhomie emanating from Paul McGinley's European camp could hardly have been more stark. Only two weeks previously, I had quoted Tony Jacklin referring to problems encountered by the 2012 US captain, Davis Love, in coping with the egos of millionaire megastars in the 2012 matches at Medinah.

From an American standpoint, there was no obvious solution to these challenges, but I suggested it would help if the team leader were given a proper job description – like, for instance, team manager.

The notion of captain in its normally accepted sporting sense is undeniably outdated where the Ryder Cup is concerned, as made abundantly clear by the sort of preparation and attention to detail outlined by Europe's leader, McGinley, at Gleneagles.

In their surprise appointment of Watson, the PGA of America believed that the power of his personality and status as an eight-time Major champion, four of which were Open titles in Scotland, would tilt the balance in a tight match. Did US officials take even a quick glance through the recent history of the Ryder Cup?

Had they done so, they would have gained some quite illuminating insight from the 1987 staging at Muirfield Village. That was where Jack Nicklaus, as US skipper and designer of the venue, spoke of how firm and fast greens, on what was essentially a second-shot golf course, were the way to 'separate good players from journeymen.' Then, regarding the strategy of his pairings, he added on the eve of battle: 'In terms of tournament performances, I could probably throw the 12 names of the US team into the air and pick them as they fall.'

By the end of the following day, the Bear had been confronted by a 6–2 deficit, including the first American whitewash in four balls. And a further 24 hours on, with Seve Ballesteros and José María Olazábal relishing every moment, his charges faced an unassailable deficit of 5½ to 10½ en route to their first US Ryder Cup defeat on home soil. All under the guidance of the greatest player and strategist in the history of the game.

Clearly, the Nicklaus charisma didn't tilt the balance on that occasion, no more than Watson's reputation did for the American cause at Gleneagles, ironically on another Nicklaus creation. And how could we have reasonably expected anything different?

I found it amazing that the PGA of America appeared to give so little thought to the impact of their captain in the team room, considering the amount of money they seemed prepared to spend elsewhere on the process. For instance, in 2006, they financed a surprise two-day visit to the K Club for Tom Lehman and his players a month before the event.

Did Lehman learn anything new from the exercise? 'Sure, I learned some stuff,' he replied guardedly. 'It was very helpful; time very well spent. It was a home run.' I speculated that the trip had cost the PGA around $300,000, but one of their officials later informed me that I had been guilty of a serious underestimate.

With the notable exception of their 2021 captain, Steve Stricker, the PGA of America traditionally insist that their Ryder Cup captain must be a Major winner. On this basis, McGinley wouldn't have qualified. Nor would Bernard Gallacher, Colin Montgomerie, Sam Torrance or Luke Donald, who have also been successful European skippers in recent years. They appear to award the distinction as something of a valedictory gesture, rather than to honour a candidate's leadership qualities.

This means that the Mickelsons of this world have no problem in voicing their disapproval – something I couldn't have imagined happening to a hard-nosed pro like Dave Stockton proved to be at Kiawah Island in 1991.

14

Seeking to Whitewash Sportswashing

Earnest journalists strove to hide their personal views as golfing millionaires were paraded before them in London. It was June 2022 and the idea was that the press could enlighten their audience as to why mountains of cash were being accepted in the name of the embryonic LIV Golf.

All this brought to mind an incident from a *News of the World* staff party some years ago that highlighted the vulnerability of the simple hack. On becoming quite drunk during the evening, nothing could stop a showbiz reporter from confronting the company's chairman, Sir William Carr.

We're told that the addled writer grabbed him by the tie and proceeded to bang his head against a wall. Then came the immortal question: 'Why are you so fucking rich and I'm so fucking poor?' As it happened, the aftermath was even more remarkable.

On returning to the office the following morning, expecting to collect his cards, the remorseful scribe walked into the lift and almost straight into the arms of his victim from the previous night, whereupon Sir William simply shook his head and said: 'Why do we do these things?'

Why indeed. The conflict between golf and mammon has been with us for decades. It gained unusually sharp focus in 1995 when Greg Norman received a reported $350,000 as an appearance fee from Murphys for playing in the Irish Open at Mount Juliet. Though the Shark eventually finished 11th behind Sam Torrance, the sponsors had reason to consider it money well spent, given that attendance figures had gone up by 27 per cent on 1994.

For his part, Norman made the memorable comment: 'You have to pay for professional talent.' The only dissenting voice among his leading colleagues came from Tom Watson, who observed: 'I probably could've earned four or five times the amount I made on the side in golf, but I chose not to, because my time was more important. You ask yourself how much is enough?'

Jack Nicklaus shared that view, even though he was badly hit financially at least twice during his tournament career. While expressing great admiration for Lee Trevino, he said earnestly: 'I don't think Lee ever played for the money.' It was invariably about the competition as far as the Bear was concerned, even though there were always financial inducements.

During the Masters a few years ago, I raised the issue of appearance fees in the US with a leading American golf writer. He was visibly shocked. How could I imagine such a thing? It simply didn't happen. All sane-thinking fans knew it didn't happen, even though they couldn't explain how leading players planned their schedules. Nor would it ever be permitted.

These days, the appearance money being paid in the millions to Rory McIlroy for committing to certain American tournaments is part of common clubhouse chat. LIV simply raised the emphasis on money in professional sports to a new level. Efforts by certain players to rationalise plain, unadulterated greed make the entire business all the more nauseating.

Leading practitioners such as Phil Mickelson, Dustin Johnson and Lee Westwood were instructed on what they should say in reply to anticipated questions, for instance, that they had made the move because it was a great opportunity to grow the game of golf. And that the 54-hole team format was new and exciting, and that while money may have been a factor in their decision, they were entitled to be recompensed for their professional skills.

They would further argue that as independent contractors, players retained the right to choose when and where they played the game. In the event, some questions were suitably probing, such as Ian Poulter being asked: 'If Vladimir Putin had a tournament, would you play there?' To which the seemingly affronted Englishman replied: 'I'm not going to comment on speculation.'

The entire process was largely predictable, simply because of the absence of a rational moral defence for the LIV enterprise. Granted, it was an interesting story at the outset, based largely on the identity of the various renegades. Taking a step back from the situation, however, and considering the implications for the actual playing of the game, it became increasingly difficult to take the issue of sportswashing seriously.

For instance, how was LIV truly going to affect the world's estimated 66.6 million golfers? Or the estimated 543,000 practitioners in this fair land? Its impact would be nil, other than the notoriety connected to the various LIV activists.

On a broader level, we could only imagine the damage being done to earnest young minds. How far removed was the influence of leading practitioners from the advice of the great Ben Hogan, 'the answer is in the dirt'?

As to the likely aftermath of events at London's Centurion GC, much of it was rich in speculation. What became immediately clear, however, was that one of the rebels, Graeme McDowell, would not be playing in the Irish Open at the end of that month.

Though he played at Mount Juliet in 2021, McDowell didn't fill the role of host en route to being tied 56th. And instead of being back at Mount Juliet for the 2022 Irish Open, he was at Pumpkin Ridge in far-off Oregon, competing in a LIV event that particular weekend – all of which was perhaps a good example of the impact the breakaway tour was likely to have on activities in Europe.

Meanwhile, we shouldn't have been surprised to find Norman heading the hunt for Arab money in golf. I can remember him talking about his favourite subject during a Dunhill Cup press conference at St Andrews. This time he got personal with the assembled media, asking us how much we earned from our golf writing.

The only scribe who was willing to answer him was Mark Garrod of the Press Association. While the rest of us silently cheered, Norman remarked dismissively: 'There are people in my office being paid more than that.' This goes some way towards explaining why the Shark has had no notable media supporter in his latest endeavours.

Colin Byrne, the Howth-based bagman of Louis Oosthuizen, claimed he had no wish to paint an unduly negative picture of how things once were in his craft. 'Things have changed dramatically since I started 35 years ago when we were treated effectively as necessary evils,' he said. 'It eventually became impossible for the authorities to ignore us.'

I remember a scandalous situation involving caddies during the 1998 US Open at the Olympic Club in San Francisco. When John O'Reilly struggled up the elevated 18th hole for the last time as Pádraig Harrington's bagman, he approached me and pleaded almost desperately: 'Is there any chance you could get me a cup of tea from the media centre? Caddies are not permitted inside the clubhouse.'

When Byrne ran away with the caddying circus, he had no illusions about the role he longed for in the world of tournament golf. He described his lowly position as among the plankton of the professional game, especially during the 1980s, a time of recession in Europe.

Now, in the twilight of a remarkably productive career, he has never been in a better place. 'Though I still expect nothing, I have been receiving an awful lot,' he said of a recent assignment. 'They've paid for my flight from Dublin; they picked me up at the airport and they've put me up in a very nice hotel. They obviously see the caddie as a key part of a golf team.'

His benefactors were the renegade LIV Tour, who were staging their last event of the season at the Trump National Doral Resort in Miami. And Byrne was there, caddying for Oosthuizen, who had been his employer for a year by that stage.

There was rich irony in all of this happening at a time when Rory McIlroy, a keen advocate of the status quo, had just regained the number one position in the world rankings. Yet Byrne was entirely comfortable being part of the perceived opposition.

'As a caddie, you get accustomed over the years to being treated with contempt,' he said. 'Things may have changed in recent years, but that's certainly the way caddying was for decades. I expected nothing and got nothing.' Later on, Byrne went on to gain a university degree in business studies.

And yet, in an unequal world, Colin Byrne wasn't afraid to stand his ground, as some individual employers discovered to their cost. At Bay Hill around 2013, on the 15th green in the second round, he grounded the bag and walked off the course, leaving Ernie Els to fend for himself. 'We all have a line, and Ernie happened to cross it on that occasion,' said Byrne. 'But we have since become friends again.'

Against this background, it wasn't difficult to understand Byrne's positivity about LIV, including the assertion that 'they can't do enough to accommodate the caddie.' But he wasn't blind to the nature of the Saudi Arabian regime that was making all of this largesse possible. As he elaborated:

> I don't quite get all of this sports-washing stuff. The Dublin Airport Authority have a five-year contract to run Jeddah Airport and I don't hear too many complaints being expressed about that. Such as threats to boycott Dublin Airport. We're all complicit. This global horse bolted years ago.
>
> We're all complicit in the trade and business we do with countries of doubtful morals. If you're so inclined, it has the makings of a very long debate. All I know is that the situation in golf became very divisive very quickly.

I was shocked by how opinionated and damning players from the PGA Tour were about colleagues who made a career decision to change. It's almost like they had forgotten that players turn professional to earn money.

It's their right to choose. I find it quite arrogant of them to be so indignant at someone considering an alternative to the PGA Tour, THEIR tour. Some of those pontificating should lay their own cards on the table. Like with appearance money, which for them seems good to take while the LIV money isn't.

In my view, they don't have the right to be calling the shots. I think it's a matter for individuals to earn money wherever they can, as professionals. And you can analyse the moral argument till the cows come home. How many of us can say that all the money we earn comes from squeaky-clean sources? It's in the nature of globalism that a lot of companies do business with Saudi Arabia. Why not golf?

He further claimed that unscripted professional golfers had become soft targets in all of this, though most of them were essentially sportspeople without political opinions. 'Whatever your view, the fact remains that a lot of lesser players on the PGA Tour have benefited greatly from the arrival of LIV,' said the Dubliner. 'Suddenly, the PGA Tour have miraculously found a bundle of cash under somebody's mattress to bolster the lot of these players.'

He described the camaraderie on the LIV Tour as 'brilliant'. Then, with a classic Byrne edge, he suggested:

There's pretty much a free bar for us in the hotel every night. And you can see how that would help camaraderie no end.

Kenny Comboy [Graeme McDowell's caddie] is an old mate and I was chatting only yesterday with Ricky Elliott [Brooks Koepka's bagman from Portrush]. We're all pretty much the same in the caddying fraternity. Being in the one hotel obviously helps us to spend more time in each other's company, rather than the normal situation of being scattered in all directions.

Caddies, Raymond Floyd once claimed, are like your wife: they're always right. By October 2004, Byrne had certainly moved above the humble menial with the launch of his first book at Royal Dublin GC, where he's a long-time member.

It had been a particularly successful season for him with his employer at the time, Retief Goosen, winning four tournaments – the US Open for a second time, the US Tour Championship, the Smurfit European Open and the Nedbank Challenge.

During World Cup week in Auckland, New Zealand, back in 1998, I approached Byrne about writing a column on his caddying experiences for the *Irish Times*, where I was a golf correspondent. A lasting memory of our discussion is that he never mentioned money.

He was caddying at the time for Greg Turner, who was also writing for publications in his native New Zealand. For Byrne, it led to the production of *Bagman* in 2006, a compilation of his columns, with the profits, incidentally, going to charity.

When we talked in Augusta National during the 2019 Masters, he was approaching his mid-fifties, working for Rafa Cabrera-Bello and looking towards retirement. Then two things happened: he was given the opportunity of sharing Oosthuizen's bag with fellow caddie, Wynand Stander – then Oosthuizen joined LIV.

'I didn't discuss the move with Louis,' said Byrne. 'The sort of relationship I have with him doesn't really extend beyond whether it's a six-iron or a seven-iron. The fact is that carrying a golf bag for a living catches up with you physically,' he went on. 'But even at 58, I could see the arrangement with Louis and LIV extending my career.'

He concluded: 'Golf needs to change, and having experienced both sides, I believe this is the way to do it.' But can it last? 'I can't say I'd bet my life on it,' he replied. 'Yet I'm beginning to think it could make for a very interesting future.' Indeed.

15

Christy O'Connor Snr

Centenary man

On the South Course at La Manga during the 1980s, I played with Christy O'Connor Snr in a pro-am event. As I recall it now, decades later, the occasion remains one of the highlights of my modest playing career, not least for a fascinating incident that occurred on the first fairway.

Having scrambled the ball nervously into play, I set off at some pace, anxious to put as much distance as possible between myself and observers of my opening drive. So, it came as a surprise when, on arriving at my ball, I noticed this stranger, dressed in a business suit, shirt and tie, standing beside me.

'Can I caddie for you?' he enquired with a soft, English accent. 'But I'm afraid I'm not much of a player,' I replied, slightly embarrassed. 'I can see that,' he responded with crushing candour. 'To be honest, the only reason I want to pull your trolley is to be close to Christy.'

He went on to introduce himself as a company director who, in younger years, would grab any opportunity to get away from his office in London, to see O'Connor in action in some tournament in the UK. 'You could say that I have been a fan of Christy's for most of my adult life,' he said proudly.

So it was that for nine holes, before he rejoined his wife in the clubhouse, our English friend was enthralled, listening to him discussing how he was going to play a particular shot, then executing it precisely as planned. It became something of a masterclass from a man totally in command of his craft, even though he would have been qualifying for the old-age pension soon.

Particularly memorable was the short fifth, listed at 201 metres off the back tee. I reckoned it at around 180 yards off our tee. Another member of our group, playing off two, happened to have played a beautiful shot comfortably on the green. 'That was a six-iron, Christy,' he helpfully told the master. Whereupon Christy asked his caddie for a four. Then, gripping the club slightly down the shaft, he proceeded to hit a low draw onto a left to right wind, sending the ball to about four feet from the pin. A real beauty!

Two things struck me from this memorable experience. The first was how totally at ease O'Connor was in his chosen working environment, where he was wonderful company. The second was the respect he had for his amateur partners, even to the point of climbing some steep hills in search of seriously stray shots from a twenty-something handicapper in our group.

This brought to mind the opening remark of a Welsh professional (no, not Ian Woosnam) to his partners, myself included, in the Carroll's pro-am at Portmarnock: 'OK guys, this is a practice round for me. I won't be looking for any balls.' And he was as good as his word.

Back at La Manga, a charming postscript to this most enjoyable little episode was that the businessman waited in the clubhouse with his wife until his idol had finished. The three of them proceeded to have a drink together.

Some years later, in the less likely setting of an obscure golf club south of Birmingham in Warwickshire, I had another enlightening chat about the great O'Connor. My informant on this occasion was another, more celebrated Englishman in the golfing domain. John Jacobs was among a gathering of the 1955 Ryder Cup team for a charity pro-am at Kilworth Springs GC, during the week of the 2002 staging at The Belfry.

Then 77, Jacobs could hardly credit that Christy, the man we had come to know as Himself, three months his senior, was still swinging the club so well.

'That was a great joy to me,' Jacobs later observed. 'I'm almost afraid to describe him as the best natural hitter of a golf ball I've ever seen, knowing the way he protests about the amount of practice he did. But it's true just the same.'

Jacobs, described as 'Dr Golf', in acknowledgement of his status among the game's leading tutors, went on:

> I could watch Christy hit golf balls forever. People often criticised him for letting the club go at the top of the backswing, but it would have killed Christy to hang onto the club with the last three fingers.
>
> Happily, the Lord took over and what we saw from there on, was absolute perfection. Not only does his swing look right to me, it remains correct in every key, technical sense. Which is truly remarkable for a man of 77.

In subsequent years, I had the opportunity of seeing Himself in his Dollymount home where he eased gently into the sunset. Through the medium of television, he would thrill to the achievements of others, especially in matters of golfing. It could be watching Annika Sörenstam in the American Skins Game or Tiger Woods in the President's Cup, or Darren Clarke's performance in capturing the NEC Invitational at Firestone.

A typical visit included him and his wife, Mary, enjoying a pre-dinner glass of wine. And as if cast in the role of intruder, I provoked a few sharp barks from beyond the French windows. This had to be the dog that took its master down to the sand dunes at Dollymount for regular morning exercise. O'Connor demurred:

> Oh no, that's Snowy. She's a half-collie. You're thinking of Woofy, who died about three years ago. She was much better bred, a lovely dog. She'd sit on a bench while I went up and down the dunes.
>
> And she'd follow me through rough a couple of feet high. That's great for your legs. Fantastic. Keep the legs active. That's the first place you get tired. And when your legs are tired, you become tired mentally. Which is the end of your concentration.

There was a pause before he added:

> Though I've no proof of it, I suspect she picked up something from the pollution down there. Anyway, I couldn't bear to lose her, but the kids had her put down and Peter [one of his twin sons] brought me this one as a replacement. But I won't take her down where Woofy would go, for fear something might happen to her, too. I couldn't do that to her.

They had moved into Blackheath Park in April 1959 when he took up an appointment as a professional at Royal Dublin. The house had cost about £2,000 and five years had passed since he and Mary were married. Looking out the rear window, he was moved to remark: 'It was never in me to want grand things. I was always happy if Mary was happy. And we've been happy here, trying to make this a friendly, family sort of home.'

So it proved to be, during a career which contained 24 European Tour victories, 10 Irish Professional Championships, a Canada Cup triumph with Harry Bradshaw in 1958, the first £1,000 first prize ever offered on this side of the Atlantic and a record £25,000 for victory in the 1970 John Player Classic.

It is still remarkable to think that as a 48-year-old, O'Connor was tied seventh behind Tom Weiskopf in the 1973 Open at Troon – his last serious tilt at what became an elusive prize. 'I remember Troon, hoping that Neil Coles [who was third] would win,' he recalled. 'I played with Jack Nicklaus on the last day, which was one of the best ball-striking rounds I've ever had. Tee to green, I reckon I was striking the ball as well as Jack, but he shot 65 to my 73. The difference was mainly on the greens.' Then there were his 10 successive Ryder Cup appearances. And as a reflection of remarkable longevity, these were followed by six PGA Senior titles and two World Senior triumphs.

Another occasion on which I called to see the head of the O'Connor golfing clan was in January 2016, after the shocking death of his nephew, Christy Jnr. His mind remained as sharp as a tack and he confounded those of us decades younger by reading without the need of glasses. But his resolute spirit seemed dented, if not broken, by Junior's untimely departure.

Four months later, he left us at the grand old age of 91. He had suffered a series of strokes and eventually succumbed, peacefully, to a major heart attack.

As we contemplated his centenary on 21 December, a glittering career was diminished in the view of many by his failure to capture the Open Championship, in which he was joint runner-up in 1965 and tied third in 1958 and 1961. Crucial breaks never seemed to go his way at critical moments down the stretch. And Peter Thomson, who was dominating the event at that time, told me: 'I believe if Christy had made the breakthrough, he would have won several Opens.'

Christy's own reaction before his passing had been: 'Sure, I'd like to have won it, but it didn't feel that important at the time. We sort of looked upon it as a pension. As for the other Majors, I tried to qualify for the US Open once and failed, but I never played the Masters, though I could have done so possibly 20 times.'

His great friend Harry Bradshaw had an interesting theory about the elusive Open. 'I always felt that Christy didn't want to win it because of the change it would have forced on his career,' he claimed. 'It would have made him an international player, with responsibility to travel the world. Christy wouldn't have wanted that.'

Jimmy Kinsella takes a much narrower view. 'Christy never seemed to have a plan, when it came to the Open,' he said. 'I always felt it was necessary to go into it specially prepared mentally. And from what I saw, Christy never put his mind to the challenge the way I felt he needed to.'

I considered it a particular honour to be able to observe O'Connor's deep, enduring love of golf, right to the end. There would be telephone chats to contemporaries like Peter Alliss, his partner in 12 Ryder Cup matches. Sadly, when Alliss phoned a week before his friend died, he was out of reach, in hospital. 'Christy was a wonderful partner and a beautiful golfer; really a genius of our sport,' said the former voice of the BBC.

In the context of all the tributes that were directed his way, I remember being very taken with O'Connor's invariably warm recollections of one-time rivals.

He described the mercurial Tommy Bolt as the finest ball-striker he had ever seen, and after watching Ben Hogan play nine holes during the 1953 Open at Carnoustie, he repaired to the practice ground, crushed that he 'knew nothing about the game' himself.

Affectionately known as 'Himself' on this side of the pond, he cast a formidable shadow over the European scene. From that shadow, champions such as Pádraig Harrington emerged as part of a glowing legacy.

When Harrington was contemplating a career as a tournament professional, he considered it appropriate to head for Royal Dublin on a bitterly cold January day to watch Christy hit practice balls.

Braving sharp winds that whipped sea sand around Dollymount's marram grasses, he came across a familiar lone figure considerably older than in the picture he had kept on his bedroom wall as a youngster. The winner of three Major championships recalled the scene:

> Most people wouldn't have let their dog out. Yet Christy was there in The Garden hitting shots. And they were beautiful shots. That's what was fascinating to me.
>
> I figured at the time that nobody in the world could have played this particular shot – a six-iron of maybe 140 yards which he was holding onto the wind with a low draw. One after the other. Then he hit a few fades. It was just spectacular. Here was a man in

his late sixties at the time, who still had the will to go out in that weather and hit those wonderful shots.

These were enduring skills with which Jimmy Kinsella was thoroughly familiar. He had become close to Christy since the spring of 1955, when they had a serious chat on the putting green at Sunningdale. Kinsella was serving his apprenticeship as a 15-year-old working at Fulwell Golf Club in London for Bill Cox, the celebrated teacher and television commentator.

'I remember on a particular Saturday, one of our customers, a reserve goalkeeper with Liverpool, was going to Sunningdale where a tournament was being played, and he offered me a lift,' the future Castle and Skerries professional recalled:

> I ended up standing by the putting green at Sunningdale where Christy spotted me. 'What are you doing here?' he asked. When I told him I was working at Fulwell he enquired 'Do you like it?' And when I replied that I didn't, Christy said: 'Then why don't you come and work with me in Bundoran? Get in touch with your dad and ask him if it's all right.' We had no phone at home at the time, so I wrote my Dad a letter from London. And he replied that it was fine.
>
> Later, Christy's wife, Mary, told me that he was soft and that he felt sorry for me. Either way, he had won the Swallow Penfold and I knew he needed somebody because he was heading for the Ryder Cup at Thunderbird CC in California in November of that year.
>
> Before he went, he sent me on my bike to the bank in Ballyshannon to withdraw £100 for the trip. He eventually spent three months over there and played a few tournaments, having met up with Ray Hayden, who was an assistant pro at Woodbrook.

According to Kinsella, he and his employer hit it off. There was no salary, but the youngster had full board and his own room in the professional's rented house, and earned enough from lessons to keep himself in pocket money.

They parted company in 1956. Kinsella had been going out with a 16-year-old local girl who decided to emigrate to Australia. Rather than being left on his own, he went home to his parents in Skerries.

The next two decades turned out to be a challenging time for any young Irish professional, not least because of the remarkable consistency of the country's top player. Results of the leading Irish events back then were replete with instances of Kinsella claiming prominent positions on the leaderboard. Almost invariably, however, the top cash, modest as it was, ended in the O'Connor homestead of Blackheath Park on the north side of Dublin.

'Another win for O'Connor' became a familiar headline in the national newspapers, not unlike the dominance that Tiger Woods exerted over colleagues on the PGA Tour in the US half a century later. 'Christy had quite a bit of success in England, but I always felt that his main objective was to be the leading Irish player,' said Kinsella.

On 4 September 1960, the *Sunday People* carried an artist's enhanced photograph of the Skerries man Kinsella standing on the 18th green of the old Dun Laoghaire course on Tivoli Road the day before. The objective was to highlight, with a white arrow, how close he had been to winning top prize in the Irish Dunlop Tournament. When the five-footer failed to drop, he had to settle for a share of first prize, despite having carded four rounds in the sixties.

It meant that instead of securing a winner's £100, he shared first and second prizes with O'Connor. Who else? The wayward putt had cost him the princely sum of £10, which was indicative of the remuneration from Irish tournaments at the time. On that occasion, incidentally, Jimmy travelled to Dun Laoghaire each day on his 250cc Royal Enfield motorbike from the family home in Skerries, with his golf clubs on his back.

By 1971, news of his challenges had become more encouraging for Kinsella, notwithstanding a sensational top prize of £25,000 the previous year by O'Connor in the John Player Classic at Hollinwell.

All the while, his admiration and affection for O'Connor never waned in the years to follow. The respect he had for him as an employer was enhanced in his capacity as a role model. Based on that formative time at Bundoran, he was under no illusions as to how good a golfer the Galwayman was.

'During the two hours I spent in Christy's bedroom before he died, we talked golf, naturally,' said Kinsella. 'But it was mainly about a caddie, not about other players. We discussed a man both of us knew only as Seamie. We didn't know his surname.

'He was a little Irishman who lived in Egham in Surrey. "That was all we knew,' said the Skerries man. 'Christy told me he gave Seamie £1,000 after winning £25,000 in the John Player Classic of 1970. I reckon he gave him more, in that 10 per cent of £25,000 would be two and a half. And Christy wasn't mean. I always found him to be a decent man and we can take it that Seamie was paid well. I suspect he got mixed up in the numbers, when we talked for the last time.'

Either way, the settlement would hardly have compared with caddie J.P. Fitzgerald's experience of a 'tsunami of dollars [$1.1 million] tumbling into my bank account' when Rory McIlroy won the FedEx Cup for the first time in 2016. Still, for that time, it seems that O'Connor was generous.

After the statutory PGA percentage had been deducted, he received a cheque for £24,375. But what to do with it? A bank strike in Ireland, which had begun on 1 May, would not end until six and a half months later on 17 November. 'I put it under the bedroom carpet until the bank strike was over,' O'Connor explained.

In the meantime, the John Player bonanza meant there were drinks to be drunk, starting in the clubhouse at Notts GC that evening and on into the night. Courtesy of the winner, there was an open-house party. In fact, the club bar was drunk dry and a van had to be sent for refreshments. Kinsella went on:

> Christy always used Seamie when playing in England. He reckoned he wasn't much of a caddie but he was a smashing little guy who

was good company and always had a smile on his face. I remember Christy telling me how, one day, he asked Seamie what club he'd need for a particular shot. The caddie replied: 'It's a four iron but a bloody good one.'

Christy said, 'Give me the seven.' We both laughed at that. When paying Seamie off, Christy told me he sort of put him into enforced retirement. He told Seamie to get out of the caddying game, buy a little van and a machine and he could do people's gardens around the area in Surrey where he lived.

Two weeks later at the Alcan Tournament in Portmarnock, Christy had his own caddie and I ended up with Seamie. He had come over to see his sister who lived in Finglas. I looked after him, took him home where Bernie [Kinsella's wife] fed him. And I collected him every morning in Finglas.

At the end of the tournament I paid him but he protested that I'd given him too much, with all the other stuff I'd done for him. Imagine a caddie saying that!

A Seamie sequel occurred a few weeks later back in England, when O'Connor went looking for a replacement caddie. Suddenly he eyed his former bagman lurking sheepishly in the background. 'I thought I told you to give this up,' he remonstrated. Seamie's head went down a few inches further. 'Where's the money?' O'Connor persisted. 'Where's the van you were to buy?' According to Kinsella, the money was gone and he returned to O'Connor's employ. The lure of a caddying life was simply too great to discard.

Testing the Great Man's Weapons

Two rather special clubs were tucked under my left arm as I approached the GUI's Academy at Carton House. First into view was national coach Neil Manchip who, on eyeing the more forbidding of the implements, exclaimed: 'I certainly wouldn't fancy that for my first shot of the day.'

The object of my visit was to place remarkable Christmas gifts into expert hands. By arrangement, Manchip's PGA colleague, Noel Fox, had agreed to compare golf clubs from another era with their modern counterparts.

Making the exercise all the more attractive from Fox's perspective was that the last player to have hit the clubs was none other than Christy O'Connor Snr. They were now my property, through the kindness of the great man's family at Christmas time 2016.

One of the clubs in question was a Fred Smyth three-iron, stamped with the famous RC10 logo commemorating Christy's 10th successive Ryder Cup appearance in 1973. Its partner was a classic persimmon driver from the MacGregor company, beautifully crafted with an unusually shallow face.

They were the sort of clubs Ben Hogan would have used when setting new standards for the professional game during the 1950s, the opening decade of O'Connor's tournament career. In this context, Hogan's famous US Open victory at Merion in 1950 was brought right back into focus by the 2013 triumph from Justin Rose in the same championship at that same, historic venue.

Merion's 18th hole measured 458 yards when Hogan set up a par as his 72nd with an iconic one-iron second shot of 200 yards, which came to rest 40 feet from the pin. When the hole was stretched to 511 yards in 2013, Rose slipped through the green with a four-iron from roughly the same position.

We're told that the lofts of irons have changed dramatically since Hogan's time, to the extent that by modern standards, the great man was probably playing a three- rather than a one-iron for that fateful approach. The same loft difference in other irons throughout the range is attributed to clever marketing by equipment manufacturers.

On seeing Christy's clubs, Fox disappeared behind a partition in the Academy from where the sound of warm-up striking was accompanied by a stream of balls penetrating the murky gloom of a winter's day. Then he returned ready for the test, saying: 'It's such a great privilege to hit these clubs that I want to give them my best shot.'

His first effort with the RC10 went 204 yards. Then, as the consequence of a much crisper strike, the second was measured at 215. The third one of 218 reflected a level of concentration you might associate with the most intense tournament play.

Fox seemed satisfied. 'Miss the middle of the blade and you know all about it,' he mused. 'Much more challenging to hit than a modern club. But catch it right and the feedback is superb – right up the shaft, through the grip and onto the hands.'

He figured he was dealing with a sweet spot about the size of a five-cent piece, compared with a two-euro piece for the modern implement. Then it was time for a modern blade which, courtesy of greater weight in the sole, resulted in a noticeably higher arc for a best hit of 221 yards.

'Far less challenging,' he declared with a smile. 'So, strictly in terms of distance, not much has changed in iron technology in the last 40 years. The key ingredient in extra distance is the ball, with help from over-size drivers.'

By way of ensuring that we were comparing like with like, he tested the clubs for loft. Christy's three-iron measured 20 degrees and the modern version, at 21, was virtually the same.

Fox then talked about a little groove left by O'Connor's left thumb in the grip of the three-iron. 'It's more to the inside than I imagined it might be, indicating quite a strong, left-hand grip which would be in line with modern coaching,' he said. 'But I would have expected a more neutral grip from Christy.'

When I asked him if the three-iron had even a hint of the forgiveness you would expect to find in abundance in the modern version, he replied: 'No. There simply isn't any.' He went on: 'That's a club only for a top amateur or a decent professional. In the hands of a handicap player, it would be an incredible experience to hit it out of the middle, maybe once a month.'

All this led Fox to reflect fondly on a Links Society outing at Royal Dublin in the late 1990s. It was an occasion when his powerful drive over the old cross-bunkers on the long 11th prompted a celebrated playing partner to enthusiastically remove his headwear and fling it to the ground with the prediction: 'I'll eat that hat if you don't make it at this game.'

Sadly for Fox and his new-found mentor, O'Connor, a sparkling amateur career was not followed by the anticipated success on the professional circuit, though he went on to establish himself as a gifted teacher with admirable insight.

Meanwhile, that treasured day on Dollymount's duneland ended in a manner befitting its resident genius. Fox explained:

> Of course, I'd heard about Christy's bush on the 18th and he wasn't far from it after a drive which, surprisingly, he drew off the ditch. Then he used the same, black Ram Zebra driver to cut the ball off the deck, sending it over the Garden to about 20 feet from the hole.
>
> He must have been in his mid-seventies at the time and I remember thinking that they were pretty amazing shots for a player of those years. Particularly the control he had over the golf ball. My brother James [winner of the 2023 North of Ireland Championship] was caddying for me and we often talk about those shots. And how Christy rebuked us for sacrificing control by using soft golf balls. Amazing.

This seemed a perfect cue for some shots with the MacGregor driver. Having searched for a tee that wasn't going to damage the precious face, Fox prepared to launch one of his finest.

Just before the crack of impact, however, he became aware of something drastically wrong. It was only on seeing his sudden dash down the range that I realised what had happened. The wooden head, which hadn't seen action for several decades, had come adrift at impact and was eventually recovered by Fox about 50 yards away.

Walking back with the separated head, concern was evident on his face. On closer inspection, however, it turned out that no damage was done, though a fine crack was visible where the whipping had once held persimmon and steel firmly in place. Putting them together again, Fox bound them loosely as a temporary fix.

Aware suddenly of greatly changed times, he went on to remark that they no longer teach the art of whipping at the professionals' training school. 'But I can still do it,' he insisted proudly. 'I learned from Peter Townsend when he was professional at Portmarnock.'

That was when the notion struck me of intervention from the other side. Maybe Christy had decided that a faithful old servant had reached the end of its working life.

Later, my grandson, Harry Osborne, a proud member of Dun Laoghaire GC, discovered the driver while rummaging in my office. And the thought struck me that I should have it repaired. But who to ask, given the lost art of whipping?

Suddenly, I thought of Jimmy Kinsella, who was only too happy to help. Admiring the highly polished head, he remarked: 'Christy must have got one of the lads, maybe Mick Murphy, to do a job on it.'

When I wondered if Jimmy would fancy the idea of returning it to action, he hesitated and in a nod to modern technology noted the decidedly neat size of the head before replying with a smile: 'I'd prefer it to be a little bigger.' A few hours later, I returned to his house and collected the finished club.

'I used all my old equipment to repair it,' Jimmy beamed, clearly pleased with his handiwork. Who knows, maybe we had indeed interfered with Christy's plans for the implement. And that it was now time to ease it into well-earned retirement in a suitable display case.

The thought would probably have appealed to Fox as an explanation for the mishap during his experiment at Carton House, lending comfortable finality to an intriguing exercise.

SIGHTING A TRUE ECCENTRIC

The sort of enduring skills one associates so readily with Christy O'Connor Snr were sparked by a remarkable sight on the practice ground at Lake Nona, Florida. It was November 1993 and eager faces had gathered to observe some remarkable ball-striking from an unlikely source.

At 63, Moe Norman was giving an impromptu demonstration, and some of the leading players involved in the World Cup of Golf later that week had gathered to watch. Standing some way back from the ball, this wild-looking character proceeded to hit draw shots and then some late fades, at will. Nick Price and Fred Couples were absolutely absorbed.

'What do you make of him?' I asked Couples. Slightly embarrassed, the American replied: 'I don't understand that sort of skill.' Mick McGinley, who had travelled to watch his son Paul represent Ireland with Ronan Rafferty, was equally absorbed with one of the game's great characters at that time.

A dedicated eccentric, Norman had started out as a gifted Canadian amateur who won his national titles in 1955 and 1956 before going on to win the Canadian PGA in 1966 and 1974. As a professional, his main aim was to make a living by playing money matches in Ontario during the Canadian summer and then on to resort areas such as Lake Nona in the US south.

Though he played in the Masters, his name doesn't appear in any of the tournament's records, simply because he decided to withdraw after moving into contention.

Then there is the story of how he was so taken by a golf tip from Byron Nelson that he proceeded to hit hundreds of balls to work the new thought into his method. The next morning, he woke up too stiff and swollen to swing a club.

On the morning of his death at 75 in September 2004, a friend of Norman's went through his belongings. In his pockets, he found a couple of Titleist golf balls, three or four tees and a watch. In the boot of his car, he discovered more than 1,000 golf balls, most of them Titleist Pro V1s, rolling around loosely.

There were also 10 pairs of golf shoes and two to three sets of irons. Elsewhere in the Cadillac was hidden $20,000 in cash.

16

Distinguished Ladies of the Links

News in late May 2024 that Irene Holland had joined her husband, Buster, in the great beyond, brought to mind a trip I had made to Tullamore GC almost 23 years previously. The memory was prompted by Irene's son, Alastair, who wrote of his mum's 'great friend and mentor, Kitty MacCann,' and a photograph he had of the two of them together as members of the Irish international team of 1958, when she was Irene Hurst.

I first got to know Buster and Irene in 1996 when he was captain of Royal County Down, which played host to the Irish Men's Amateur Close Championship that year. While watching Peter Lawrie claim the title, I happened to be about to undergo heart bypass surgery and Buster, an eminent gynaecologist, gave me wonderful advice on what to expect, having himself come through the same surgery some years earlier.

We corresponded quite a bit and I retain a beautiful Christmas card in aid of the Newry Hospice titled 'Winter in the Mournes', from a painting by William McAlpine.

Meanwhile, the occasion I attended in June 2001 marked the golden jubilee of Ms MacCann's remarkable victory in the British Women's

Championship at Broadstone, Dorset. Irene was among the guests while Kitty filled the position of honour, somewhat bemused, it seemed, by all the attention she was receiving.

The presence of so many old friends, admirers and former rivals left the organisers in no doubt about the merit of the venture. I learned later that Tullamore GC had encountered predictable difficulty in persuading their most famous member to agree to a special function to mark her greatest triumph. However, though famously shy about her golfing achievements, she eventually agreed to the celebration.

So it was, in the wonderful tradition of sporting friends, that she was reunited with Moira Earner, Irene Holland, Anne Crowley and Roly O'Neill, four colleagues on Tullamore's triumphant Irish Senior Cup team of 1958. Grace O'Brien, the sixth member of the group, sent apologies.

Her distinguished contemporaries Philomena Garvey and Clarrie Reddan also sent apologies. But Lillian Behan was there, 16 years to the day after she had become the last Irish winner of the British Match-play title, at Ganton. Earlier that month, Ms MacCann had watched Ms Behan lose the final of the Midland Championship on a sixth tie hole at Tullamore.

Ms MacCann's one-time caddie, Dinny White, was also present. So was her former Irish international colleague Aileen McCarthy, who had proved to be an unavailing challenge at Broadstone. Finally Cathy Smith, president of the Irish Ladies Golf Union, also attended, as did Leinster Branch chairman Albert Lee, representing the Golfing Union of Ireland, all through the organisational skills of Tullamore's Leonard Dolan.

It was a time for fond reminiscences by Ms Holland who, as I have indicated, was guided by Ms MacCann during her formative golfing years at Tullamore. And Ms MacCann recalled a 'very happy foursomes partnership' with Ms Earner at international level.

As a footnote to the events at Broadstone all those years ago, the *Sunday Press* of 10 June 1951, carried this fascinating little tale: 'Proud father of Kitty, Mr G.S. Smye, timed his retirement as manager, Bank of Ireland, for last Wednesday. He chartered a plane for a family party to see Kitty play, but the plane landed at an unauthorised British airport and there was hell to pay.' It concluded: 'After placating angry officials, Mr Smye saw his daughter win after being two over fours for the last 15 of the 36-hole final.'

The private aircraft reference was only part of a fascinating string of events that brought the championship to Ireland for the first time since May Hezlet had won the last of her three titles in 1907. In the five years leading up to Ms MacCann's triumph, there had been final defeats for Ms Garvey in 1946 and Ms Reddan in 1949. As it happened, Ms Garvey eventually triumphed in 1957.

Born in Clonmel in 1922 as Katherine Smye, Kitty married Pat MacCann, a veterinary surgeon, in February 1950, sixteen months before Broadstone. As mentioned above, her father, Gerard Smye, retired from being a Tullamore bank manager on the Wednesday of championship week. At 64, he reckoned he had earned himself the luxury of chartering a plane when his daughter reached the final. So he rose at 5.00 a.m. on the Thursday morning to catch the aircraft bound for Hurn Airport, along with other family members and friends.

This, apparently, was the first aircraft available and we're told that it discharged its passengers just before lunch, to the news that their heroine was five up. And though she proceeded to lose the next two holes, she went into the afternoon round three holes to the good and won eventually by 4 and 3.

Towards evening, family and friends arrived back at what was then Collinstown Airport, with the champion 'tanned and smiling.' She then disclosed that she had entered the event only at the 11th hour, adding, 'I didn't think I had any chance.' Her husband, apparently, had convinced her to enter.

After some initial celebrating, the triumphant party was honoured with a civic reception in Tullamore 24 hours later.

We're told that members of the Tullamore club in 'a hundred tricolour bedecked cars, met the champion on the outskirts of the town, accompanied by the St Columcille Pipers' Band and a tremendous number of the general public'. A report in the *Midland Tribune, Tipperary Sentinel and Offaly Co. Vindicator* went on:

> A blazing bonfire lit up O'Connor Square to where she was escorted from the urban boundary by a procession of cars and cheering crowds. Here, over a thousand people thronged the square to take part in the celebrations, which included the presentation of an illuminated address of welcome by the Urban Council.
>
> The entire town was en fete for the occasion and Tullamore can be justly proud of the tribute they paid their townswoman on her magnificent achievement.

In acknowledgement of what appears to have been a wonderfully warm occasion, Kitty said: 'This is the proudest moment of my life, and I would like to thank you all for this wonderful welcome. I am very proud to have won the British Ladies Open Championship, but I am prouder still to have put Tullamore in the news for a day or two.' To this, a voice from the crowd shouted: 'Glory to you.' Reportedly the crowd then sang 'For She's a Jolly Good Fellow' and the proceedings in the square were concluded with the playing of the national anthem.

I've always felt that the events surrounding Kitty's success gave a charming insight into the importance of sport, especially in our rural communities. And Kitty, who was 88 when she died in April 2010, was keenly aware of this, despite her natural shyness.

Some years had passed after Broadstone before I got to know her on a personal level and I found her to be delightful company. A colleague and I took advantage of her kindness when, during a championship in Carlow, she loaned us her car for overnight trips back to Dublin. We had the effrontery to give it back to her with hardly a drop of petrol in the tank. Typically, she later shrugged off our apology with a hearty laugh.

As it happened, Kitty had died several months before Lillian Behan eventually realised a lifetime ambition in golf. She won the 2010 Lady Captain's Prize at Royal Curragh under extraordinary circumstances.

One could sense her frustration in July 2001 when she said, reflecting on a remarkable career in golf:

> If I can just win the Captain's Prize, that would cap it all. It may seem funny after winning the British in 1985 and playing on the winning Curtis Cup team in Kansas a year later. But all I want to win in golf is the Captain's Prize at the Curragh.
>
> Watching people going up to claim the prize over the years and the fun they get from it makes me want to experience it!

In 2001, she shot rounds of 71 and 72 for a total of 143 to win the gross prize by a whopping 17 strokes from club secretary Mary McNally. She added:

> I have won the gross a number of times, but it is going to take a pair of 66s playing off my handicap of +1 to win it. I guess I put too much pressure on myself each year and I should maybe relax a little bit. I'm certainly capable of doing it and hopefully it will happen in the next few years.

When the breakthrough came eventually, the nature of winning the actual prize from Maggy McElroy made for a memorable story. On her way to victory, playing off one-handicap, Lillian hit a splendid drive, all of 300 yards, down the long dog-leg 13th which had been redesigned by Patrick Merrigan. And her reward? A beautiful painting of that particular hole by the distinguished local artist Rosemary Burns. Her playing partner that day was Anne Delaney, who would become lady captain four years later.

'Winning that captain's prize crowned my golfing career,' Lillian recalled recently. 'And it was made all the more special by the fact that my mother, Bernadette, had died on January 6th of that year. She had been my mentor, along with Dick Collins. Though my drive down 13 was long, I still had to settle for a par there. It's beautiful but a difficult hole. My overall scoring was 70, 71, one under par for the 36 holes.'

Golf historians reasonably took the view that Old Tom Morris had a lot to answer for concerning a decidedly sexist comment at St Andrews in 1899. That was when he had exclaimed: 'I'll no' be licked by a lassie.'

Since then, some male golfers have quaked at the possibility of being outscored by a woman, while the notion of actually being outdriven by one has been too grave to even contemplate.

The outburst from 77-year-old Morris occurred midway through a 36-hole challenge match with Rhona Adair, who had been runner-up to her great rival May Hezlet in the Irish Championship that year. As it happened, he had to withstand a spirited rally before winning the match on the final green.

Royal Curragh GC would have a number of male members, however, who were not quite so fortunate in friendly matches with Ms Behan. And at the highest level of the modern game, quite a few male eyebrows were raised by Annika Sörenstam's 59 on the LPGA Tour.

In my view, it is arguable whether this country has produced a player, man or woman, more naturally gifted than Lillian, who was born on 12 January 1965. Among her wealth of skills is an ability to work the ball in either direction at will, which she displayed to particularly fine effect in the 1986 Home Internationals at Whittington Barracks, where dog legs abound. As she explained to me years later, there was no mechanical adjustment. And she added proudly:

> After I had played with Christy O'Connor Snr in a pro-am in Bandama in the Canaries, he complimented me on the quality of my ball-striking. That's when I told him I could move the ball either way by picturing the shot in my head. My hands do the rest. He said that's exactly what he did.

American Stacey Shinnick from El Cajon, California, also enjoyed her golf, especially when playing against men. 'I played with a guy once and he told me GOLF stood for "Gentlemen only, ladies forbidden,"' she said. 'Then I outdrove him and he got real quiet.' At 6ft 2ins, Shinnick used her physique to launch the ball impressive distances away. In the World Long Drive Championship in Nevada, she won the women's section with a launch of 249 yards into a 20mph wind, having hit a qualifying effort of exactly 300 yards earlier.

And we shouldn't be surprised. The great Glenna Collett-Vare recorded a 307-yard drive prior to the 1922 US Women's Amateur. And Babe Zaharias was through the green with a four-iron second shot at a 540-yard hole in the 1947 British Women's at Gullane Number 1, an event in which Clarrie Reddan competed.

But what of Rhona Adair? She, too, was remarkably tall, given the time and the restrictive clothing she was expected to wear. On a trip to the US at the beginning of the last century, she drove a ball across the expanse of a river – a carry of 170 yards. Small wonder Old Tom was worried!

Looking back to Ganton in 1985, the triumph of 20-year-old Lillian became a wonderful story, given that her success was totally unexpected, though she had captured the Leinster Championship the year before with a 19th-hole victory in the final over Maureen Madill.

Let us consider the fact that she progressed from a 27 handicap in 1981 to British champion four years later, at the first attempt. Against this background, it doesn't diminish her achievement in any way to attribute significant credit to the instructional and emotional support of Evelyn Hearn, the Waterford schoolteacher who caddied for her over the closing stages.

I wasn't at Ganton, but I remember much talk at the time about Ms Hearn's role in her eventual success, specifically her advice on shot-making and general clubbing. Almost 40 years on, however, I could sense Lillian bristling at this suggestion, to which I admit to having contributed myself. She explained:

> People talked about me having fun on the golf course, but I went out there to win. Don't ever forget that. By the time I went to Ganton, my game was based on feel and visual assessment. I was fully aware of how far I hit every club.
>
> That was my first time to compete in the British and I travelled with Katherine MacCann. Evelyn was with another group. We went by boat from Rosslare and when I reached a certain point in the championship, we talked about caddies.

> Though I was new to the British, I had played in the Girls Home Internationals in '82 and won a few events, including Leinster. So there was no question of Evelyn telling me what to do. I trained myself to know the importance of club selection. I considered myself to be a feel golfer and a visual golfer. Evelyn was a great companion but I had confidence in what I could do.

Purely from observation, I could see a wonderful freedom, a refreshing innocence about her game, which she had developed by playing mainly with men off the men's tees, over her home course. And she was tall. Well-built and with strong arms developed through working with horses at the Lisieux Stud on the Curragh, her game was technically sound, with admirable freedom about everything she did. I remember meeting her during international matches in Stavanger, Norway, a few weeks after her Ganton success. With local admirers gathered around to watch her tee-off in practice, she remarked cheerily: 'I'm still only a novice at this level and there's nothing like a few hours with the yard brush for bringing you back to earth.' I suspect that this sort of self-deprecation had the effect of exaggerating the fun-loving image emanating from Ganton.

A year later, she experienced the joy of sharing a marvellous Curtis Cup triumph with compatriots Mary McKenna and Claire Dowling. It marked the first occasion when Britain and Ireland had won on American soil and with two foursomes and a singles win, Lillian contributed three points to a historic 13–5 triumph at Prairie Dunes, Kansas.

Her foursomes partner was the experienced Englishwoman Jill Thornhill. The matches were played in extreme heat and Lillian blamed the effects of sunburn and losing three pounds weight per day on her 18th hole singles defeat to America's Kim Gardener, on the afternoon of the second day. Reflecting on a marvellous team effort, Scottish veteran Belle Robertson later remarked: 'Lillian has the look of a champion.'

Still only 21, her decision to turn professional came as a shock – especially to those of us who had been captivated by the fresh innocence of her talent, at a time when the European women's tournament scene had very little to offer – certainly compared with her male counterparts. For instance, at the end of the 1987 season, which was Lillian's first as a professional, Dale Reid led the order of merit with earnings of £53,815 from 19 events. Lillian's reward was £3,398 from 15 events, which left her 52nd on the list.

By comparison, Ian Woosnam led the men's list with £253,717 from 21 European Tour events. The 52nd man, fellow Welshman David Llewellyn, earned £33,461, ten times Lillian's return. Even with sponsorship, it simply didn't make sense as a worthwhile career for a woman, particularly the lonely existence for someone like Lillian, who seemed to thrive in a home environment. So, it seemed entirely predictable that she would seek to regain her amateur status, which she did in 1992.

With so much movement by players at that time, Lillian was made to pay quite a heavy price by the Royal and Ancient. It took more than three years to recover her amateur status, which she celebrated by reaching the final of the Irish Women's Close in 1996, only to be beaten 3 and 2 by Barbara Hackett at Tramore.

She declined to discuss her tournament career, other than to admit that her best performance was a seventh-place finish in a Northern Ireland event at Belvoir Park. 'Obviously, there wasn't really any money in it, unlike the men's game,' she said. 'But I've no regrets. I made a lot of friends who are still friends to this day. People like Trish Johnson, who was in the Curtis Cup in Kansas.'

Then there was Jean Rudgard, who played with Lillian as a marker for the stroke-play qualifying at Ganton. 'Seeing that I played with a number one ball all week, she gave me the gift of a number one Titleist for the final,' Lillian said. 'We then exchanged Christmas cards and I still send a card to the Ganton club every year.'

The culmination of her return to amateur ranks was what she described as 'a fantastic year.' It was 1998 when she was nominated as the ILGU's Golfer of the Year in recognition of capturing the Irish Close Championship at Clandeboye, where she beat Co. Louth's Oonagh Purfield on the 19th hole of a thrilling final. Additional successes in the Hermitage, Curragh, Heath and Waterford Scratch Cups meant generous compensation for her controversial omission from the Ireland team for the Home Internationals the previous year.

Meanwhile, she dominated Leinster golf as a member of the side that secured its fourth successive Inter-Provincial women's title. All this meant a return to Ireland selection for the Home Internationals at Burnham and Berrow GC.

'It takes a while to get over the need to be on an Irish team,' she said. 'I played top golf for nearly 20 years and the aim was always to play good enough to be selected. I'm now getting used to playing just for fun and I think I'm playing better than I ever did.'

Her adult life turning full circle, she returned to working with horses and playing golf a few times a week, maintaining the friendships she had made along the way. As proof, her handicap is a very respectable 2.7, after being cut by 0.2 in late June 2024.

Now, in her 60th year, she has embarked on another exciting phase to a fascinating career by joining Gerry Byrne's green-keeping staff at The K Club. 'With the Irish Open last year, I realised I was working on hallowed ground,' she said with an impish smile. 'It's a whole golfing world that I never really appreciated. A wonderful new adventure.'

High-flying in Honolulu

When Muriel Spark's celebrated schoolmistress, Miss Jean Brodie, addressed her pupils, among her more sage remarks was this: 'One's prime is elusive. You little girls, when you grow up, must be on the alert to recognise your prime at whatever time of your life it may occur.' From a golfing perspective, one sensed that Michelle Wie's prime was destined to occur early.

Having begun playing golf at the age of four, she went on as a 10-year-old in 2000 to become the youngest player ever to qualify for the US Women's Amateur Public Links Championship.

My first trip to Hawaii was in January 2004, prompted by Darren Clarke's qualification for the Mercedes Championships at Kapalua through his victory the previous August in the Firestone Invitational.

A week after Clarke finished third on Maui's Plantation Course for a reward of $400,000 behind Stuart Appleby, a 14-year-old schoolgirl took golf by storm.

Michelle Wie was competing in the Sony Open, a PGA Tour event at Waialae Country Club on the outskirts of Honolulu.

For me, her appearance held the promise of the greatest impact by a teenager since the emergence of Ronan Rafferty on the British and Irish scene, 25 years previously. In the late afternoon of Friday 16 January, she duly lit up the gathering darkness with the most amazing smile. After sinking a five-foot birdie putt for a remarkable second-round 68, she believed she had made history and survived the halfway cut in the $4.8 million tournament.

On reaching the recorder's cabin, however, her tender world was suddenly crushed. An official informed her that she was just a stroke away from one of the most astonishing achievements in golfing history. Yet typically, she betrayed no signs of disappointment: there were no tears, only further smiles.

With rounds of 72 and 68, she had completed 36 holes in level par, playing alongside male professionals on a par-70 course measuring 7,080 yards off the back tees. Irrespective of her failure to make the cut, it was a performance of unparalleled maturity from a player so young. And she did it by covering the last three holes in two under par.

'I think I played really great today,' she said afterwards. 'One more shot ... It's killing me. I just wish I didn't push that shot at number nine. I could have made a birdie.' She was referring to a badly blocked three-iron from a downhill lie in the middle of the fairway, followed by a duffed chip, leading to a scrambled par.

Yet such recriminations had seemed highly improbable the previous day, when more than a dozen pairs of eyes had peered through the glare from a burning sun, anxious to see the figures on the hand-held score-board. All activity on the practice range at Waialae had stopped as Ms Wie stepped onto the first tee, close by.

It should be noted that, having started her opening round on the 10th, she had covered the back nine in one over par. And nodding their heads, the pros had seemed to acknowledge an outstanding effort which, as yet, wasn't going to embarrass them.

That's when she forced them to think again. 'I never felt I was out of place,' she claimed after her opening round. And at the end of 36 holes, when asked if she would echo the words of Annika Sörenstam by admitting that she didn't belong on a men's tour, she replied confidently: 'I think I belong in both the LPGA and the PGA. I was confident I could shoot 68 in both rounds.' On the evidence of two memorable days, one didn't dare challenge that view. Indeed that 68 remains the record score for a woman in a PGA Tour event.

British and Irish enthusiasts could look forward to the chance of seeing her in action in the Curtis Cup at Formby in June of that year when, as the US Public Links champion, she would become the youngest-ever member of the visiting team. And her father, BJ, revealed that she was anxious to expand her experience of links terrain.

'I looked into the possibility of getting Michelle into the British Open but females aren't permitted,' he said. And when told that the same applied to the European Tour, he replied: 'That's a pity. It would be cool if she got a sponsor's invitation to the Irish Open [at Baltray].'

Back in Hawaii, Wie's performance came in the wake of Sörenstam's failure to survive the halfway cut at the Colonial Tournament, from which she had departed in tears the previous May, having carded rounds of 71 and 74. Then came the unavailing effort of America's Suzy Whaley in the Greater Hartford Open in July 2003, when a 36-hole aggregate of 153 left her 13 strokes outside the cut.

When Mses Wie and Sörenstam played in the Mercedes Championships pro-am on the Plantation Course in those early weeks of 2004, the Swede said of her younger colleague's prospects in the Sony: 'Experience matters a lot, and she doesn't have experience. One day, she's going to have a ton of experience to match her game. But in the meantime, we must remember she's only 14. Let her learn and have fun.'

So, how good was Ms Wie at that stage of her development? By any standards she was very good; indeed, by the standards of a 14-year-old, she was absolutely magnificent. Compared with Ernie Els, winner of that particular Sony two days later, there were undoubted similarities even to the point of being labelled The Big Wiesy, especially in the way she made an exaggerated finish to her follow-through, just like the gifted South African.

At 6ft tall, she was not your classic, string bean teenager. Rather, she presented herself as a very elegant young woman, beautifully proportioned, with a size four (US) figure which wouldn't be out of place on a fashion catwalk. She also exuded a charming, confident manner while her on-course etiquette was faultless.

As a golfer with an interlocking grip, there was evidence of expert tuition in her exemplary posture and balance, while a delightfully rhythmic swing delivered regular drives of over 300 yards.

Her iron play, surprisingly with blades, was somewhat questionable – a fault she acknowledged. And from my observations, her chipping and pitching could have been improved. But she putted very well in the second round, when nine single putts included efforts of 58 feet, 52 feet and two from 12 feet. And her five-footer at the last was stroked confidently into the centre of the cup.

At various stages of the exercise, her swing quickened somewhat from the practice rounds, but comparisons between her and the field tell their own story.

- Driving distance: Wie – 275 yds; the field – 279.9 yds
- Driving accuracy: Wie – 79%; the field – 54%
- Greens in Regulation: Wie – 67%; the field – 65%
- Par-3 average: Wie – 3.25; the field – 2.98
- Par-4: Wie – 4.17; the field – 4.10
- Par-5 – Wie – 4.50; the field – 4.46
- Average approach shot: Wie – 33ft 8ins; the field – 21ft 11ins

On the downside, there were other, slightly disturbing aspects to her Tour debut, notably in the area of commercialism – such as her Adidas golf shoes and shirts, her Astra, hipster slacks and the way she managed to have a Titleist baseball cap to match each ensemble.

Meanwhile, she found herself in the amusing position of signing autographs for her fellow pupils at the local Punahou High School, where she was a freshman. She also acknowledged the support of her playing partners, Craig Bowden, a graduate of the Nationwide Tour, and local professional Kevin Hayashi, whom she affectionately described as 'Uncle Kevin.'

His admiration was evident in a red-and-white badge he wore on his hat, carrying the legend 'Michelle No Ka Oi', which translates as 'Michelle, you're the best.' The previous week in Maui, her pro-am partners carried a huge sign that read 'Wie are so excited.' Amid all this fuss, one could easily imagine salivating management companies calculating her potential, even at that early stage.

Still, Sergio Garcia remained the only 14-year-old on either side of the Atlantic to have made the cut in a premier professional tournament. He did it in the 1995 Turespana Open Mediterrania at Escorpión in his native Valencia. Tiger Woods was 16 before dipping his toes in these particular waters in 1992, when he missed the cut in the Los Angeles Open.

Assessing precocious skills, we in Ireland remember Killarney's Bridget Gleeson, against players twice her age. Unlike Ms Wie, however, she developed only very modest power and relied mainly on a short game to compete successfully beyond her years.

Michelle's Korean-born father, BJ, was a professor of transportation at the University of Hawaii. Having migrated to the US to be educated in Pennsylvania, where his height of 6ft 2ins belied his oriental origins, he married his wife, Bo, and moved to Hawaii in 1988. Michelle was their only child. He explained:

> Some members of our extended family view me as being pushy where Michelle is concerned, but I prefer to think of myself as encouraging. Whether a child's talent happens to lie in sport or music or whatever, it's a parent's duty to ensure that it isn't lost.
>
> So, I encourage Michelle to practise hard at her golf. But at the same time, I try to make sure that she doesn't lose touch with her friends. And, of course, to be aware that she's only 14, with

everything that that entails. Like indulging her love of television and of shopping for jewellery items, especially earrings.

Two years later, in 2006, I was back in Honolulu to watch another attempt by Wie in the Sony. This time, I noted that she was unable to hold back the tears, like a bewildered teenager who had just been ditched by her high-school sweetheart. Her reaction to a first-round 79 on the Thursday became an enduring image, even though seven sparking birdies gave hope of a miracle en route to a second-round 68 – two under par.

The 11-stroke improvement for a halfway total of 147 included her worst and equal-best rounds in a PGA Tour event and saw her miss the cut by four strokes. Since I had first seen her in 2004, she had been transformed into a 16-year-old $10 million commodity with a Hollywood agent. And we were assured that this weekend's effort, which contained some wonderful driving on Waialae's wind-swept stretch, didn't really matter in terms of her long-term development.

The juxtaposition of two comments on Friday evening captured the novelty of her situation. 'I would love to play in another couple of men's events this year,' she said. Then, when asked what her next assignment was, she replied: 'I have to study.'

Modelling Nike Golf's spring line, which was due in the stores six months later, she was making her seventh appearance in a men's tournament, ranging from events in the US, Canada and Japan to the US Nationwide Tour, without ever making the cut.

Taken at face value, her latest incarnation could have been viewed as a fascinating project, a classic exercise in modern commercialism. What might be termed the Wie for All reminded me of the 1970s and the then Manchester United manager, Tommy Docherty, referring to the chase for the signature of Home Farm player Martin Murray as the 'Murray-go-round.'

In one crucial respect, however, this was disturbingly different. Her press conferences made me decidedly uncomfortable for having us observe a gifted girl being thrust into a man's world with no apparent thought for her vulnerable youth. Her previous appearances in the Sony were entirely different for the fact that she made them as an amateur with no strings attached.

Tom Lehman endorsed this view, giving her the charming nickname 'The Big Wiesy' on first setting eyes on her in the Maui pro-am. 'The pressures on her are greater now than they were in 2004, simply because the expectations are higher,' he said. 'My opinion is that you need to grow and I kind of think Michelle has skipped a couple of steps. In the short term it's going to hurt her because she's got to learn how to win things. That's very important, whatever age you are.' Wie hadn't won anything since capturing the 2003 US Women's Amateur Public Links Championship, which had become somewhat devalued by that stage.

The most recent memories were of an unfortunate professional debut in the women's Samsung World Championship in the US in October 2005, when she was disqualified for an illegal drop.

One mischievous US scribe had a bit of fun at her expense, by writing about 'a tall, beautiful and very wealthy princess' who was the 'rock star of the realm,' and how she made 'a correctable error, if only her royal advisers had told her about it in time, because beautiful princesses employ many royal advisers who do this sort of thing for them so they can concentrate on being beautiful, wealthy and tall.'

Wie was not short of advisers. 'This week is no big deal in her life,' insisted her mind coach Dr Jim Loehr. Then there was swing coach David Leadbetter, who famously guided Nick Faldo to major triumphs and claimed to have given her a tighter swing and a better short game. The swing had certainly improved but her putting was decidedly streaky, betraying sharp fluctuations in feel.

For instance, when carding 79 on the Thursday, she three-putted twice and an average of no better than 2.0 putts for every green hit in regulation ranked her 105th in a field of 144. Meanwhile, average drives of 272 yards left her ranked last in the field and a formidable 66.2 yards behind the leader Jeff Gove (338.6).

Leadbetter, who prompted her to read a biography of Babe Zaharias, the last woman to make the cut in the US PGA tour event in 1945, turned to the reliable old 'learning curve' to explain her lack of success. 'She's a pioneer and there's no doubt she's going to win and win a lot,' he said. 'But when you're limited in how many events you play in – as she is – and against the best players in the world, men and women, the chances of winning are less.'

Therein lay Wie's biggest problem. Her father, a university lecturer, and mother, a former Korean beauty pageant winner, seemed determined that their daughter should finish high school and go on to Stanford University, which Tiger Woods attended before turning professional as a 20-year-old. Apart from her undoubted golfing talent, she was clearly a very bright girl, who spoke Korean, English and Japanese and was in the process of learning Mandarin.

All this seemed to have been of no concern, however, to Nike and Sony, who were reported to have signed her on contracts worth $10 million between them. For reference, this was $2 million more than Sörenstam commanded in endorsements. And Sony reaped a dividend even before the deal, in that Wie had boosted attendances at their Hawaii tournament by up to 30 per cent over three years.

'In the spotlight by playing tournaments from when I was 12, I grew up a lot faster than maybe I had to,' Wie said. 'Going to college helped me be a normal 18-year-old and that was something I needed. I could keep training, but I needed something more to help me be well-rounded. I dreamed all my life about going to Stanford.'

She went on to win five LPGA events including the 2014 US Women's Open, her only Major. Having fallen a stroke behind Stacy Lewis through a double-bogey on the 70th, she birdied the next and parred the last hole for a par-70 final round and a two-stroke triumph. She made only one cut in a men's tournament: at the rain-shortened 2006 SK Telecom Open on the Asian Tour. Her last appearance in a men's professional event was at the 2008 Legends Reno-Tahoe Open on the PGA Tour, where she shot rounds of 73 and 80 to miss the cut by nine strokes.

Her presence on the US Solheim Cup team at Killeen Castle in 2011 enhanced the event's appeal significantly. Especially when she battled for a decisive point against Suzann Pettersen, one of the strongest competitors in Solheim history. As it happened, the irrepressible Norwegian gained a superb victory by winning the last three holes with birdies to edge clear by one hole.

In March 2019, Wie announced that she was engaged to Jonnie West, Director of Basketball Operations for the Golden State Warriors and the son of national basketball legend Jerry West. They married on 10 August 2019, at a private home in Beverly Hills, California. Five months later, she declared she was pregnant and expressed interest in eventually returning to competitive golf. On 19 June 2020, she gave birth to a daughter named Makenna and in May 2022, Wie said she would be stepping away from the game following the US Women's Open at Pebble Beach in July.

She made a surprise return in June 2024 at Pinehurst, the scene of her US Women's Open triumph 10 years before. This time, it was in a ceremonial capacity. Attired in a long black dress which accentuated her height, she formally invited the 13 legendary women who had launched the LPGA Tour back in 1950, some decades before she was born, into the Golf Hall of Fame. The honouring of Pádraig Harrington would come later in the evening.

As I was subsequently discussing the evening's events with the golf broadcaster, Shane O'Donoghue, he suggested to me that the 13 inductees honoured by Ms Wie could have been 14, had Philomena Garvey succumbed to a tempting inducement when the LPGA was being formed. Apparently, Fred Corcoran, the highly regarded American agent, wanted Ms Garvey to join his professional team. She had been strongly recommended to him by none other than the great Babe Zaharias.

They had clashed in a transatlantic match on which the *Washington Post* reported: 'America's women completed a clear 9-0 sweep over the International women's team led by Diane Critchley at Sunningdale. Fair-haired Philomena Garvey, 24-year-old Irish champion, was the only member of the home side to offer serious resistance. Miss Zaharias won by one hole over 36 holes.' Typically modest, Phil later remarked: 'I was always put at the top of the order to be devoured.' The match with the Babe was supposed to have been over 18 holes, which Phil won one-up, but they played again in the afternoon, this time with victory going to the American.

Sixty years on, and with the experience of having worked for an extended period with Ms Wie, Leadbetter was prompted to make this expansive prediction: 'Once she starts putting well, watch out!' Sadly, his confidence served only to confirm Lee Trevino's famous claim that when God hands out skills in golf, he always holds something back.

For all her gifts, the most remarkable young player I have ever seen didn't have the putting skill to allow her to reach her full potential. It was the one visible gift that God denied her.

17

Bowing to a Demanding Craft

On a bleak morning that somehow managed to escape mid-winter, they stood as lonely figures on the practice ground at Killeen Castle. Looking at the Maguire twins, an immediate thought was of sacrifice and dedication. And the phenomenon of precocious talent.

There was something decidedly odd about 14-year-olds wanting to be so engaged with golf during a break from school rather than lounging at home, listening to pop music and making phone calls to their friends. But this was clearly what Leona and Lisa Maguire wanted to be doing, as a build-up to the 2009 Lancôme Irish Ladies Close Championship that was going to start a few days later at Fota Island.

Their father, Declan, was also there, and their seven-year-old brother, Odhran, who seemed determined to upstage his sisters with some truly remarkable ball-striking for one so young. Completing the intimate gathering was the girls' coach, Shane O'Grady.

In his book *In Search of the Tiger*, Tom Callahan quotes Jack Nicklaus remembering his tutor, Jack Grout, in similar circumstances. 'I'd hit balls for an hour and he wouldn't say a word,' recalled the Bear. 'Then he'd say,

"Looks good, Jackie Buck. Maybe we ought to take that left hand and just slip it over a little bit ....'"

More recently, there had also been the celebrated relationship between Tiger Woods and his coach Butch Harmon, arranged by the player's father, Earl. The prodigy was 17 at the time and viewed by the coach as 'that once-in-a-lifetime dream guy.'

But let us return to the Maguire twins. 'From the first day Declan came to me, I was conscious of the huge responsibility I had been handed,' O'Grady recalled. 'The girls were ten-and-a-half at the time and I saw instantly their potential. Serious talent. Then, when he came to me again, he seemed happy that we got on together, especially the interaction between us.'

The resident professional at Black Bush GC, outside Dunshaughlin, went on:

> We sat down and outlined a plan in which I assured him that nothing would be overlooked. Then, in the course of further lessons, their special qualities were reinforced. Potential world beaters. From the outset, they were easy to teach, but their development had to be taken one stage at a time. And they understood that.
>
> Technically, they're not the same. They're individuals with two different swings and I allowed them to develop that way. Lisa, for instance, has a slightly brisker action. And their chipping and putting actions are also different. Even though they're twins, you can see the difference if you stand and watch them.
>
> Even with all the success they've had at such a young age, they want to get better. Which is great fun for me, instead of having to battle with pupils who think they're better than they are. But there have been differences along the way. We've fallen out on occasions, though thankfully, not for long.

It struck me that we sometimes take our mentors lightly, overlooking their remarkable patience and attention to detail. In this respect, Declan

Maguire reflects the best qualities of his profession as a schoolteacher – a quiet, thoughtful man who wants only the right things for his girls.

So what is it like, raising remarkably gifted children? 'I've found that the real challenge is to balance everything,' he replied. 'As schoolgirls, their first priority has to be the Junior Cert next year. Schooling must come first, yet their golf is very much a part of it, because if they weren't golfing, they probably wouldn't be happy at school. So, you've got to keep everything in tandem, which can be difficult.'

He continued:

> The type of characters they are, they're perfectionists in everything they do. At school, their work has to be done to perfection. They won't go into school with things half done. Of course this can be a cross; setting very high standards for yourself and feeling unfulfilled if you don't achieve them.
>
> But that's their nature; something in them that just can't be changed. And to be honest, I wouldn't want to change them. I see it as a part of them which must be nurtured.
>
> I'm essentially a facilitator, taking a back seat as much as possible and allowing them to become more independent; to be able to make decisions for themselves. Myself and Breda [his wife, who is also a schoolteacher] are in the background doing the planning. Breda probably does most of it. Arranging flights and accommodation when they're playing abroad.
>
> Shane [O'Grady] and I tend to plan their playing schedule, conscious of what's in their best interests. There are lots of times when they're pulled from all sides; when they get too much golf. That's a danger for players so young. But at the same time I've got to keep them challenged; raising the bar for them, but not so high that they'll be overwhelmed.

Their first exposure to golf occurred when Declan brought them to the North West of Ireland Open at Slieve Russell, their present club, not far from their home in Ballyhugh, Co. Cavan. That was in August 2000, when Henrik Stenson, who later captured the 2016 Open Championship at Royal Troon, was in the field. So was another future Major winner, Justin Rose. And the Maguires gave Scott Drummond a bed for the week.

Swimming was still their main sport, however, until a fateful weekend in Enniskillen, when Lisa fell in a playground and cracked her elbow. This put her out of swimming for eight weeks and when Declan brought her for a return visit, the specialist suggested that while the arm had healed perfectly, she was protecting it, and he should encourage her to try some racket sports to increase her mobility.

'That's how golf came into their lives,' he recalled:

> That summer, they joined a par-three course and I bought just three clubs because, it being August, I thought they'd do it for a little time and then lose interest. But they eagerly went back for a second week. Then they went to Castle Hulme [a golf club in Enniskillen] where they played in a four-hole competition which Leona won.
>
> This was 2004, when they were nine going on 10. They were due to go to Mosney for the all-Ireland swimming on a Saturday but there was a par-three competition in which Leona wanted to play. They're the type of girls who, when they get an interest in something, they want to perfect it.

So it was that they embarked on a sport which could not be perfected. But as with the great Ben Hogan, who vainly sought golfing perfection, everything had to be right, even to the point of treating practice rounds as an important tournament.

As often happens with twins, Leona is right-handed and Lisa is left-handed. They both play right-handed, though Lisa had a left-handed club that she often hit shots with. 'Dad just started us right-handed and I'm told that if you're left-handed with your left hand at the top of the club, it's a wee bit stronger that way,' she said.

Lisa wore a blue cap and Leona a white one; otherwise, they were dressed identically. The previous year at Westport, Leona beat her sister in the final of the Irish Close, though Lisa had the consolation of winning the Leitrim Cup as leading qualifier. Trophies then continued to pile up for both of them.

Getting her revenge for Westport, Lisa beat Leona in the final of the 2008 Irish Girls Championship before going on to win the European Girls' title in France, in which Leona was runner-up. They then went to Louisville, Kentucky as members of the European Junior Ryder.

In 2009, Leona won the French Under-21 title and the Scottish Ladies for the Helen Holm Championship, in which Lisa won third place. Then Lisa became Close champion, and they combined to retain the Irish Schools title for Loreto, Cavan. A year on, they both gained Curtis Cup honours at the tender age of 15.

Almost inevitably, the question arose as to who the better player was, but such assessments seemed insensitive at best. Instead, I asked them about their rivalry. Here's how they responded:

> *Lisa*: 'I suppose we're a little like the Williams sisters who seem fierce when they're playing against each other in Wimbledon and US Open matches. But off court, they're still best friends. It's kinda the same with us, though we're not on their level yet.' This latter line was delivered with a modest smile.
>
> *Leona*: 'People say that twins know how each other is feeling, but I don't really think that's true. I'd know Lisa's weaknesses and strengths mainly from practising so much together and playing foursomes with her. And I'm able to use that to my advantage in a match.' And exploit a perceived weakness? 'Well, you're trying to win.' At this, both girls laughed.
>
> *Lisa*: 'Playing against each other is very much like playing against anybody else. You're out to win. Perhaps you might be more competitive against somebody else, but you're still out to win. We might talk to each other going around, but at the end of the day

your target is to win more holes than she's going to win. You have to treat it like any other match.'

'So, it's not that you necessarily want Leona to lose, it's that you want to win?' I asked. 'Yes, that's it.'

Leona: 'Playing each other doesn't bother me. Nobody is going to remember whether it was Lisa you were playing against or not. But the nice thing is that if we're in the final, the cup is going back to the house at the end of the day.'

Finally, I wondered about having both parents as teachers. 'Well, they make sure you get your schoolwork done,' replied Lisa with a wry smile. 'Like after being in Scotland recently, they made sure we caught up on all our schoolwork before we went back out on the golf course. It's great that they're off in the summer to bring us to tournaments, but they have to sacrifice a lot, bringing us all over the place.'

Soon they were back hitting shots, smashing drives more than 240 yards into the cold Meath air. You couldn't help but marvel at what they had achieved at such a young age, and how they would be coming to full bloom.

It was more than 12 years later when I met them together again. They were at Rathfarnham GC and Leona was doing a business day, fresh from her base in the US where she had recorded a stunning 4.5 points on a Solheim Cup debut in Toledo. Like the rest of us, Lisa had now become an interested observer.

Without prompting, she remembered that Killeen practice-ground meeting with herself and her sister as 14-year-olds. 'My plan now is to enjoy my golf as a social outlet,' she said. It had been thirteen months since her decision to quit the professional scene to study dentistry at University College Cork.

'I'm still competitive and I plan to continue playing for the rest of my life. In due course, I'll probably apply for my amateur status back.' On this point, I imagined the authorities treating her gently, given that she was a professional for only seventeen months.

Did she see herself playing amateur for Ireland again? 'I honestly don't know,' she replied:

> The main thing is getting back into the game as a club member and enjoying it. I don't even know what my handicap would be. I'll probably start at inter-club level then work my way to interprovincial again. Through the ranks. I'm definitely not finished with competitive golf.
>
> I've seen Leona at all the levels. Very successful amateur and very successful in college. That's the way Leona does things. Achieves the highest level at whatever she sets her mind to, then moves on to the next challenge.
>
> The really nice thing about the Solheim was the exposure it got all over the world, including here in Ireland. It gave people the chance of seeing a side of Leona they hadn't seen before. They could see how she belongs among the best players in the world.

She paused before saying with some emphasis:

> I'm not jealous of Leona. I'm 100 per cent behind everything she does. Would I like to be in her shoes? Absolutely. But I made a decision based on what I knew I was capable of.
>
> I had seen players hang on for longer than they should have and I promised myself it wouldn't happen to me. Golf has been good to us and I believe it will continue to be good to all of us.

Before departing Rathfarnham, I happened to see the two sisters having afternoon tea in the corner of the lounge. They seemed eagerly engaged with each other, chatting animatedly.

A demanding game may have sent them down separate paths, but now they were back on a shared objective, going home for Christmas.

A few months later, in February 2022, Leona became the first Irish winner on the LPGA Tour, capturing the Drive On Championship in Fort Myers by three strokes from Lexi Thomson. In early July 2024, she made the breakthrough on the LET, the European equivalent, with an eagle on the final hole for a spectacular victory in the Aramco Team Series at the Centurion Club in London.

Appropriately, Lisa was there to see her do it and spray her triumphant sister with champagne.

18

Verbal Masters

A great joy during one of my longer journeys was meeting with the celebrated American broadcaster, Jack Whitaker. He proved to be marvellous company, very much at odds with the image conveyed by a notorious episode during the Masters at Augusta National.

We met at Gulf Harbour GC, on the outskirts of Auckland, New Zealand in November 1998, when Paul McGinley and Pádraig Harrington were attempting to defend the World Cup they had captured at Kiawah Island 12 months previously. On this occasion, the Dubliners finished sixth for a reward of $30,000 each, a combined four strokes behind the victorious English duo of Nick Faldo and David Carter.

Were he around now, with much focus on the D-Day landings through the 80th anniversary celebrations, chances are that the international media would list Whitaker among those American heroes who fought in the Normandy campaign, where he was wounded by an artillery strike.

Instead, he remains the broadcaster who was banned from a primary role in covering the Masters for CBS after Augusta's chairman, Clifford Roberts, took offence at the expression 'Here comes the mob'. It was a simple, spontaneous reference to the arrival of the gallery at the 18th hole at the end of a playoff in 1966, which led indirectly to the current clichéd references to 'patrons' for Masters spectators.

Six years later, Whitaker was invited by CBS to attend the 1972 Masters as a guest, essentially a spectator. Clearly the network felt bad about what had happened, and their one-time star was happy to let them off the hook. 'I said okay,' was his reaction:

> So I went back and I'm up on the second floor of the clubhouse having breakfast with Claude Harmon and Cary Middlecoff. And Claude's telling us some of those marvellous stories of his. Suddenly, there was a tap on my shoulder and Frank Chirkinian [the long-time CBS golf producer, now retired] says: 'Henry Longhurst has just gone to the hospital and you're going to do 16. So we'd better go down and talk to the old man [Roberts].'

Whitaker was understandably apprehensive:

> Down we went to the man, the ogre who had banned me and who used to critique every telecast. As I walked in, Chirkinian said 'Mr Roberts, this is Jack Whitaker.' And he got up and said: 'Young man. We're very fortunate that you're here. Welcome.' And that was it. I was back. And I remember thinking that maybe he wasn't such a bad guy after all.

But there was still a price to be paid. Longhurst, a treasured English voice at the Masters, returned to broadcasting action the following day and though Whitaker was retained for the 14th hole that year, he had lost the anchor position to Pat Summerall. He would never regain that coveted seat of broadcasting authority.

On meeting him that day in New Zealand, the first thing I noticed were the two obtrusive hearing aids that allowed a greater clarity of speech when engaging him in conversation. For his part, the famous voice had retained the authoritative vigour that held such appeal for CBS and ABC network audiences over 40 years.

At one time, he was as familiar a figure around the upper room of the old colonial clubhouse as the game's leading competitors. But Jack

Whitaker had no plans for a return to Augusta National. 'They got tougher on the badges a few years ago and I couldn't get beyond the ropes and into the clubhouse,' he informed me. 'It's a lot different going to the Masters if you can't do that.' A view with which I had no difficulty empathising.

Whitaker entered network sports with CBS in 1961, when he did play-by-play for the Philadelphia Eagles of the NFL and hosted the anthology series, CBS Sports Spectacular, among other duties. He worked for CBS for more than two decades and was probably best remembered for his coverage of golf and horse racing.

Now, he was with his wife, Nancy Chaffee, a three-time former US indoor tennis champion, who also reached the semi-finals of the Wimbledon mixed doubles with Tony Trabert. 'She got to be number four in the world,' he said with obvious pride.

He continued: 'She was married at one stage to a famous baseball player in the United States – Ralph Kiner, a Hall-of-Famer. We had known each other and after she had been divorced about 20 years and I had been divorced about 18, we just met one time and decided, "Let's go". So that was how we got married in 1989. It's great.'

Wearing a collar and tie, a sports jacket and twill slacks, the only informal piece of his outfit was a somewhat incongruous baseball cap. Otherwise, this legend of American broadcasting was very much a product of the old school. And looking back, I wonder what he would have made of the informality of modern attire, even in golf clubs.

Humility, they say, is truth. After only a short time in Whitaker's company, I sensed that there would be no false modesty when discussing his chosen craft.

'I've got to accept that I belong to another generation, but I still think aspects of sport have got out of hand,' he said.

> We have basketball and baseball players and footballers being paid a king's ransom while we can't pay our schoolteachers and sanitation engineers a decent salary.
>
> People will tell you it's what the marketplace will bear. But I don't understand the enormous prices they pay for the franchises

> in the United States and then they keep paying more money to the players while they complain about the money the players are getting. It's like *Alice in Wonderland*.

As for his own craft, he went on: 'In the old days, a network was known by its news department which gave it its character and personality. Now it's known by its sports department. I don't think that's an advance.'

Had he become a crotchety old man? 'I hope not,' he replied:

> I think that players today are better, no question about that. There is a greater depth of talent, but where stars are concerned, I believe Ben Hogan would dominate golf now just as he did in his day. Just as [Gene] Sarazen, [Walter] Hagen and [Bobby] Jones would do.
>
> The current generation have been raised differently to the way we were raised. Their values are different. I like to watch good football and I applaud the achievement of Mark McGwire and Sammy Sosa because they're decent people. One's an Irish Catholic and the other's a Dominican Republic Catholic. There was a joy in their performance that appealed to me. But that's so obviously lacking in the fellows who are there just to take the money.'

And what was the essence of good broadcasting in his experience? He didn't hesitate:

> Preparation, a command of the English language, a love of what you're doing and an innate sense of knowing when to speak and when to shut up. Obviously, preparation is very important. If you try to be the best you can and it's not good enough, well that's okay in my book.
>
> I've been in the business for 50 years and I find that discipline is an ongoing challenge. I think people talk too much most of the time.

Against this background, he appeared to have no regrets about incurring the wrath of golf's most ruthless autocrat. This was long before a CBS successor, Gary McCord, had been shown the door for references to body-bags and bikini wax.

With no hint of wishing to bypass this painful episode, he volunteered: 'Yes, I said there was a mob scene at the 18th when they all broke ...'. He paused to gather his thoughts. 'It had been a very long day, a Monday play-off and if you go over 6.00 on American television with a sporting event you're into the local news which is a no-no. An absolute no-no. This was going over 7.00 o'clock, which was the network news with Walter Cronkite and that was absolutely anathema.'

As it happened, there was a good number of first-time spectators there that day, using passes they had acquired from regular ticket holders who couldn't wait for the play-off. And as the three contestants, Jack Nicklaus, Gay Brewer and Tommy Jacobs, approached the final green, Whitaker was concerned that the crowd's unruly behaviour could cause a further delay.

'I was rushing to get off the air as Nicklaus sank the winning putt and I said, "Here comes the mob."' he recalled. Clifford Roberts was so incensed by the remark that he instructed CBS to remove Whitaker from future Masters telecasts. As Whitaker explained:

> When they told me six or seven months later that I wasn't going to be back at the Masters, the reason they gave me was that I called the gallery a mob. I was also told that I had failed to inform the viewers that there would be a green-jacket ceremony on the putting green.
>
> It really stung. But I was more angry with CBS than I was with the Masters for not notifying me earlier about my so-called fall from grace. I never quite believed the reasons they gave me. When it came down to it, I think it must have been that they just didn't like me.

Adopting a philosophical tone, he continued: 'But it turned out to be a good thing for me in that I got a lot of sympathy afterwards.'

Later on, he was assigned to cover the spectacular long 13th, which he loved. 'In the tower there, you're back away from the people,' he explained. 'It's a lovely site and so many dramatic things tend to happen there. So I stayed there until I left for ABC in 1982.'

When I was indelicate enough to enquire about his age, the reply came in horse-racing terms. 'I'm rising to my 74th fence,' he replied proudly. 'And I've been in the broadcasting business since I got out of college in 1937 and went into radio. In 1950, I joined television where I've been ever since.'

Lowering his voice as if in wistful memory of happy bygone days, he went on: 'My first TV job was in Philadelphia at the local CBS station and I moved from there to the CBS network in New York, 12 years later. I was there until 1982 when I moved over to ABC. Six years ago, I retired from ABC and I'm now on my own, I suppose you could say freelancing.'

He then described the varied nature of his work:

> From an early stage, it became apparent to me that television had a great appetite for sport. And sure enough, I found myself doing everything from ice skating to American football, baseball, track and field – athletics as you call them – and soccer.
>
> When the first great experience with soccer in the United States was led by the New York Cosmos, I had the enormous pleasure of seeing Pele play. Even though he was nearing the end of his career you could see that he was something special.
>
> In later years, from about 1977 on, I concentrated mainly on golf and horse-racing. Along with baseball, they became my three great loves. Nowadays I don't do the horses anymore, but I do five Shell Wonderful World of Golf programmes every year.
>
> My heroes? Joe DiMaggio and a great football player from Notre Dame by the name of Charlie Lujack. Charlie and me are now good friends and I see him in the desert every winter, in the Palm Springs area.

In fact, all those heroes of my college football days, Glenn Davis and Lujack, they're all kind of pals now. And it all happened because of somebody asking me when a certain sportscaster quit, if I knew anything about sport. I didn't know half as much as I pretended, but of course I said yes.

I often wonder what would have happened had I stayed in news. I wouldn't have had as much fun, but it might have been more interesting. But no. I've no regrets.

From a professional standpoint, few gaps needed to be filled. He won three Emmy Awards: for Outstanding Host or Commentator in 1979, for writing in 1990 and the Lifetime Achievement award in 2012. The Broadcast Pioneers of Philadelphia, his native city, named Whitaker their Person of the Year in 1981 and inducted him into their Hall of Fame in 2003.

Over the years, he established first-name relationships with some of golf's greatest names. During the 1987 Masters, when he was passing the ninth green at Augusta, this voice with a familiar colonial twang rang out: 'Jack, who's going to win the [Kentucky] Derby?' Whitaker replied that he liked a horse called Indian Charlie. Then he and Gary Player continued to talk about horse-racing on the walk to the 10th tee. He considers himself similarly fortunate in becoming acquainted with Ben Hogan, Gene Sarazen, Byron Nelson and, of course, Jack Nicklaus and Arnold Palmer.

'I never got to know Hogan well, but I was in his company about four or five times,' he recalled:

> One such occasion was a dinner in Fort Worth at the Colonial and I sat between him and Valerie and had a great evening.
>
> Ben was funny and marvellous company. I would love to have got to know him, but I never really had the chance. Either way, I found him to be completely different from his popular, media image. Nicklaus I was fortunate enough to cover in his hey-day. ABC hired him as an analyst, and we worked the Major championships together. I remember the 1982 US Open [at Pebble Beach]

when I did an interview with him on the edge of the bay while Watson was walking to his ball on 17.

Jack had had five birdies on the front nine and having finished his round, he was now tied with [Tom] Watson. And when Watson hit it in the heavy rough at 17, it looked as if Nicklaus was certain of at least a tie. I know that was the way Nicklaus was thinking.

From the tower, we watched as Watson sank that famous chip on 17 and Jack just sagged beside me. Finally, he said, 'that's the second time the sonofabitch has done that to me.' Which, of course, was a reference to the 1977 British Open at Turnberry. It was quite a moment, and I was amazed at the way he carried it off.

There was no way of knowing how much it hurt him. Shortly afterwards he was congratulating Tom and being his usual, charming self. It must have hurt him desperately to see the record fifth US Open being torn from his grasp but you would never have known.

I think most golfers do that very well – the good ones certainly. It's part of the game. To be a good golfer, the first thing you've got to learn is patience and not to get mad at yourself like I do. Cover your emotions. I think it's remarkable and I wish we all had their level of self-control.

His thoughts then drifted back to Augusta National and a special golfing week which has had a profound impact on his career. 'Golf is a lot like horse-racing,' he mused. 'You lose more often than you win. Golf teaches you to take the knocks and move on to the next shot.'

There wasn't a hint of rancour as he concluded: 'I've done enough Masters. Even with all that's happened there, I've enough nice memories from the place to see me out. It's been a great experience.'

And what of sporting events in general? 'My outstanding memory of covering a sports event was Secretariat winning the Belmont Stakes by 31 lengths in 1973,' he said. 'That was a much more dominant achievement, in my view, than the 1997 Masters win by Tiger Woods [by a 12-shot margin].'

Warming to what was clearly one of his favourite sporting decades, he openly expressed his enthusiasm for this remarkable racehorse:

> Secretariat was a good-looking horse. He seemed to be able to win off the pace or when setting the pace.
>
> His sire was Bold Lad which never could go the distance and Secretariat always had detractors because of this, despite all the records he smashed, including the Kentucky Derby. They said he would never make the distance in the Preakness Stakes, which is the second in our triple crown series.
>
> When he got to Belmont, it was right in the middle of our Watergate scandal and the country desperately needed a hero, from wherever. And Secretariat was it. He was the people's horse and to prove it, his picture was on the cover of *Time*. And when he delivered this smashing performance, the response was amazing.
>
> People began to cry and jump up and down with emotion. I suppose it would have been a bit like the reaction to Red Rum in the English Grand National, except more so. You may question whether it's possible to feel that way about a horse. Believe me it is. I didn't think so at first, but I soon became a convert.
>
> Secretariat was easy to like, a feisty horse with a personality. He could be friendly, but he could also nip you if the mood took him. He had that look about him as if he understood you and everything about you. Yes, I can become attached to horses.

From there, the conversation turned to Muhammed Ali and how Whitaker became involved in broadcasts of three Ali fights:

> They weren't the great ones but at a time when Ali still had enormous appeal. It was a time when CBS was weak in its evening programming, so they put on an Ali fight against Jean-Pierre Coopnan, the so-called Lion of Flanders.
>
> It took place down in the ballroom of a hotel in Puerto Rico and was transmitted in primetime. It was a terrible fight, with

Ali carrying him for five rounds before it came to its inevitable end. But it took us through the primetime period and carried the ratings for a whole month at CBS.

In fact, it was so successful that they decided to do it again. And so, we went to Las Vegas where Ali met Leon Spinks – and got beaten. Then he won the title back and we did another fight in Yankee Stadium against Ken Norton. It was a heck of a fight which, if memory serves me correctly, Norton won. That was my experience with Ali when he was effectively carrying the CBS Network.

When I asked about his favourite sportsperson, there was no attempt at being accommodating to a non-American. 'I have two favourites,' he replied. 'Art Rooney was just a delight. I wish you had known him. He was the owner of the Pittsburgh Steelers in the NFL and was probably the nicest gentleman that I ever met in sport.

'The other one happened to be Wathen Knebelkamp, who was president of Churchill Downs. He left a distillery business to run a baseball team in Louisville and from there he went to become president of Churchill Downs. And he was a gentleman to his fingertips. A great administrator but a gentleman.'

Whitaker was born in Philadelphia on 18 May 1924, and it was also in Pennsylvania that he died on 18 August 2019. I find it interesting that he emphasised the importance of gentlemanly behaviour in others because that's the characteristic I best remember about his treatment of me, a total stranger, on a golf course in New Zealand 26 years ago.

'They think it's all over ...'

The death of Mícheál Ó Muircheartaigh in June 2024 was a reminder of the countless broadcasters who lent their voices to GAA commentary over the years. Some enthused us, others irritated and others still simply bored us. Only a select few have remained in our memory as experts in their craft.

Among that group was Kenneth Wolstenholme – the same man who claimed a unique place in broadcasting history through an unforgettable finale to his commentary on England's triumph over West Germany in the 1966 soccer World Cup final.

That was when he captured the sporting dreams of a generation in the iconic phrase: 'They think it's all over ... it is now.' Indeed, we may describe these words as immortal, given that Wolstenholme passed from us in March 2002.

I had caught up with him a while before when, as a 75-year-old, he could still be heard on the Italian soccer segment on RTE and Channel 4's Gazzetta d'Italia. The splendid voice had softened pleasantly over the years and a sharp memory allowed him to reflect on visits to Croke Park for BBC commentaries on All-Ireland finals.

'I have fond memories of the 1958 World Cup finals in Sweden, where Northern Ireland made such a wonderful impact,' he said. 'You probably know that Sweden is a very Protestant country: religion seems to be very important there. Anyway, they concluded that the reason Northern Ireland were doing so well was because they were playing for the Pope.

> That raised a great laugh because, as I remember it, Peter Docherty, the manager of the side, was their only Catholic. But with a view to taking a rise out of their hosts, the entire Northern Ireland party went to church the following Sunday. Eventually, the Swedes learned the truth and they loved it.

By 1959, when I was learning my craft as a copy boy at the *Evening Press*, Wolstenholme was considered a sufficiently experienced broadcaster to attempt his first All-Ireland final. He covered both finals that year, including a replay in the hurling in which Waterford ultimately triumphed.

Smiling warmly at the memory, he said: 'The football [between Kerry and Galway] was straightforward enough, but the hurling was a different matter. Michael O'Hehir, who was commentating of course for

Radio Éireann at the time, was a great help, acquainting me with established cliches of the game, such as "the clash of the ash".'

He further recalled that as a gesture to their visitor from the BBC, Croke Park officials presented him with a hurley. It happened to be the one used by Waterford's great midfielder Seamus Power in scoring the equalising goal. And, of course, Waterford went on to win the replay.

'I enjoyed my visits to Dublin, particularly my meetings with Pádraig Ó Caoimh, the secretary of the GAA,' Wolstenholme added. 'His liberal attitude to sport surprised me at a time when I was aware of the GAA ban against "foreign games".

> But there were a few embarrassing moments. Like when I was offered a drink and replied 'Scotch and water', which brought the gentle reproach that the only whiskey they had was Irish. Another was the occasion when my report on one of the matches was edited for *Sportsview* and the director devoted quite a bit of time to players fighting. I know the Irish blamed me for that, but, in fact, the matter was outside my control.

When I discussed my Wolstenholme interview with a respected colleague, David Guiney, he recalled 'a great buzz at Croke Park over the fact that the BBC had sent an outside broadcast unit to cover the All-Irelands.' Soon, with the establishment of Teilifís Éireann and O'Hehir's appointment as its first head of sport, the country was in a position to provide its own service in televised sport. However, Wolstenholme remained a highly influential figure.

Dramatically, at the height of his powers, he parted with the BBC. His last broadcast for them was the 1971 European Cup final. 'My contract had expired and there was a disagreement over its renewal,' he explained. 'Of course I was disappointed. In those days everyone wanted to work for the BBC.'

He achieved renewed popularity through the famous phrase mentioned earlier, however, particularly from its use as the title of a BBC sports-comedy quiz programme, headed by Nick Hancock. This offended him. 'I hate to see it being trivialised in this way, not least because I suspect it doesn't mean anything to the people involved,' he said.

Then, presumably for the umpteenth time, he revisited those fateful moments in extra time at Wembley, where England were leading by 3–2. He recalls:

> There was only a short time remaining, and I can remember a lot of whistling around the ground. Then I noticed some spectators coming onto the pitch and I said on the air 'they think it's all over.'
>
> As I spoke those words, I could see Bobby Moore passing the ball to Geoff Hurst and as Hurst shot for goal, I finished the phrase 'it is now.' Instinctively, I knew he was going to score. In fact, there's a marvellous picture of that shot, taken by a photographer from behind the goal.

In addition to the crushing disappointment of his break with the BBC, Wolstenholme tragically lost one of his two daughters to leukaemia. However, he could reflect on the enormous personal satisfaction of becoming virtually a household name to successive generations, even in GAA circles in this country.

'Of course I'm glad I said it,' he acknowledged of a phrase that is quite correctly regarded as the most famous in the history of sports broadcasting. 'The BBC have been very good in allowing the particular segment to be shown in all sorts of circumstances. Which means that through royalties, I have made a lot of money out of it.'

Then came a gentle chuckle as he mused: 'I've often wondered why some newspaper has never bothered to track down and interview one of those people who encroached on the Wembley pitch. Without them, you know, I would never have said it.'

19

Tragedy and Triumph for the Foley Family

2021

This is a story about the Foley family from Clontarf in north Dublin. It's about Irish Close champion, Hugh, who found a new focus on his golfing endeavours following the serious illness which eventually took the life of his father.

It's also about David Foley, who gained remarkable solace from golf through horrendous times. And it's about his wife, Oonagh, and their daughter, Ally, who followed her father into medicine.

Based in Beaumont Hospital, Professor Foley's expertise in stenting made him one of the country's leading cardiologists. He could also be described as a fanatical golfer, who won the President's Prize at Bally-bunion before going on to capture the Healy Matchplay Cup at Royal Dublin in 2017.

He and I had become friends in recent years, which caused me to watch his funeral Mass online during Covid. As part of the service, Hugh and Ally sang Sting's iconic 'Fields of Gold' as a duet. When they had performed it on the occasion of the death of their grandfather, Michael

Foley, in Askeaton in 2015, their dad had liked it. And you can imagine how the opening lines about the wind blowing through fields of barley would appeal to farming people from Co. Limerick.

On 11 October 2020, I found myself sending a text to the professor that read: 'Hi David. What's this I hear about Hugh?' To which came the reply: 'He just won the Close in Rosapenna, Dermot ... by 10 shots. Truly surreal. Not there. Virtually never go watch in case he notices me, haha, and it might distract him.'

To win a national championship by such a margin was remarkable. Only two comparable achievements come to mind in an Irish context. One was by Niall Kearney, another Royal Dublin member, who triumphed by 14 strokes in the 2015 Irish PGA Championship at Dundalk, also in October, when three players were tied for second place. Before that, Des Smyth had set a target which has never been matched when, in 1980 at Headfort, he won the Irish Dunlop Tournament by a staggering margin of 16 strokes. And the runner-up happened to be former Walker Cup and Ryder Cup player Peter Townsend.

From a weak start of 77, culminating in four bogeys in the last five holes, Hugh Foley proceeded to sparkle with second and third rounds of 66 and 67 on the formidable Sandy Hills stretch for a six-under-par aggregate of 210 in the 54-hole event. As Hugh recalled:

> I drove home that evening with Patrick Keeling from Roganstown and Richard Knightly and Robbie Hynes from Royal Dublin, three of the lads I had shared digs with in Rosapenna. The car was a bit of a squeeze, with all our gear and the trophy in its protective box. We got back about nine.
>
> It was all a bit surreal. Dad stayed up making us sandwiches until two or three in the morning. I have a picture of him drinking from the cup, which became a bit of a struggle, it's so big. The occasion brought home to me what a close family we are, which had never really hit me until my dad got ill.

Two months later, the newly crowned champion was at Roganstown GC with his coach, Geoff Loughrey, for a rather special practice session. Through medical connections at Ardglass GC, the Professor had lined up his son with Loughrey during Hugh's Leaving Certificate year in 2015. That was also when he first met Michael Bannon.

His father compared the challenge Hugh was facing in golf to the years of work he had to put into becoming an established cardiologist. 'He trusted Geoff and Michael to guide me along the right road,' said Hugh:

> Part of the arrangement is that I see Michael five or six times a year. When we met last 12 December [2020], he had already sent me a very nice congratulatory text about Rosapenna. He was in Florida, working with Rory McIlroy at the time.
>
> He and Geoff bounce off each other very well. Michael is great on detail, which I imagine comes from working with a world-class player. Suggested changes may appear minor, but can make a big difference. A little tweak from a different set of eyes.
>
> He has a great memory, quiet and detailed. Five or six months on from his previous visit, he will remember what we were working on when we last met. Out of the blue, he'll ask, 'Why are you doing that?'

On 1 August 2019, David Foley collapsed suddenly, fracturing the back of his skull. After being monitored in hospital for a few weeks, a cancerous brain tumour was diagnosed, leading to surgery. Hugh explained:

> Seeing him attached to all sorts of tubes in Beaumont Hospital was harrowing. I tried not to dwell on it but I remember stopping golf for two or three weeks when he was in there. Of course, it meant missing our annual involvement in the Father and Son Tournament in Waterville, but we learned that they said prayers for Dad during the week. Which was lovely.

When I resumed competition in the Interpros, I played great. Without touching a club. In fact, I got down to plus-four [handicap] without really practising.

Dad's illness gave me a fresh perspective on life in general. On what's really important, not the silly little things that can get to you on a golf course. I know I became a calmer, more focused player during 2020.

Calmness on a golf course is a great thing to have. All the while, I was optimistic dad would pull through. Though I became aware that brain tumours don't tend to have good outcomes, I was convinced he would be in the one per cent who would survive for 10 or 15 years.

As for him, his attitude was incredible. He had great surgery followed by expert treatment and would show us he was getting better, especially by never complaining. He must have known what the prognosis was, but he gave the impression that his treatment had beaten it. It was like he wrapped it all up like a grenade and threw it over the wall where it would go off, whenever it went off. The words 'tumour' and 'death' were never mentioned.

As a professional golf writer, it is intimidating to be confronted by someone who is better informed than you are about the finer points of the modern game. David Foley posed such a problem for me. I could only smile when Hugh talked about what they found on his father's mobile phone after he had died – close to 200 videos, mainly from Sky Sport where *Nick Dougherty's Tee Time Tips* were among his favourites. According to Hugh, these were to help restore the single-figure handicap he had treasured for most of his golfing life.

When illness struck, he drifted out to 15 but then managed to work his way back to 11, at a time in life when most players are headed in the opposite direction.

He had grumbled to me quite a few times about ill-informed medics closing down golf courses (during Covid) before delivering his grand finale in August 2020. That was at a return to the Father and Son at

Waterville, which Covid made a quieter affair. There, with typical grit and bloody-mindedness, Foley Snr made a handsome contribution to their victory in the Gross section by a significant eight-stroke margin. Particularly impressive was a better-ball 71 on the final day.

He later texted me: 'We were just so glad to be there ... to get involved in social aspects and the craic/interaction as compared to last year at this time. Small, intimate crowd and great hospitality by Marty Carr. The Gross Award is becoming the main prize actually ...' Wonderful, I thought.

My last text to him was on 1 January 2021, wishing him 'A better year in 2021.' The reply came from Hugh on 14 January, preparing me for the worst. The cancer had returned, and he died two days later. He was 59.

Hugh, who by then played off plus-six under the new world scheme, was going to be 24 on 9 May, his father's birthday. 'I'm definitely turning professional, but I've no idea when,' he said. 'I tend to set goals as I go along.'

Then, wistfully: 'I keep thinking about the 2023 Walker Cup at St Andrews. Dad always felt there couldn't be a better place to wrap up my amateur career.'

The idea of excellence appealed to him. As a one-time golfing patient of his recalled him saying in the operating theatre: 'I may be five-handicap at golf, but I'm scratch at this stuff.' And he surely was.

Postscript: Hugh didn't make the Walker Cup, which was going to lead to a move to professional ranks. But there were compensations, like winning the West of Ireland only a few months after his father's death and then emulating the achievement of Darren Clarke in 1990, by completing the double of the North of Ireland and South of Ireland titles.

20

When Golf Can Help with Gaping Wounds

Trusting the passage of time to have eased the terrible hurt, I spoke with Lindsay Hall about the Omagh bomb. It was 20 years since we had met at Portmarnock Links, where golfers from all over these islands and further afield came together in solidarity with those affected by the outrage.

For the Hall family, Saturday, 15 August 1998 became a day for tidying up some loose ends for their youngest son, Alastair, as the summer holidays drew to a close. 'His mother took him into town to get a pair of trousers for back to school,' the father recalled. There was a pause.

'She sustained a fractured skull and compound leg fractures,' he went on. 'In fact, she got the hearing back in her right ear only about six months ago from new technology that's come out. Alastair lost his right leg.'

Acceptance has come to replace the raw emotion of a dreadful time when a devastated father could utter only the plaintive plea: 'He was just a boy. How can they do this? He loved playing rugby, but he was only 12, for God's sake. I am 57. Why didn't it happen to me?'

The idea for the Portmarnock gathering came to Dungannon native Darren Clarke during the Smurfit European Open at The K Club in late August. 'I suppose it was prompted by the fact that on the day of the bomb, Heather [his wife, who died of cancer in August 2006], brought our son, Tyrone, home from hospital,' said Clarke at the time.

> The response has been wonderful. Apart from the 27 teams who played, we had 29 waiting in the wings for the chance to play. I realise that money is not going to bring back those loved ones who have gone, but I hope it can help the survivors in some small way.

He was right. As Hall put it: 'It helped people. Made life a bit easier.'

The event took place on Monday, 14 September, the day after the All-Ireland Hurling Final in which Offaly beat Kilkenny by 2-16 to 1-13. Having scored an unavailing 0-5, DJ Carey endured the physical discomfort of broken toes inflicted by a rival. But he still turned up for this special golfing day.

Des Smyth sat beside him in the locker room where they changed into their golf shoes. 'As DJ struggled to get a sock off, I could see that his foot was in a terrible state,' said Smyth. 'And I can remember saying to him "Do you think you should be playing today?"

> I'll never forget his reply – 'Aw Jesus, Des, you couldn't let Darren down on a day like this.' Which left me with a new respect for the toughness of Kilkenny sportsmen. DJ was determined to honour a commitment, whatever the circumstances.

Carey's reaction was typical of the tremendously uplifting atmosphere I remember around the links clubhouse that day. Like the fact that a private whip-around among the staff of the adjoining hotel realised £4,000 for the fund. Then there was a personalised golf bag which arrived from Ernie Els, including balls, visors and gloves autographed by Els, Mark O'Meara and Nick Price. And Australia's Stuart Appleby saw fit to make a contribution, only a short time after his young wife was killed in a car accident.

Europe's number one, Colin Montgomerie, was among the playing professionals to respond to the call, direct from his win in the British Masters. And he brought with him a print of a Keith Fearon painting of himself and Scott Hoch at the Ryder Cup at Valderrama 12 months previously, which was auctioned for £2,000.

José María Olazábal, whose roots in the Basque region of Spain would have made him sadly familiar with terrorism, was there to honour the Spanish dead of Omagh. Ian Woosnam was also there, to show solidarity with his Irish colleague.

Clarke's initial target was a modest £40,000 but the final figure of £348,000 reflected the wonder of sportspeople pulling together in a common cause. Though Aer Lingus didn't want it mentioned, they gave free flights to visiting professionals.

Later in the day, as the shotgun start culminated in some of Europe's leading players streaming in together from the course, there were appreciative looks from Hall and from another Omagh resident, Sammy Jameson, who spoke of the pain the bomb had inflicted on his nephew and sister-in-law. 'Omagh is a good town and it's the feeling of solidarity that's so important,' said Jameson, who died in 2006.

Meanwhile, Hall noted that the broad sweep of the sporting response included Eddie Jordan and former Formula One world champion Damon Hill, who went from Portmarnock to the Altnagelvin Hospital in Derry, so as to visit his son.

And he talked of the support from the world of rugby. 'I got a beautiful letter from Tony Ward,' he said back then, 'which I read three or four times every day.'

Brian Mellon, the 2018 president of Omagh GC, recalled how the words of Longfellow – 'There is no grief like the grief which does not speak' – inspired his club to organise their own event that autumn, so that 'action might help lessen despair.' So it was that £150,000 was raised in a golf classic on 10 and 11 October, when a special limited-edition plate donated by Belleek Pottery was presented to each of the 92 competing teams.

A retired bank manager, Hall enjoyed golf as a member of Newtownstewart GC until 2015. That was when a torn Achilles tendon, accompanied by a diagnosis of Parkinson's disease, caused him to pack the clubs away.

'I couldn't get about,' he explained, before adding almost offhandedly, 'I'm just taking the tablets now.' Then, looking back once more to Portmarnock Links, he seemed to be especially taken by the presence there of Christy O'Connor Jnr, who passed from us in January 2016.

'He had lost his son [Darren] in a car accident only the previous week,' he said, as if consoling himself that Alastair's plight could have been a lot worse.

As it happened, Christy's wife, Ann, was also there with their elder son, Nigel, who caddied for his father. And I remember the player saying to me with typical, wide-eyed enthusiasm: 'I can't believe shooting 68. It must be Darren's putter. I took it out of his bag coming here and holed everything.'

And there was an Omagh connection in the appearance of Christy Senior, going back more than 40 years to his time as professional at Bundoran. 'I used to go regularly to Omagh to play in exhibitions and they always treated me very well,' he said. 'So many members became friends that when I heard about this, I immediately wanted to become involved.'

Alastair Hall is now married and living in Wales, and while he never found a place in active sport, he is a season ticket holder at Cardiff Blues RFC. 'There was a busy time in the early part of 1999, by which stage he had a prosthesis,' his father recalled.

> Especially memorable was a visit to Old Trafford, for my wife, myself and Alastair as guests of Manchester United. That was the year they won the treble and we were there on the Sunday they beat Tottenham Hotspur to secure the Premier League title.
>
> We met Roy Keane. I like Roy. He's a rough diamond but he's honest; he says what he thinks. And he was more than nice to us.

We also met Bobby Charlton who told Alastair that he once had a terrible experience [the Munich air disaster] but he didn't want to talk about it. "Maybe your dad will tell you about it some time in the future," he said.

I have the match programme with a wee note in it about us. All signed. And a real collector's item in a shirt autographed by all the players. Earlier that year, on an invitation from the IRFU, Alastair had appeared as a mascot for the rugby international against England at Lansdowne Road. And he walked onto the pitch, as he promised himself he would do.

Though dates have changed, the link with the 2018 happenings at Croke Park didn't escape this member of Omagh RFC. 'I never thought Limerick had the sort of strength to win a hurling All-Ireland,' he remarked. 'Mind you, Munster people love their sport.'

Pausing to gather his thoughts, he concluded: 'Sport can be a great comfort.'

Which you sensed was something that wasn't said lightly.

21

Golf's Great Dreamer

Less than a year into my retirement, I've learned that a significant element of my golf-writing activities over a period of 30 years are set to come to an end. This was Pat Ruddy's disclosure that he was selling the European Club, which he officially opened on St Stephen's Day 1992.

'If I was guaranteed another 10 years of life, I'd stay with it', he said. 'But the way things are, it's for sale, to secure the future of my family.'

The news brought me back to one of my first visits to Rosses Point, covering the West of Ireland Championship for the *Daily Mail*. That was where a youthful Ruddy declared to the rest of the press crew: 'One day I will design and build a course of my own.' And we smiled indulgently at the innocence of those words.

Later, I was to learn that the first seeds of golf course design were planted in Ruddy while watching celebrated exponents like Joe Carr, Cecil Ewing, Guy Wolstenholme and Gerald Micklem competing in the West of Ireland Championship on the County Sligo links. They were simple times, when the sight of a bulldozer was confined to the activities of the local county council and, through family membership of Co. Sligo, there was always the opportunity of seeing golfers of contrasting skill applying club to ball. As Ruddy said:

> I was taught everything there, and if you're infected from childhood, there's really no escape. Johnny McGonigle [resident professional] was the fount of all knowledge, and I remember occasions when Christy O'Connor Snr would come down from Bundoran and they'd play together. All of which gave me a huge appreciation of people's enthusiasm for this amazing game.

A growing awareness of course design came in his first golf book, *My Golfing Album* by Henry Cotton, which he acquired in 1958.

It imparted a knowledge of the great architects like Harry Colt and two key design concepts of his at Rosses Point: cross-bunkering, which was generally popular at his time, and straightaway lines off the tee. Colt's straight-line philosophy was clearly productive at a time when the rough at Rosses Point was quite punishing.

In the meantime, Ruddy kept body and soul together through golf writing for the *Evening Herald*. And when I was recently writing *Links of Love* about Jimmy Kinsella, my research uncovered pieces of his concerning Kinsella's triumph in the 1972 Madrid Open on the newly created European Tour.

All the while, the wild dream remained. Then, to our enduring surprise, Ruddy proceeded to make it glorious reality, taking a daunting project through every stage from buying the land to designing the layout and supervising its construction among breathtaking dunes. He discovered the site of his dream course in the early 1980s, while surveying the country's eastern seaboard by helicopter. There he found the desired terrain, 200 acres which only locals were aware actually existed, and he went to work, moulding and shaping it until the prototype was ready for play.

It was a bit like a playwright buying his own theatre. Or, in an Irish context, like car enthusiast Eddie Jordan putting together his own Grand Prix team. And journalistic colleagues, myself included, couldn't but admire the courage and ambition of a man I came to refer to as the European Club's commander-in-chief.

Meanwhile, distinguished visitors liked what they saw. Among them was NBC's golf anchorman, Johnny Miller, who went there to broaden his knowledge of links design. Describing it as 'the toughest links I've played', Royal Birkdale's Open champion of 1976 added: 'Man, with at least eight par fives, I shouldn't have left my one and two irons at home. This is way ahead of Carnoustie.'

As a further endorsement, Miller agreed to lend his name to the 415-yard 16th, following a line of other distinguished associates of the links, as in Sam Snead (fourth), Peter Thomson (fifth), Lee Trevino (sixth), Arnold Palmer (seventh), Fred Daly (eighth), Gary Player (11th), Billy Casper (12th) and Tony Jacklin (13th).

Another notable occasion found Ruddy standing as a fascinated host on the elevated tee of the par-four 12th. Alongside Mark O'Meara and Scott McCarron, he watched the world number one study the beckoning shoreline in the right, with the Irish Sea beyond. Ideally, Ruddy suggested, Tiger Woods should draw his drive off the fairway bunker on the right. To which O'Meara made the memorable response: 'Tell him where, not how.'

Then there was the 2006 Irish Amateur Close in which the European Club delivered the sort of quality champion observers had anticipated, when Rory McIlroy retained the national crown. McIlroy was joint leader of the stroke play qualifiers with Andrew Pitcher of The Island after sharply contrasting rounds of 70 and 80. Indeed, there was a remarkable number of 80s among the qualifiers, despite reasonable conditions.

From the outset, Ruddy's handiwork found a great admirer in Pádraig Harrington, who made regular visits there as an accomplished amateur. Remarkably, the handicap system simply didn't allow him as a player of plus-three status to win a net prize in his home club, Stackstown. So, were there any circumstances in which he felt he could concede the full complement of shots to a middle- or high-handicapper and still have a reasonable chance of winning? 'Yes,' he replied. 'At the European Club on a windy day.'

And its mystique was further embellished in 2007 and 2008 when Harrington captured the Irish Professional Championship there, the week before winning successive Open titles at Carnoustie and Birkdale.

****

If a deal goes through, visitors are going to miss the mannerly warmth of the Ruddy children, Gerry, Patrick and Sidon, who have invariably been delightful hosts through the years. The remaining offspring, Bernardine and Zilla, have been engaged in other pursuits.

For his part, their father is certain to miss a challenge where, he predicted: 'The shot-maker and thinker will thrive on coming to terms with a primeval piece of ground. And the less adept should enjoy the odd flash of brilliance and the sheer beauty of nature in the raw.' But he warned: 'The unthinking golfer may suffer.' Indeed.